IMAGES
of America

ALONG DELAWARE'S OLD POST ROAD

FROM CLAYMONT TO IRON HILL

On the Cover: Pictured is the Grand Opera House on Markey Street in Wilmington in 1971, lit up by Delmarva Power and Light for its centennial celebration. (Courtesy National Register of Historic Places, National Park Service.)

IMAGES
of America

ALONG DELAWARE'S OLD POST ROAD

FROM CLAYMONT TO IRON HILL

Kenneth Baumgardt

ARCADIA
PUBLISHING

ISBN 978-1-4671-2273-3

Published by Arcadia Publishing
Charleston, South Carolina

Printed in the United States of America

Library of Congress Control Number: 2014942488

For all general information, please contact Arcadia Publishing:
Telephone 843-853-2070
Fax 843-853-0044
E-mail sales@arcadiapublishing.com
For customer service and orders:
Toll-Free 1-888-313-2665

Visit us on the Internet at www.arcadiapublishing.com

For all my family and friends, who are still writing their own history along the Old Post Road.

Contents

Acknowledgments

I would like to thank the Christiana Historical Society and the Pencader Historical Society for their dedication to preserving the history of the area. I would also like to thank Neal Davis for his memories of the Richardson Park area.

I have had a unique relationship with this particular road. Both my grandparents lived on it—my paternal grandparents lived in Elmhurst and my maternal grandparents in Richardson Park. Some of my earliest memories are of traveling up and down the road to visit them. My parents grew up, met, and married in the Richardson Park Methodist Church.

Growing up, we would shop at the old ShopRite in Stanton and go to the Pleasant Hill Drive-In in Newport to lie on the roof of my father's station wagon and watch the first releases of movies like the Disney classics *The Shaggy Dog* and *Herbie, the Love Bug.* As a teen, I would join the Armstrong Lodge No. 3 in Newport as a junior member of the Masons, the DeMoley.

My first job in my chosen profession of history was as a volunteer tour guide in the Iron Hill Museum of Natural History. There, I would take children around the museum and then inside the room filled with phosphorescent geodes and show them how they would glow under black lights. A few years later, I was employed by an archaeological company, and my first task was cleaning artifacts dug from the Mendenhall House on Front Street in Wilmington. My second task was cleaning artifacts from the Indian site dug up for the Route 7 expansion in Stanton.

I lived in Iron Hill and then Richardson Park, and after a decade in Pennsylvania, I returned and bought a house in Christiana. Even today, I travel down Old Baltimore Pike through Cooch's Bridge every day, passing by the monument there to the September 1777 Revolutionary War battle. This road is not only a part of Delaware history, but also a very personal part of my own history, filled with memories of what was, what is, and what could be.

Introduction

The Old Post Road, also known as the King's Highway, was built in the late 17th century to connect the new town of Philadelphia with points south. Baltimore and Washington would eventually be situated along its path, and this was the corridor mainly used by travelers during the 18th and 19th centuries.

The road has evolved and been given a plethora of names as it winds through Pennsylvania, Delaware, and Maryland. In Delaware, the Post Road is now known as Philadelphia Pike north of Wilmington, Maryland Avenue between Wilmington and Christiana, and Old Baltimore Pike from Christiana to the state line.

It was along this route that George Washington traveled many times as he passed from his home at Mount Vernon in Fairfax County, Virginia, to the seat of the new country in Philadelphia. It was along this path that Caesar Rodney made his famous midnight ride to Philadelphia to sign the Constitution and make Delaware the first state. It was also here that American and British troops fought in the only Revolutionary War battle fought on Delaware soil.

The Post Road was a critical element in the development of Delaware, but it was largely bypassed by first the railroad and then by road improvements, which were laid out as faster, more efficient modes of transport. Because it became a forgotten byway, many of the historic places have missed the destruction that is inherent with dualizing a colonial road for the sake of improved mobility.

A majority of these photographs were from publicly available sources, such as the Historic American Building Survey, conducted as part of the Works Progress Administration during the Depression and now housed at the Library of Congress; the records of the National Register of Historic Places; and the Delaware Public Archives. By necessity, modern photographs were taken when earlier photographs were not available for use in this publication.

One

Philadelphia Pike

The King's Highway is known as Philadelphia Pike, or Business Route 13, from the city of Wilmington to the state line and was established in 1666. This portion of the road is largely developed with an array of businesses and neighborhoods, but intermixed are the forgotten homes and businesses that made it a popular route to Philadelphia.

The area around Claymont was inhabited at least as early as AD 1200 by the Middle Woodland Indians, who had a large village on the banks of Naaman's Creek. The town of Claymont was originally known as Naaman's until 1852. Well into the 20th century, the stop on the railroad was still called the Naaman's Station. It was an agricultural area in the 18th century, a popular resort area for wealthy Philadelphians in the 19th century, and an important industrial center in the 20th century. Claymont derives its name from the wife of Reverend Clemsen, pastor of the Episcopal church there. The Claymonts relocated from their family plantation, Claymont Court, in Charles Town, West Virginia.

Farther down Philadelphia Pike are the communities of Belvidere, Penny Hill, and Edgemore. Like so many areas, these small communities began as little crossroads and railroad stops, never evolving into larger towns before they became eclipsed by the suburban sprawl that left them with little individual identity of place.

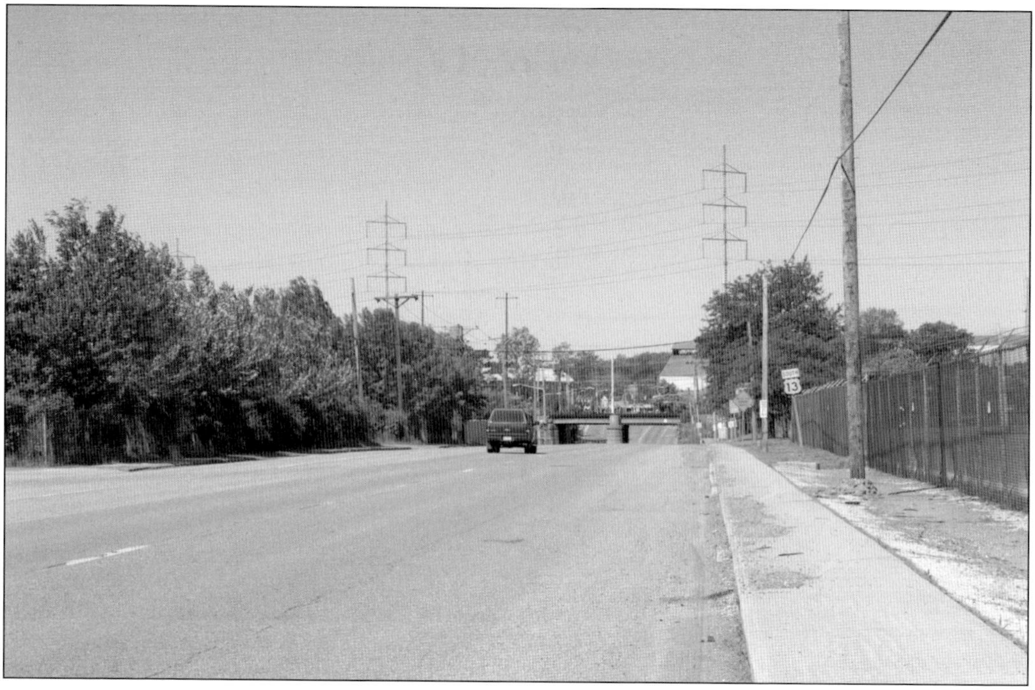

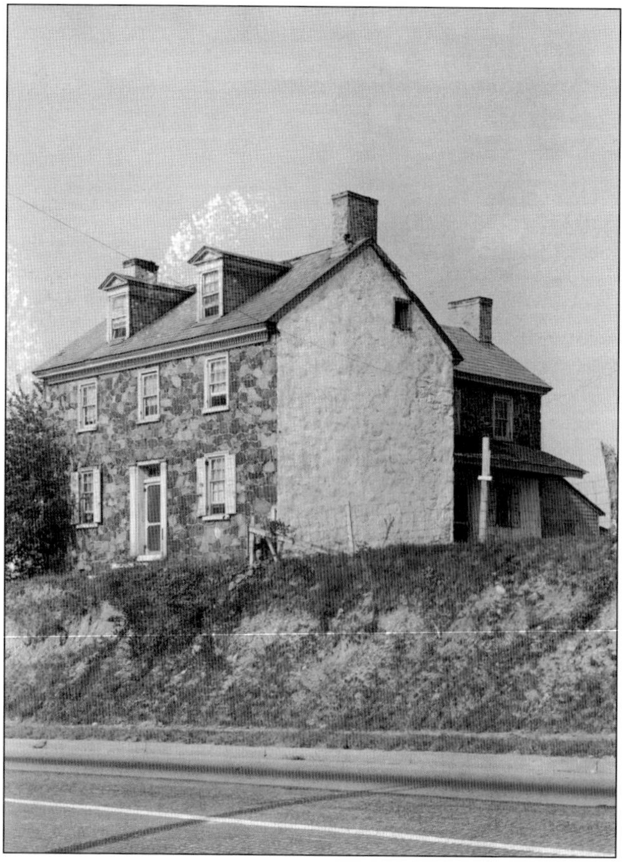

This is a view of where Philadelphia Pike crosses into Delaware north of Claymont and begins its circuitous 13-mile route through New Castle County. (Courtesy personal collection.)

The Old Lodge, formerly a half mile south of Grubb Road on Philadelphia Pike, was left perched high above the road when it was paved. The front part of the house was thought to have been built by Daniel Buckley in 1700. It was demolished in the 1930s when Philadelphia Pike was widened. It was owned for a time by novelist Anne Parrish, who lived in an adjacent house. (Courtesy Historic American Building Survey, Library of Congress.)

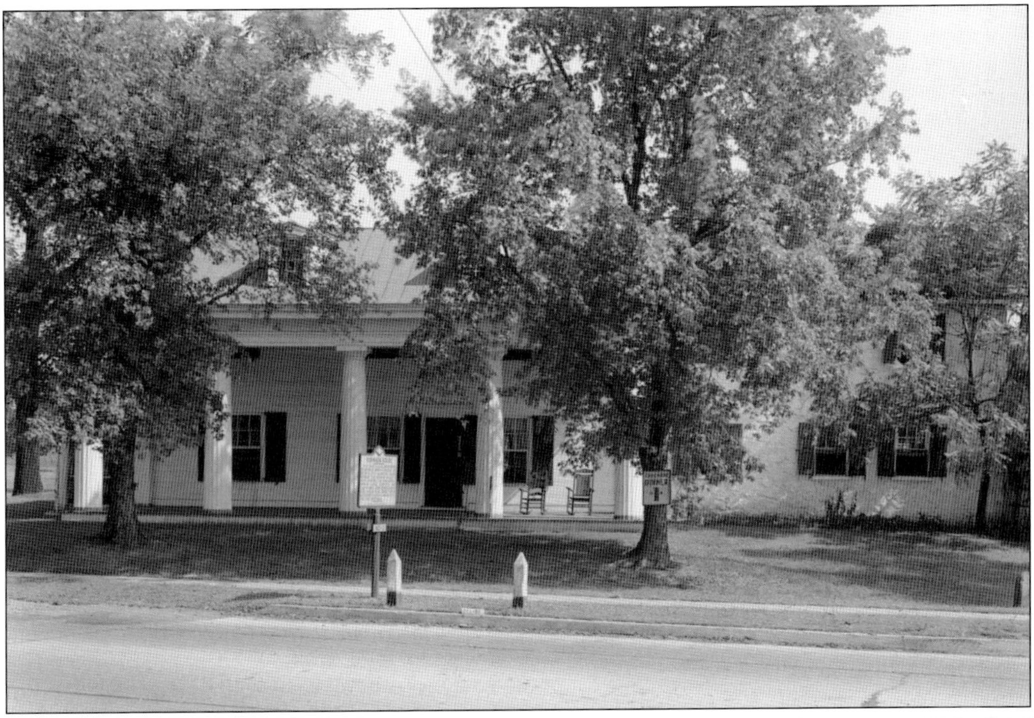

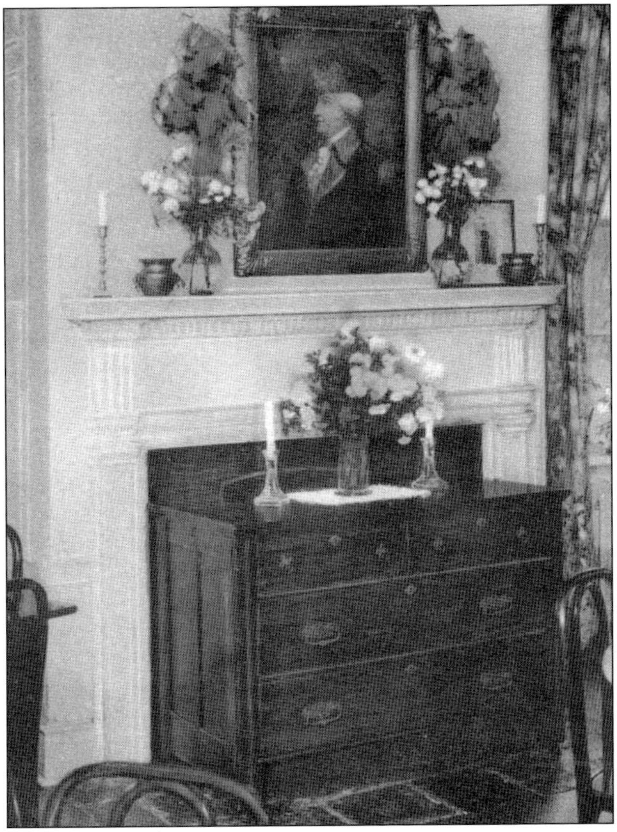

The Robinson House was built around 1723. It became a famous inn and teahouse, host to George Washington, General "Mad Anthony" Wayne, and others. In the 1740s, the house was sold to Philadelphia merchant Thomas Robinson. There was also a mill on nearby Naaman's Creek. Thomas Robinson Jr. became famous during the Revolution. (Courtesy National Register of Historic Places, National Park Service.)

The proximity of the Robinson House to Philadelphia Pike made it a landmark for passing travelers, and it is believed that many prominent figures stopped to visit. For a time during the 20th century, it was operated as a restaurant known as Naaman's Tea House. The Robinson House was listed in the National Register of Historic Places in 1971. (Courtesy National Register of Historic Places, National Park Service.)

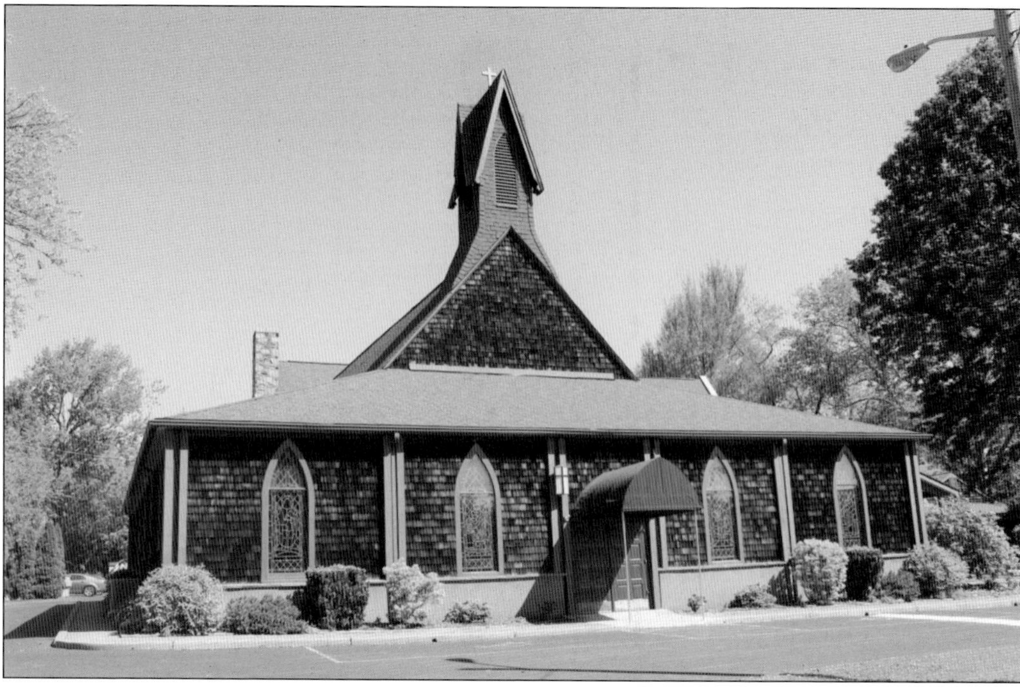

The Church of the Ascension was originally built across the street in 1854 but moved to this location in 1927, and at the same time, a new stone parish hall was added. It was named after the Church of the Ascension in New York City, one of the first to offer Sunday school to black children. (Courtesy personal collection.)

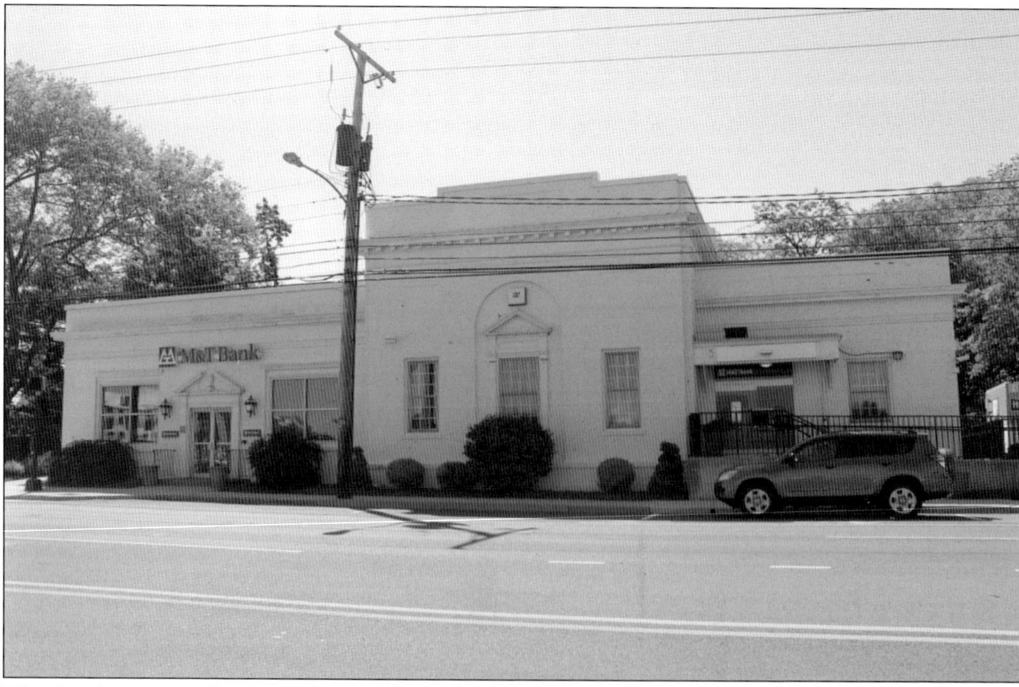

This bank is across the street from the Church of the Ascension and was built in the Greek Revival style with classic porticos over the doors and a flat roof. (Courtesy personal collection.)

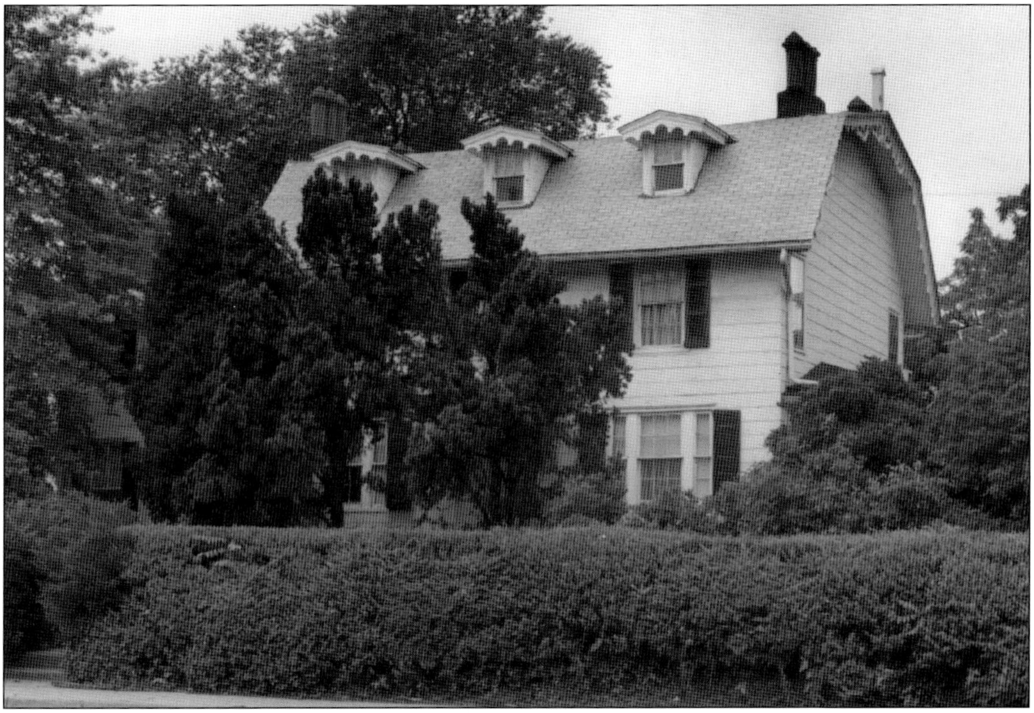

Wren's Nest, or the Darley Mansion, was owned by well-known illustrator Felix O.C. Darley (1822–1888). It was built in the late 18th century and enlarged several times during the first half of the 19th century. The house was purchased by Darley in 1863 and renamed Wren's Nest. The house was placed in the National Register of Historic Places in 1974. (Courtesy National Register of Historic Places, National Park Service.)

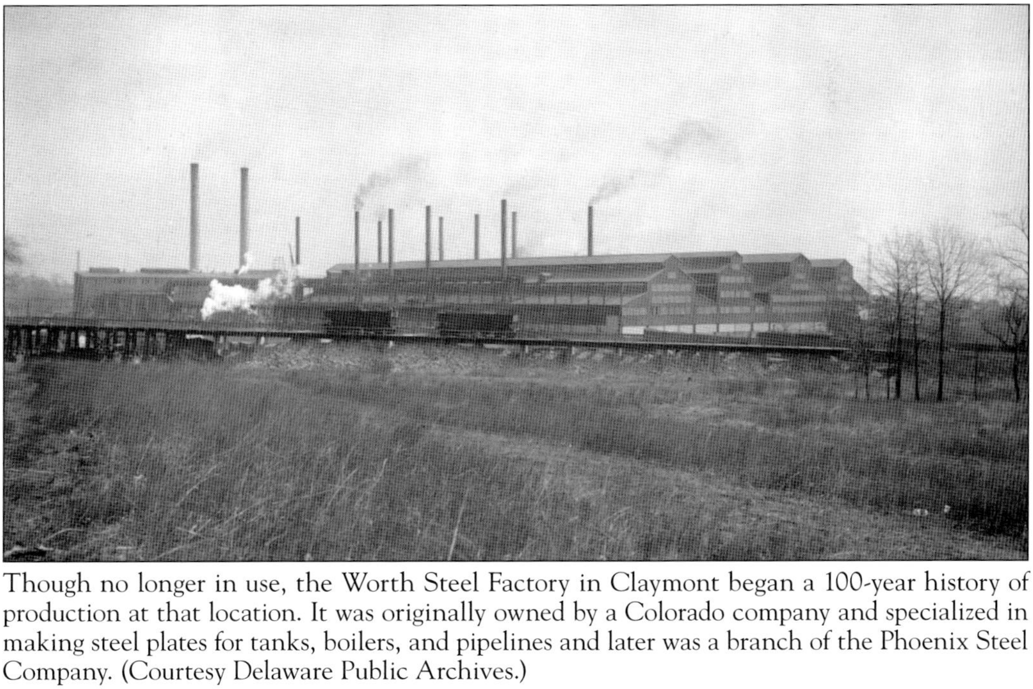

Though no longer in use, the Worth Steel Factory in Claymont began a 100-year history of production at that location. It was originally owned by a Colorado company and specialized in making steel plates for tanks, boilers, and pipelines and later was a branch of the Phoenix Steel Company. (Courtesy Delaware Public Archives.)

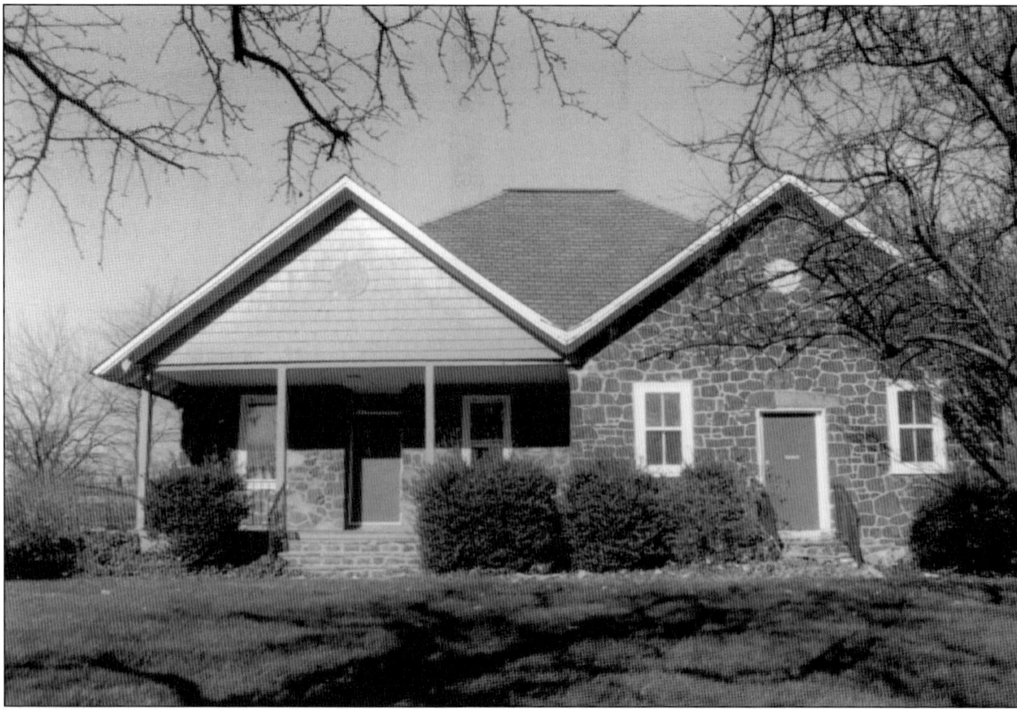

The Claymont Stone School, also known as Naaman's Creek School No. 1, was built on land donated by John Dickinson, the "Penman of the American Revolution," in 1805. Evidence suggests that it may have been the first racially integrated public school in the state. (Courtesy National Register of Historic Places, National Park Service.)

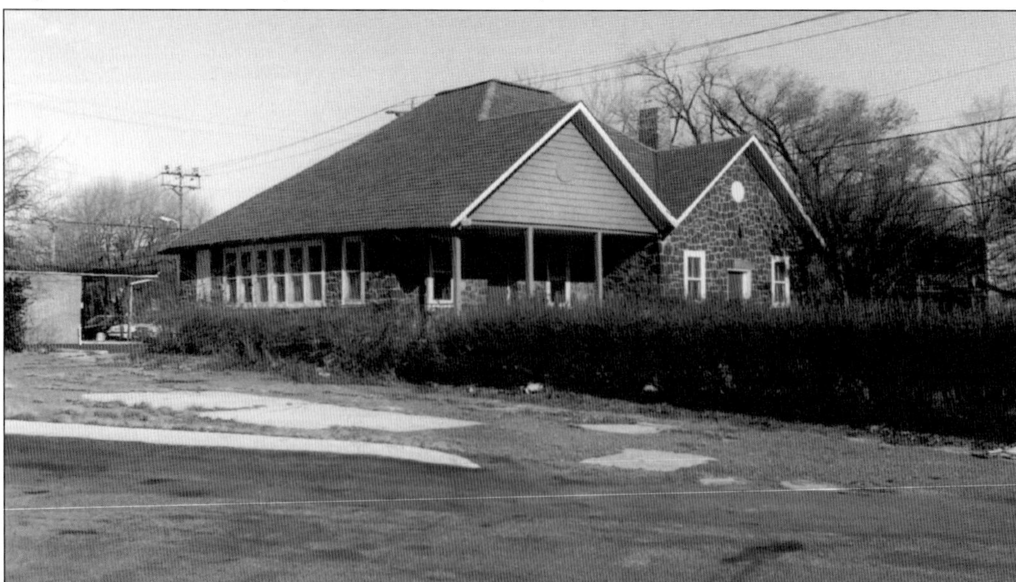

The school was renovated in 1905 into a two-room school and served the Naaman's Creek community until 1924. In 1928, it was converted into a community center and library, but by 1988, it had become structurally unsound. A community effort led to its renovation and reuse as a museum. (Courtesy National Register of Historic Places, National Park Service.)

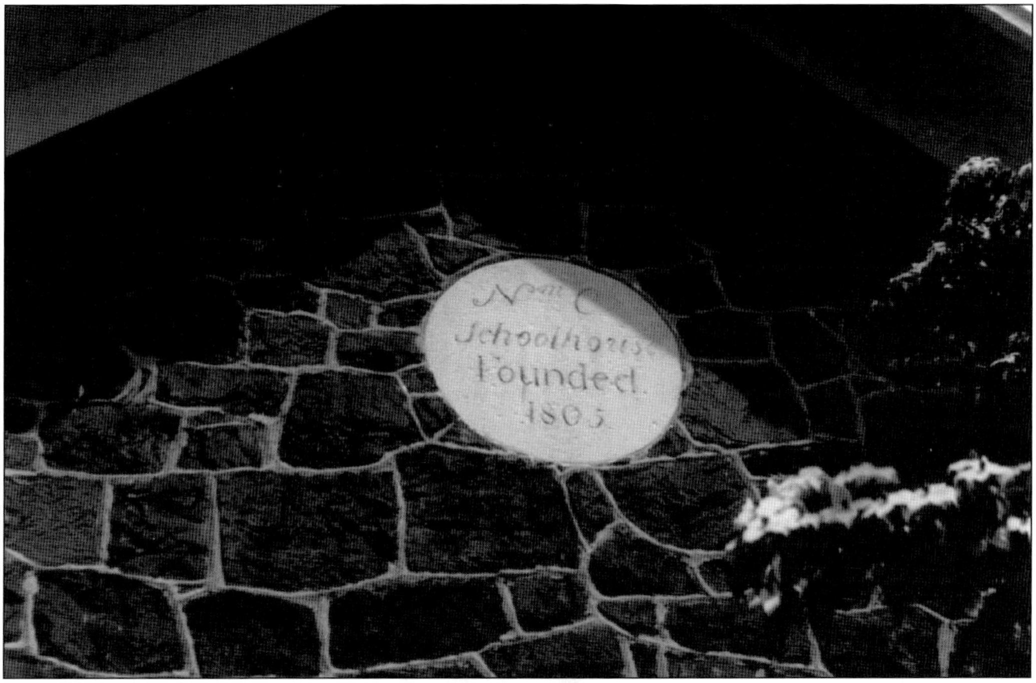

This date stone, in limestone and set into the gable end of the Claymont Stone School, demonstrates its construction in 1805. The Claymont Stone School was listed in the National Register of Historic Places in 1990. (Courtesy National Register of Historic Places, National Park Service.)

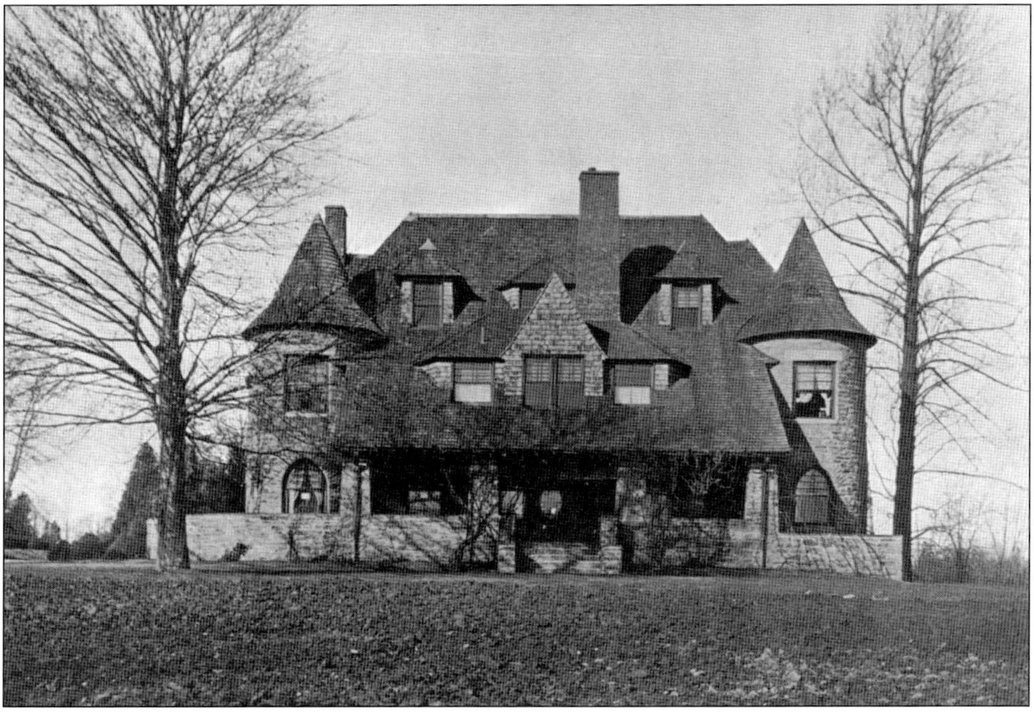

This stone house with flanking towers and slate roof, featured in 1902, was one of Claymont's most illustrious and was then owned by J. Edward Addick. (Courtesy personal collection.)

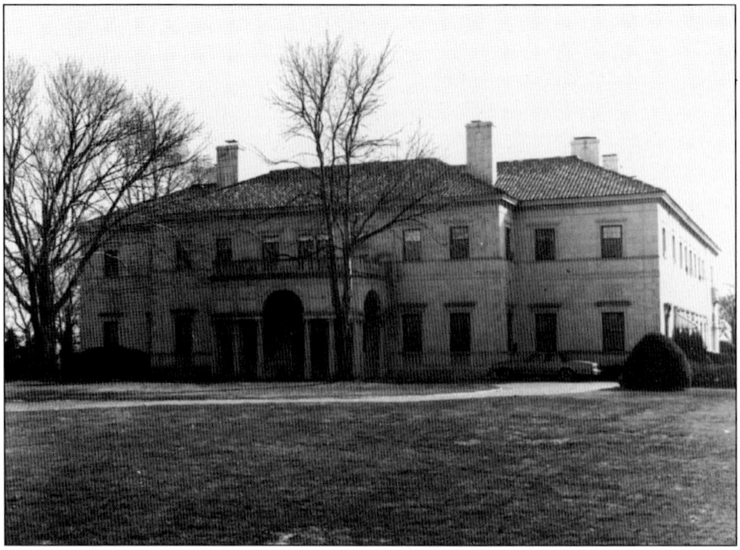

Archmere Academy was the former estate of John Jacob Raskob. Raskob was vice president of General Motors and the chairman of the National Democratic Committee in 1928, and he was a prime backer of Alfred E. Smith for president. A devout Catholic, he left his home to the church for a school. (Courtesy National Register of Historic Places, National Park Service.)

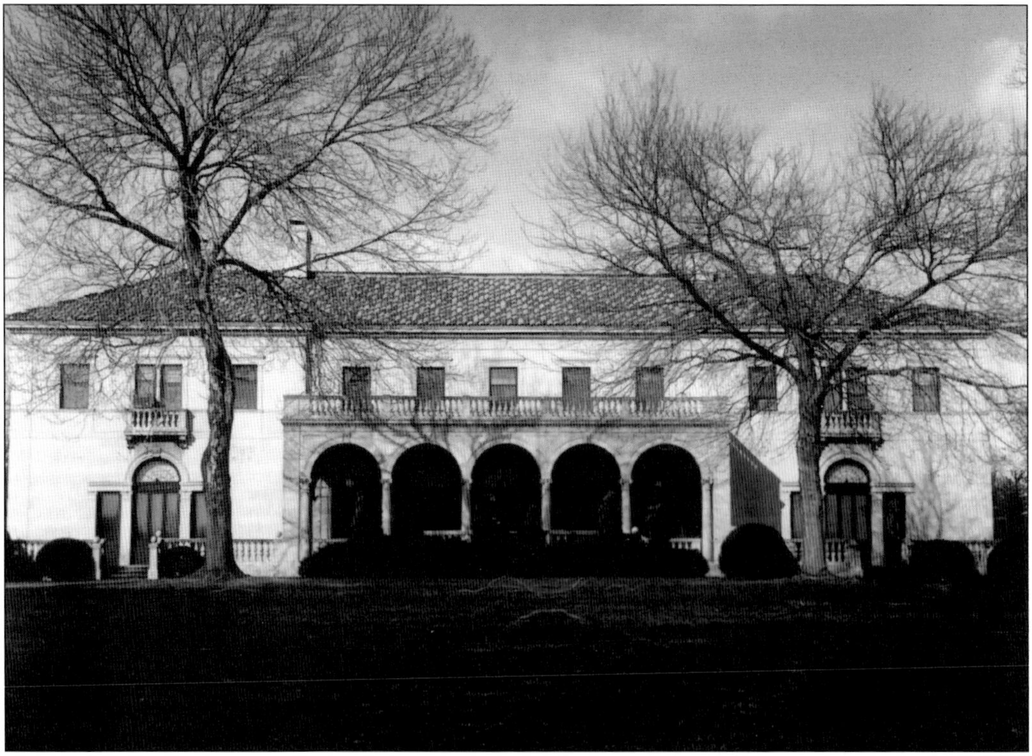

Archmere Academy was founded in 1932 as a boy's boarding school under the direction of Premonstratensian Fathers of the Roman Catholic Church. Among its graduates are Vice President Joseph R. Biden, his son Beau Biden, and Thomas Capano, former deputy attorney general of Delaware who was convicted of the murder of Anne Marie Fahey. (Courtesy National Register of Historic Places, National Park Service.)

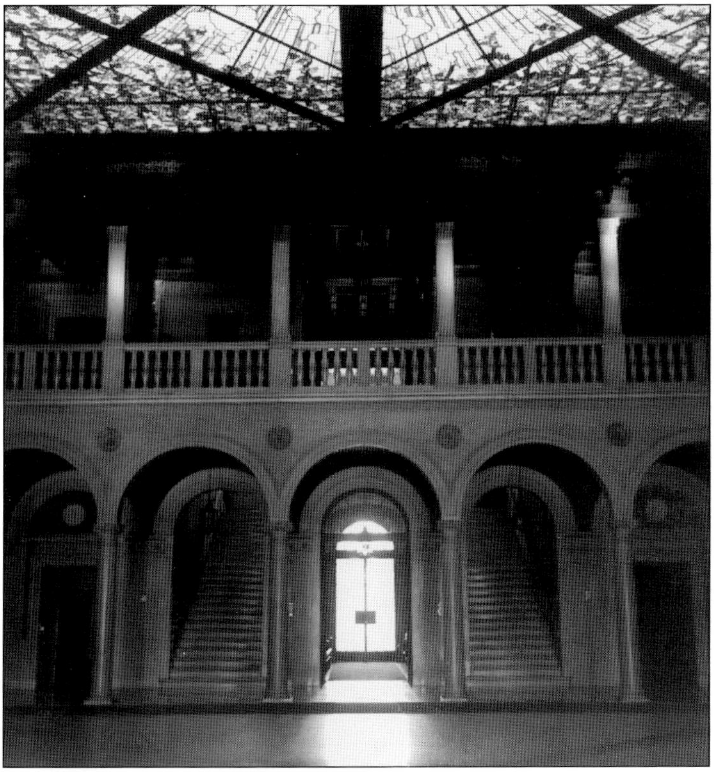

Archmere was built in 1918 in the manner of an Italian Renaissance villa, decorated with lavish interior arches and a central plaza. It features a glass-covered patio of 2,000 square feet that can be entirely opened. The architects were McClure and Harper of New York City. (Both, courtesy National Register of Historic Places, National Park Service.)

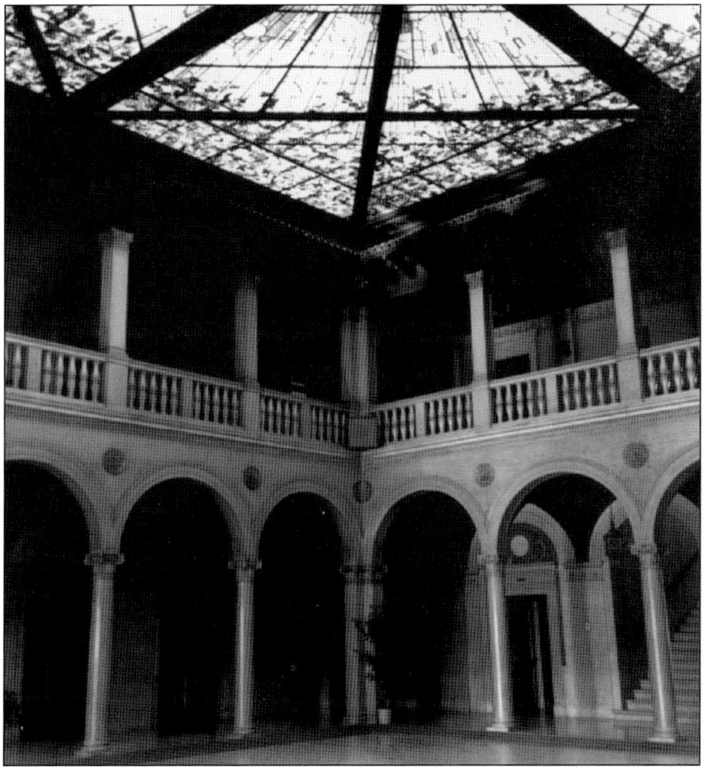

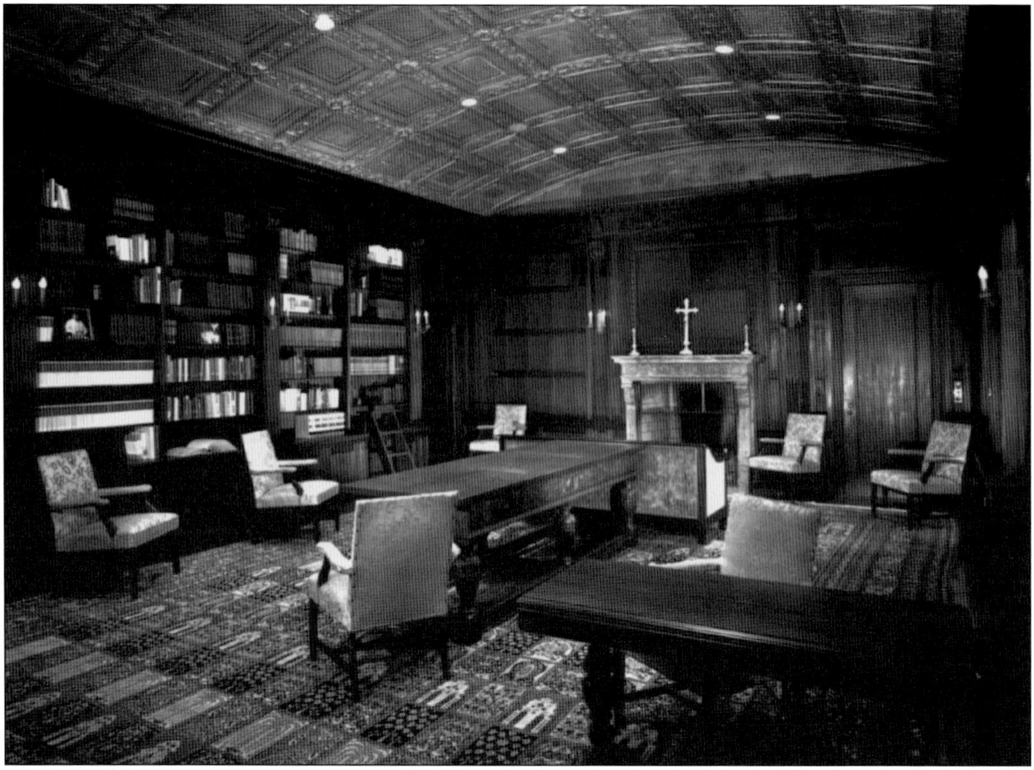

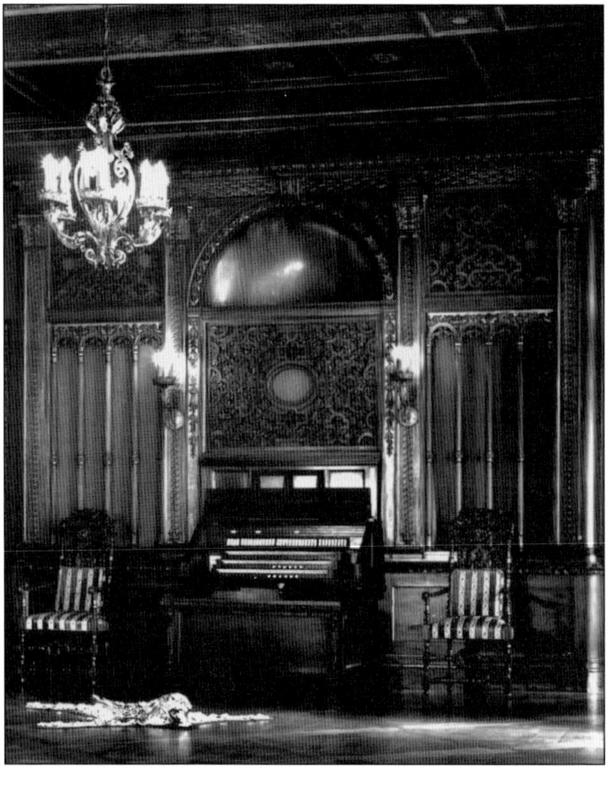

The inside of Archmere is lavishly decorated in the finest inlaid woods and carpeting. Archmere Academy prides itself on being one of the best parochial schools in the country. The photograph above is of the library, and the photograph at left is the music room. (Both, courtesy National Register of Historic Places, National Park Service.)

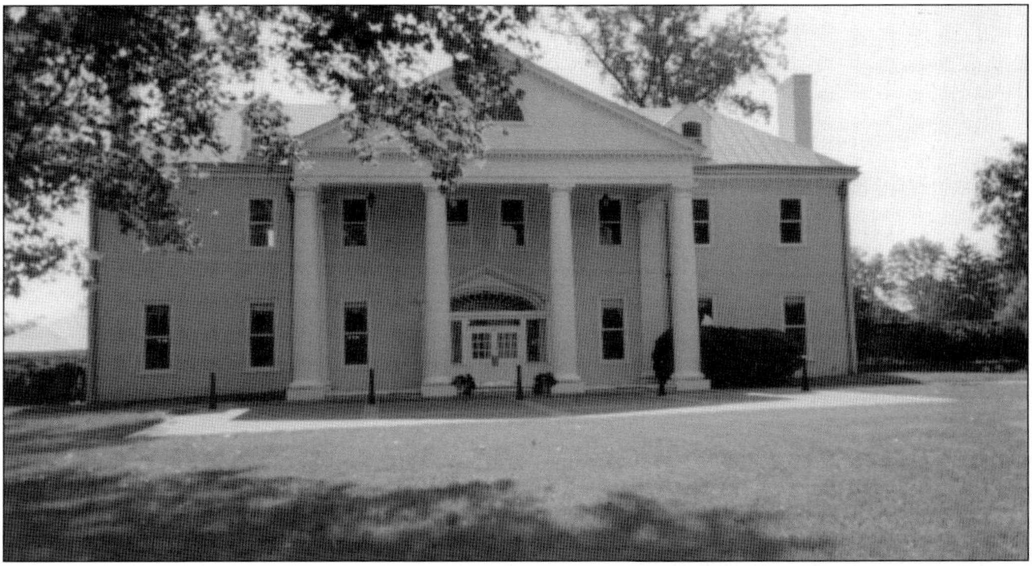

Bellevue, formerly the William DuPont Farm, was home of the banker William DuPont and had its own private horse racing track and stables. William DuPont was the president of the Delaware Trust Company and devoted his free time to promoting sporting throughout Delaware. He was the founder of the Delaware Park Racetrack in Stanton and Fair Hill Stables in Cecil County. (Courtesy personal collection.)

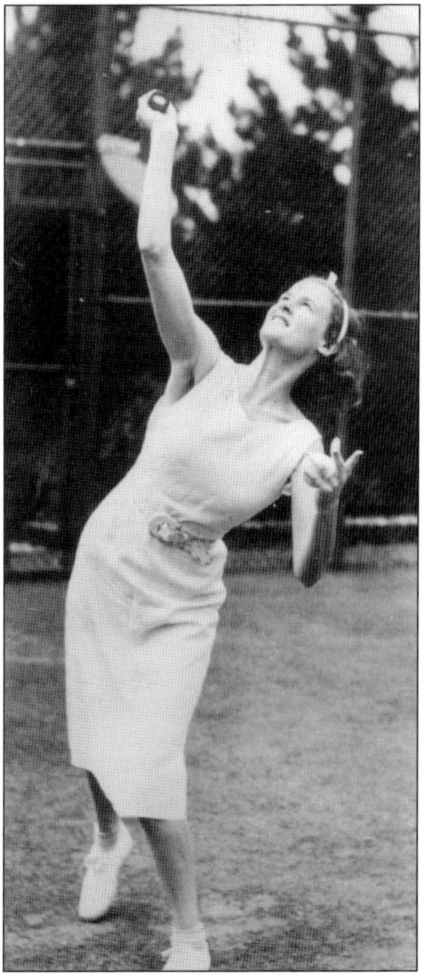

Pictured in 1947, William DuPont's second wife, Margaret Osborne DuPont (1918–2012), was a former star professional tennis player, and DuPont built her a number of courts at Bellevue. He also donated substantial funds to built free courts in Wilmington. DuPont won a total of 37 singles, women's doubles, and mixed doubles Grand Slam titles, winning 25 of her Grand Slam titles at the US Championships, which is an all-time record. After William DuPont died, his estate was donated to the state, and it became a state park and is a popular place for weddings and other formal gatherings. (Courtesy personal collection.)

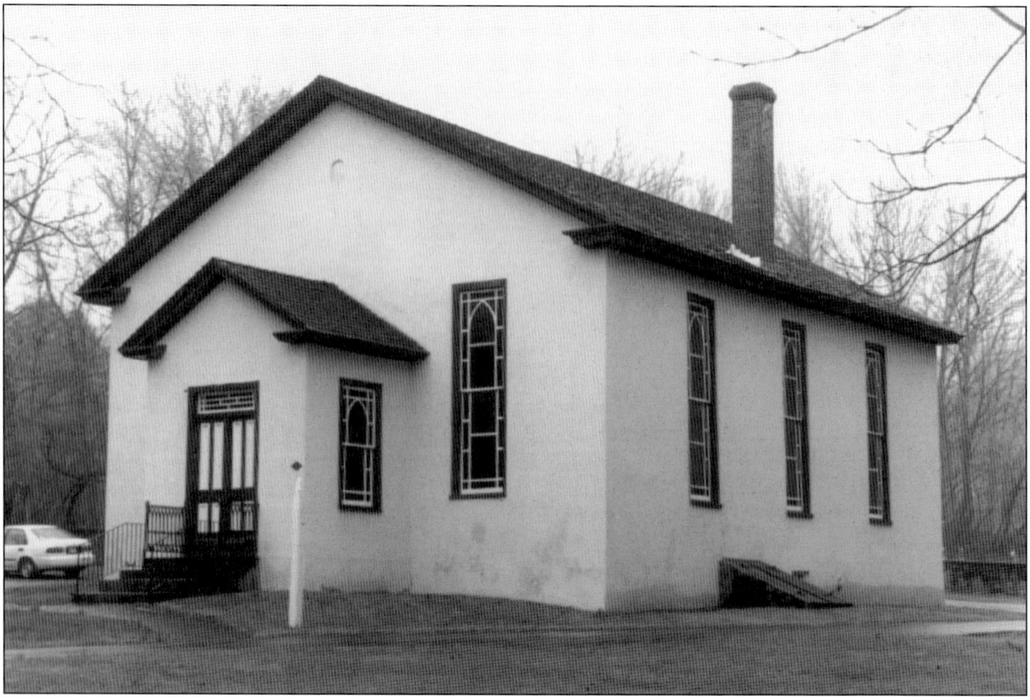

The Mount Pleasant Methodist Episcopal Church was built in 1838 and is a one-story, stuccoed stone structure with gable roof. The church and associated parsonage are at the Bellevue State Park. It was listed in the National Register of Historic Places in 1998. (Courtesy National Register of Historic Places, National Park Service.)

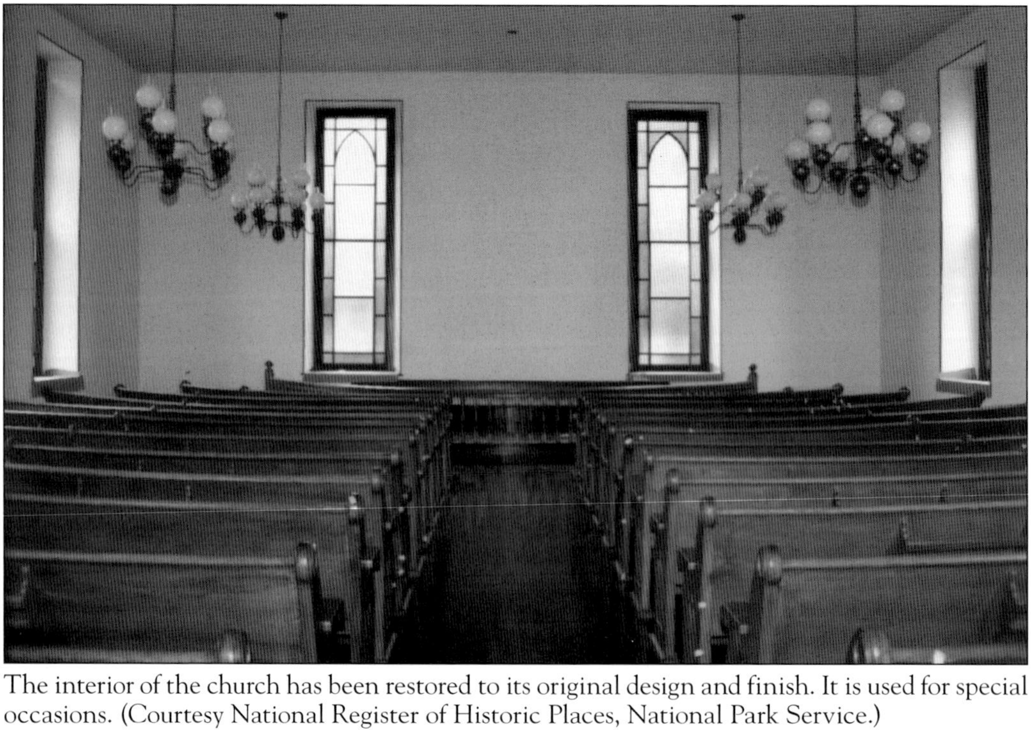

The interior of the church has been restored to its original design and finish. It is used for special occasions. (Courtesy National Register of Historic Places, National Park Service.)

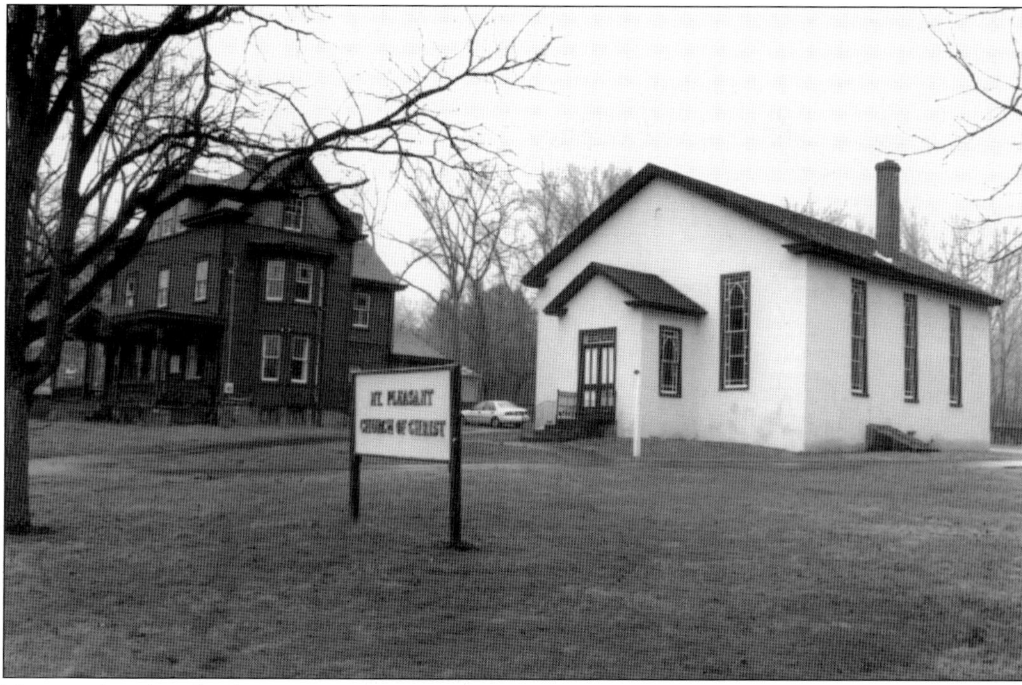

Next to the church, the parsonage was built in 1894. It is a two-and-a-half story, four bay, L-shaped frame dwelling in the Queen Anne style. (Courtesy National Register of Historic Places, National Park Service.)

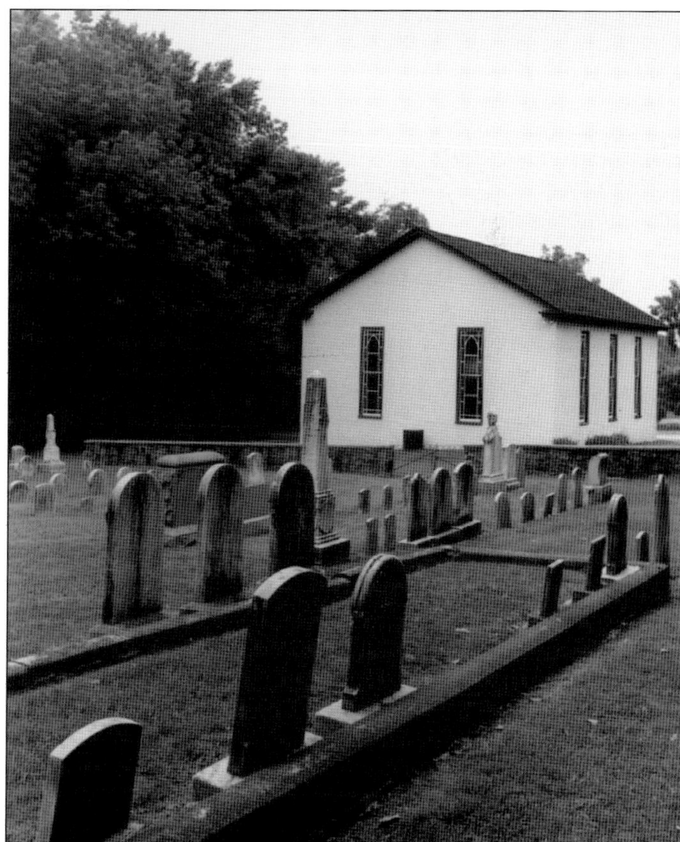

There is also a large cemetery associated with the church. The church holds many prominent members of the local community. (Courtesy National Register of Historic Places, National Park Service.)

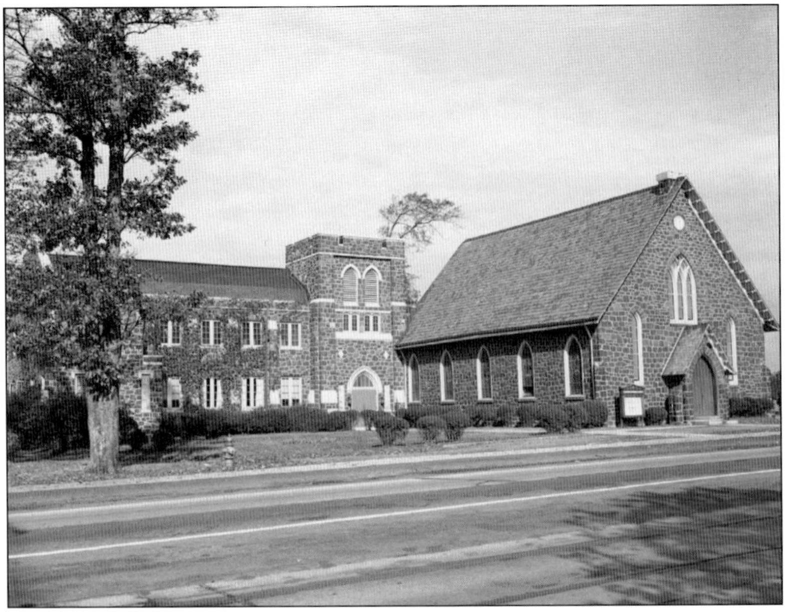

The Church of the Atonement United Methodist Church on Penny Hill was constructed in 1866 and remodeled in 1949. The impressive stone structure is still actively used for religious services. This photograph dates to its centennial in 1966. (Courtesy National Register of Historic Places, National Park Service.)

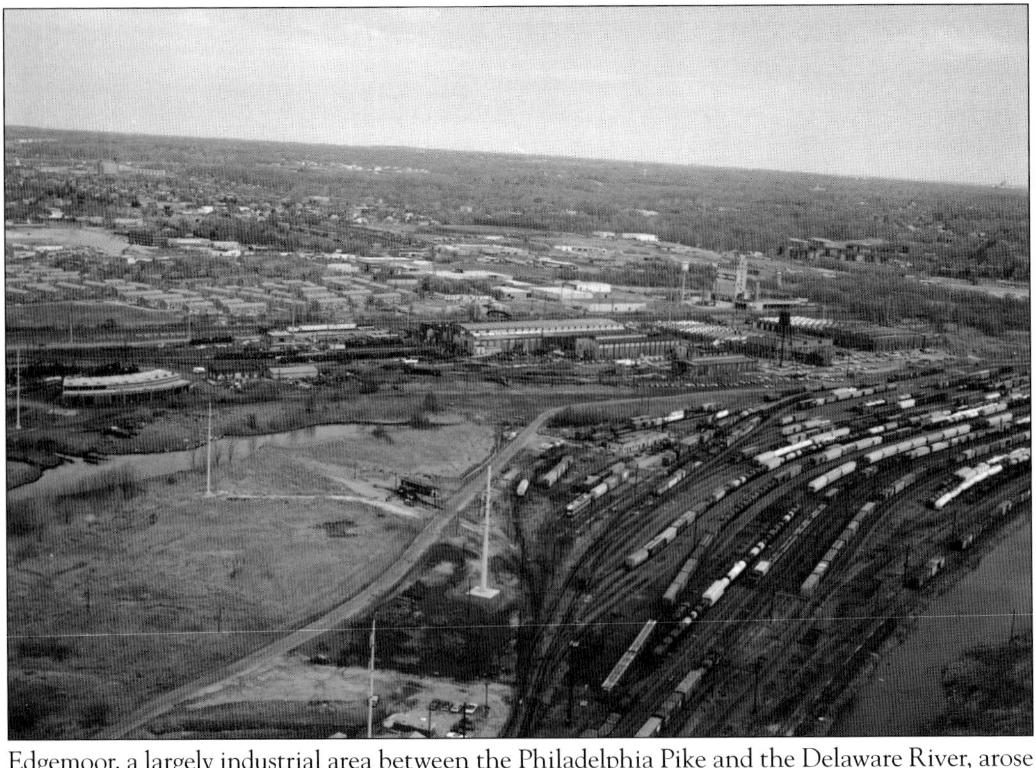

Edgemoor, a largely industrial area between the Philadelphia Pike and the Delaware River, arose because of the need for shipping materials on the river to ports in Philadelphia and Baltimore. It was surrounded by blue-collar neighborhoods, whose people relied on heavy industry for income. (Courtesy Delaware Public Archives.)

Two

BRANDYWINE VILLAGE

Mills began to be built along the banks of the Brandywine River as early as 1740. The river was prized because it fell a dramatic 124 feet in its last five miles, and the strength of the river was able to support a number of milling operations at the same time.

In 1799, the small town built a community center and school, and by 1820, fine mill owners' houses had been constructed along the lower part of Market Street in Brandywine Village. The side streets were populated with a wide variety of tradesmen, including coopers, blacksmiths, leather workers, carpenters, and numerous millworkers.

The Brandywine Village mills began to falter with the beginning of the industrial age and fell into disuse. Redevelopment in the 1940s allowed the formation of Brandywine Park, a scenic riverside attraction with walkways and pavilions and the Brandywine Zoo on its western end. But the village was listed in the National Register of Historic Places in 1971, and the boundaries of the district were increased in 1976. This prestige helped inventors turn the abandoned mills into a complex of upscale housing along the banks of the Brandywine, bringing new life into the community.

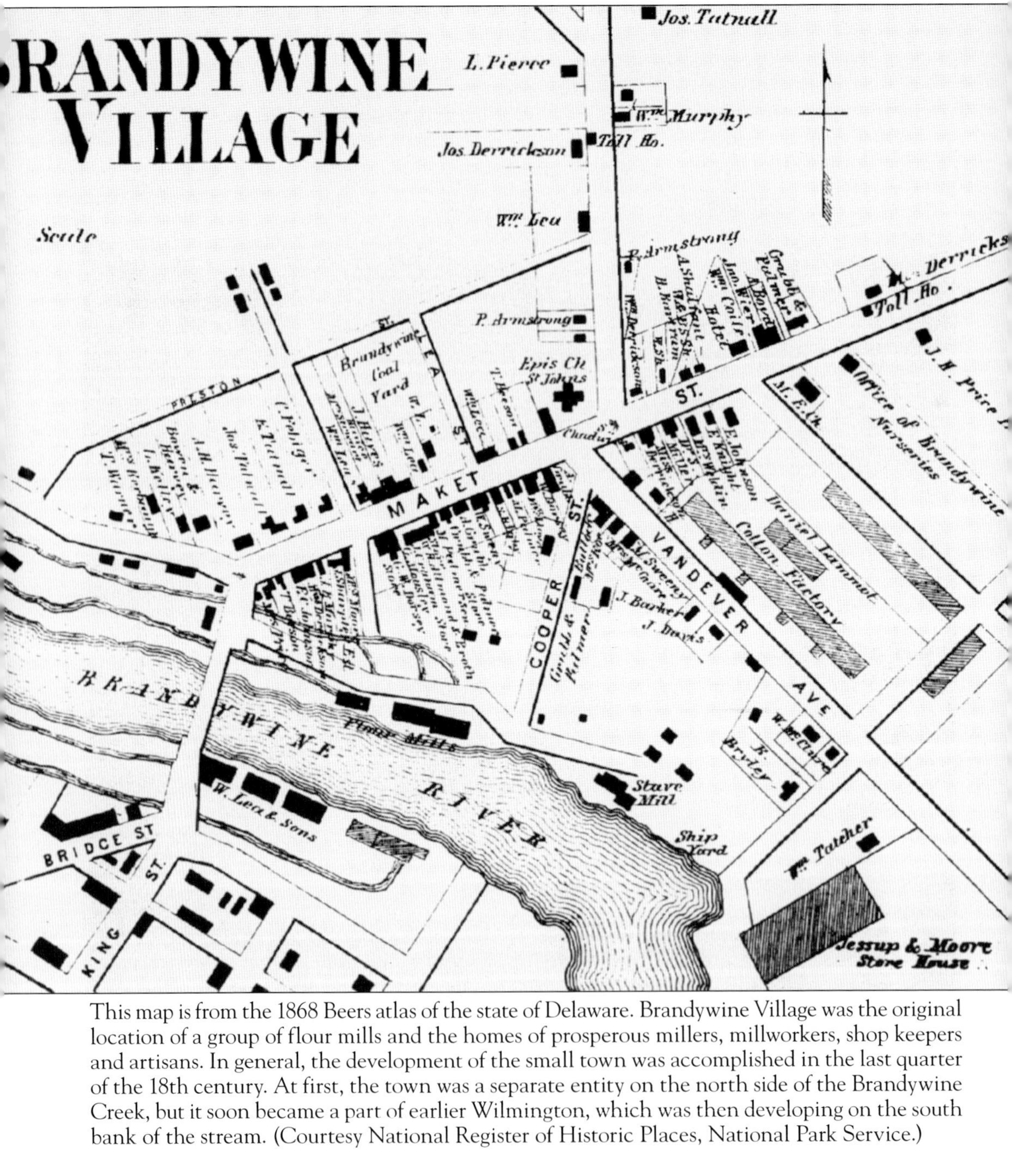

This map is from the 1868 Beers atlas of the state of Delaware. Brandywine Village was the original location of a group of flour mills and the homes of prosperous millers, millworkers, shop keepers and artisans. In general, the development of the small town was accomplished in the last quarter of the 18th century. At first, the town was a separate entity on the north side of the Brandywine Creek, but it soon became a part of earlier Wilmington, which was then developing on the south bank of the stream. (Courtesy National Register of Historic Places, National Park Service.)

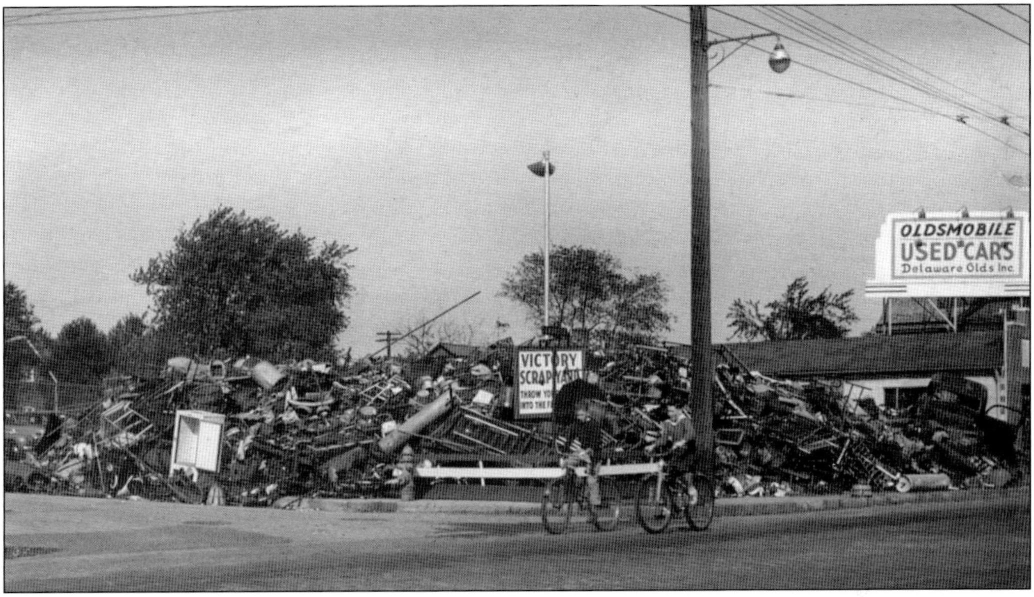

A large metal scrap yard was established along North Market Street during World War II for the collection of metal for the war effort. (Courtesy Library of Congress.)

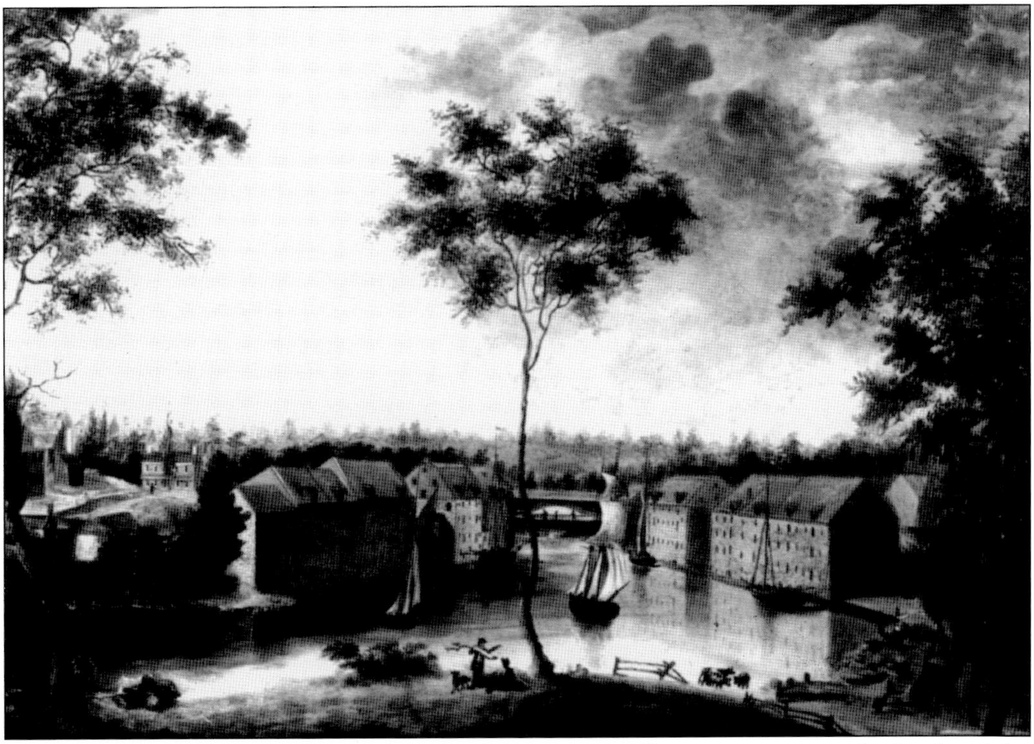

The Brandywine Flour Mill was a large and important milling operation on the banks of the Brandywine. Thomas Shipley and several others had a three-mile race dug and, by 1762, had completed two of four mills along the south bank between the terminations of French and Market Streets. This is an 18th-century painting of the mills along the Brandywine River. (Courtesy Delaware Public Archives.)

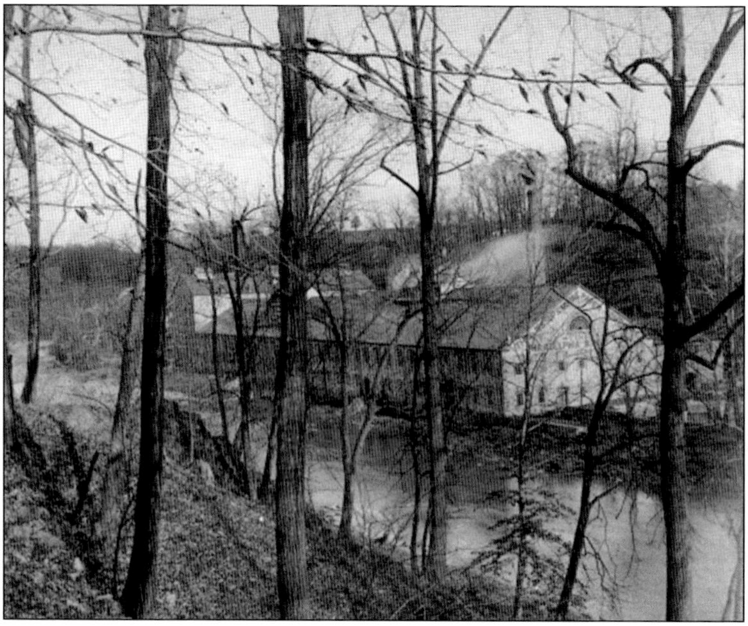

This photograph by Charles Madison in 1898 shows the paper mills along the Brandywine River. However, the era of the mills' real importance began in 1770. In that year, Joseph Tatnall, Delaware's first great industrialist, had a millrace dug along the north bank, a feat that had been considered impossible. Between 1770 and 1820, the number of mills increased from 8 to 14. (Courtesy Delaware Public Archives.)

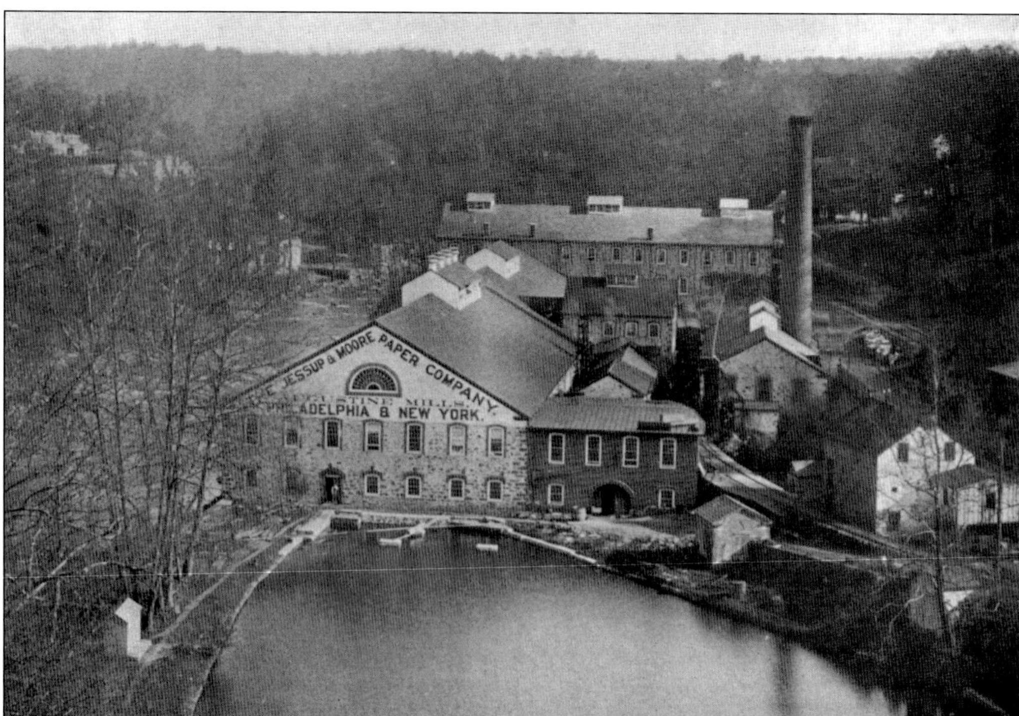

This image, from 1902, shows the Jessup and Moore Augustine Paper Mill on the Brandywine. (Courtesy personal collection)

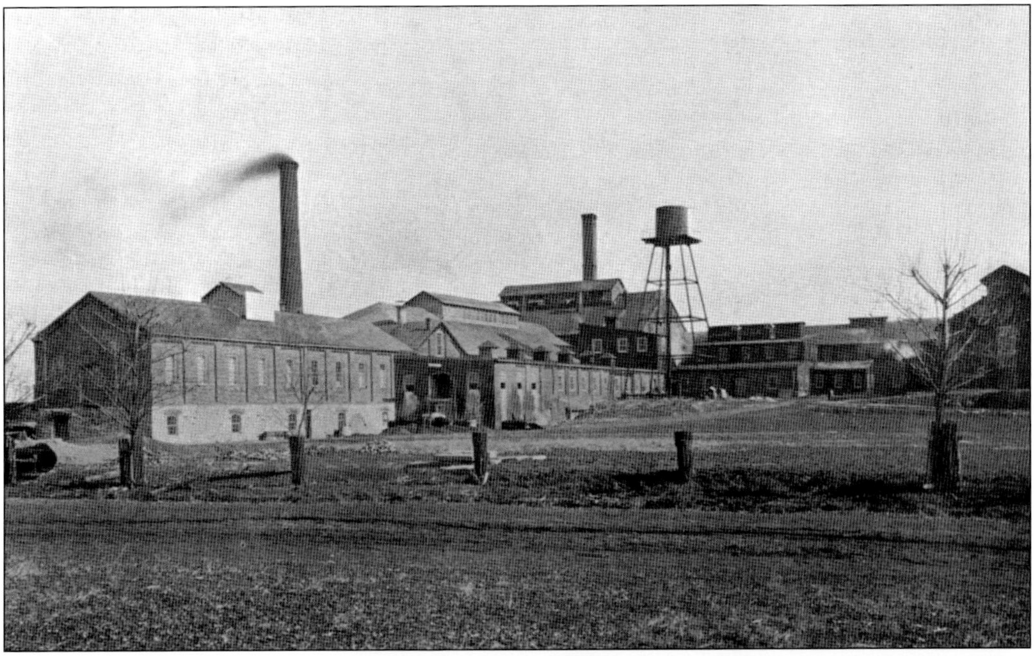

This view, also from 1902, shows the Jessup and Moore Pulp Works on the Brandywine, which was famed for the quality of paper produced there. (Courtesy personal collection.)

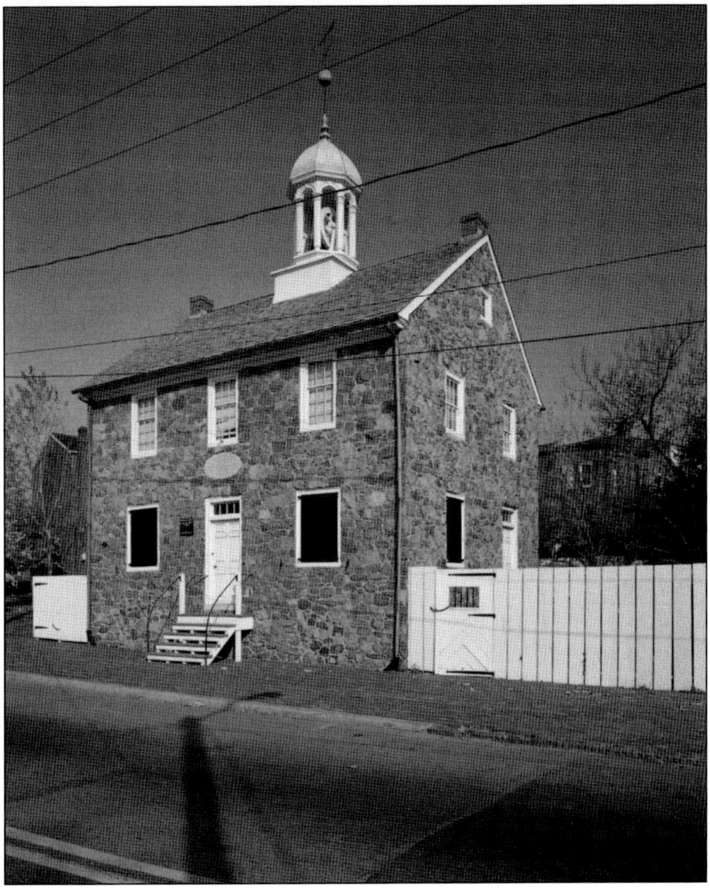

The Old Brandywine Academy at 5 Vandever Avenue was founded in 1796 after the land was purchased from Delaware senator John Dickinson. It was originally a school and later became a branch of the Wilmington Free Library. The wheel-bell cupola was added in 1820, and it rang joyfully when Lafayette returned for a triumphant visit in 1824. (Courtesy National Register of Historic Places, National Park Service.)

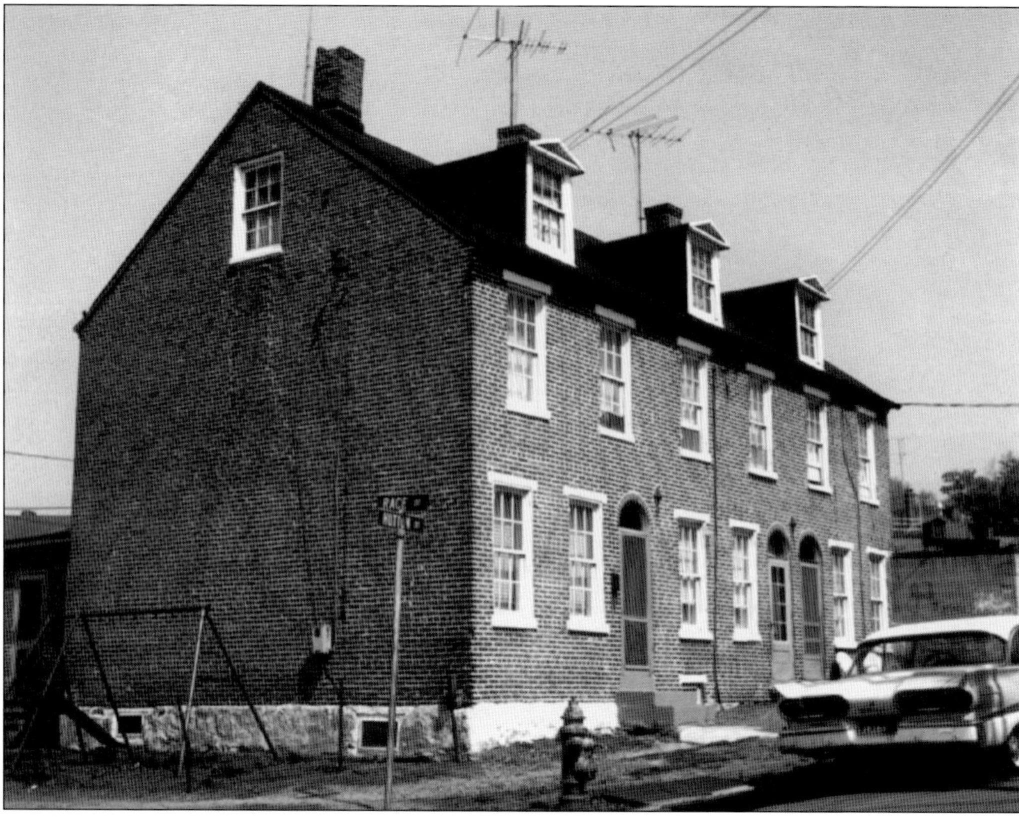

Workers' housing dominates the side streets in Brandywine Village. The opposite side of Market Street is lined with small stores and other commercial activities housed within the walls of the old shops and homes of the less affluent members of the mill community, some of brick and some of frame construction. Store fronts and signs of the last century have, in general, obscured the original buildings. However, in many instances, second-story windows and pitched roofs above the first stories attest to the former character of the row. The workers were mostly employed in the mills, which were located an easy walk from their homes. Cooper Street is above, Buena Vista Street below. (Both, courtesy National Register of Historic Places, National Park Service.)

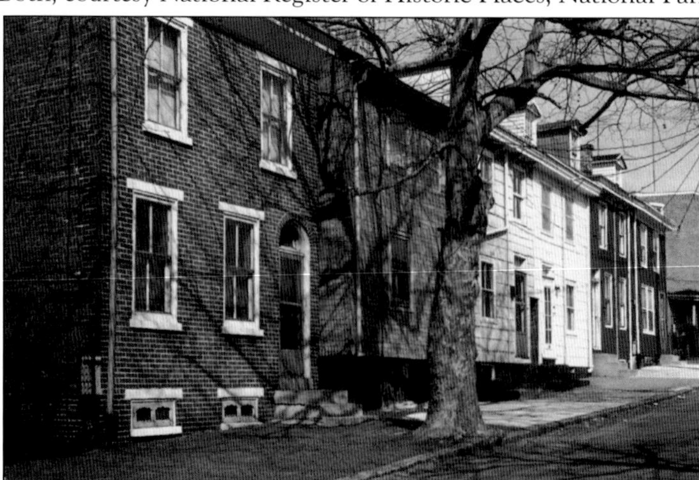

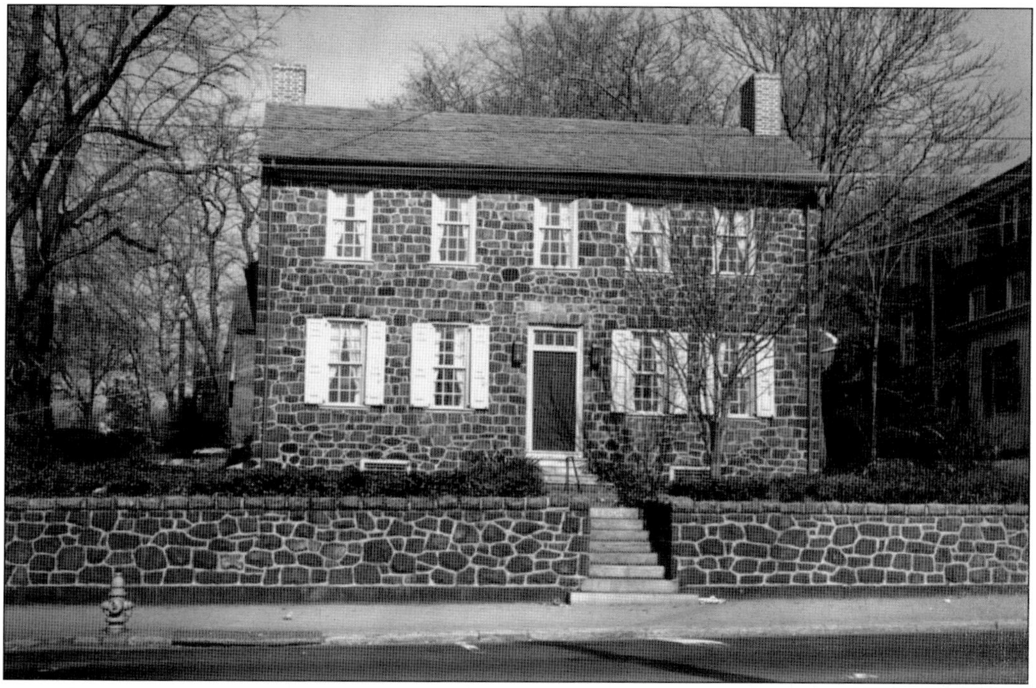

The Derrickson House—at 1801 North Market Street, along a row of other fine stone, 18th-century mill owners' houses—was built about 1771 by James Marshall and named after Jacob Derrickson, a descendant of the original Swedes who settled Wilmington. The house is built in the Greek Revival style. (Courtesy National Register of Historic Places, National Park Service.)

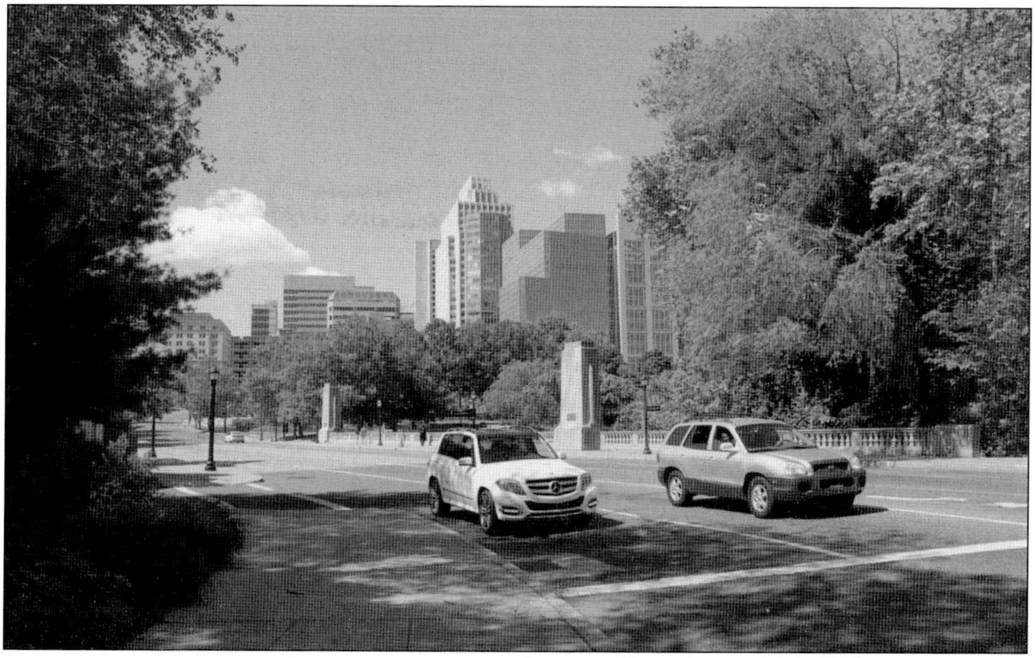

The current concrete Market Street Bridge, is a three-span, 213-foot-long steel girder bridge with cantilevered end spans, dating to 1928. It is considered eligible for the National Register of Historic Places because it was designed by a notable engineering firm. (Courtesy personal collection.)

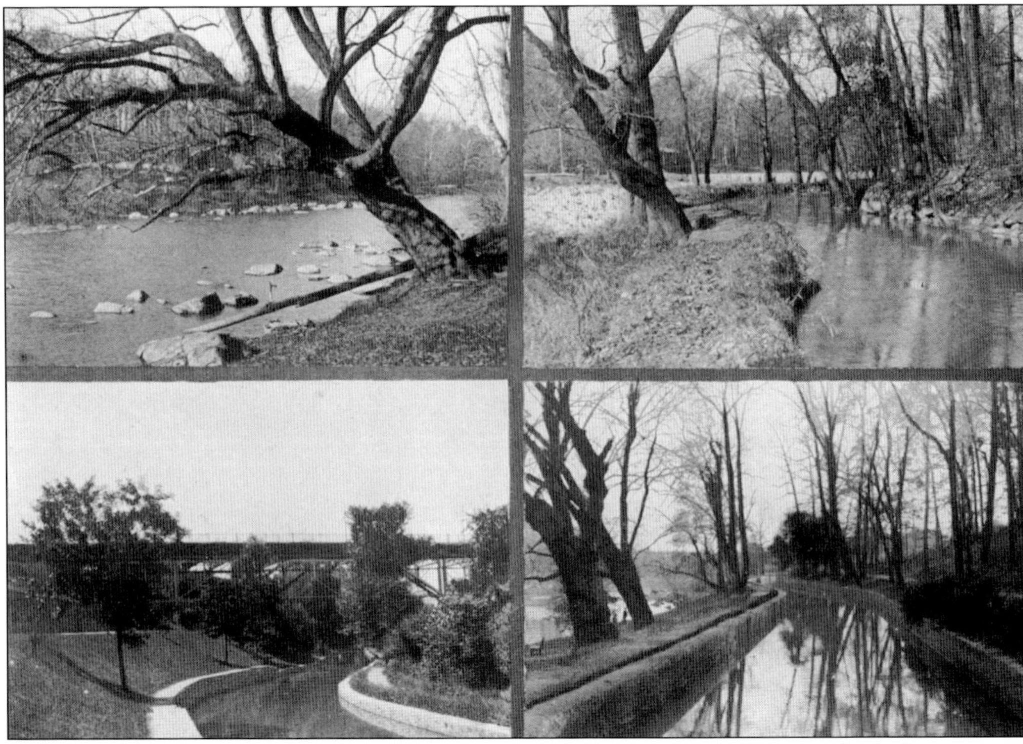

These four views, from 1902, show the Brandywine River Park after it had been developed into a scenic escape for the residents of the city. (Courtesy personal collection.)

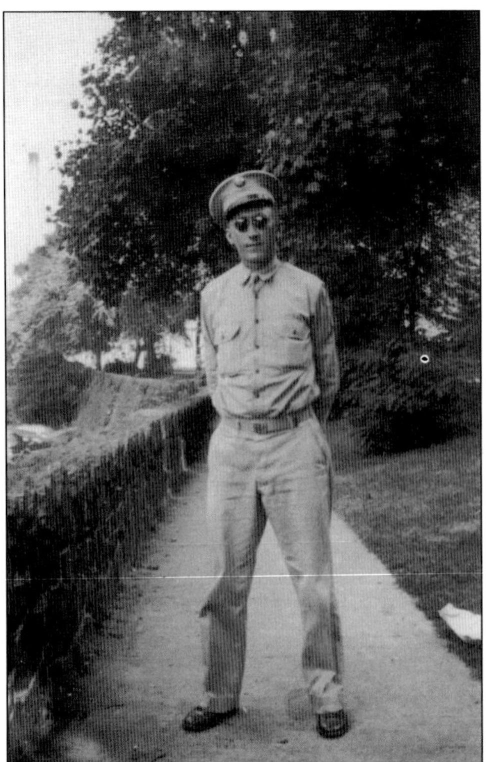

This soldier, stationed in Delaware during World War II, is seen visiting Brandywine Park. (Courtesy personal collection.)

Three

Wilmington

The first Swedish settlement of what is now Wilmington occurred in 1638, when Peter Minuit landed at the "Rocks" just west of the Amtrak Train Station. Minuit built Fort Christina there, naming the fort and the adjacent river after the current queen of Sweden. A small Swedish community of settlers grew up around the fort.

In 1655, Dutch governor Stuyvesant captured the fort and changed its name to Fort Altena. It remained in Dutch control for a short time, but the English, under the Duke of York, claimed the entire region for England and thereafter pushed the Dutch and Swedish settlers farther inland. Near Stanton, an early town called Bread and Cheese Island was first settled by these Scandinavians around 1683 after they were pushed inland.

Little happened until 1730, when Andrew Justison laid out a town on the banks of the Christina River. It developed slowly and came under the control of his son-in-law Thomas Willing. Willing began to call the area Willing's Town and that became Wilmington. By 1735, there was a small community of 15 or 20 houses, mostly along Market and Second Streets. To the north of Brandywine Creek, Brandywine Village also became an important milling center in the 18th century.

Wilmington grew throughout the 18th century to become an important town, with its focus on shipbuilding and commerce. The Old Post Road runs through the center of town, where it is now called Market Street, and then turns west as Front Street and Lancaster Avenue before it turns south again as Maryland Avenue. Thus, many of the oldest and most important landmarks along the Old Post Road in Wilmington are central to the community.

In the city of Wilmington, Philadelphia Pike becomes Market Street and crosses the Brandywine River on the Brandywine River Bridge. The Old Post Road runs along Market Street and then turns west along what is now Martin Luther King Boulevard. At Interstate 95, the road turns south again as Maryland Avenue.

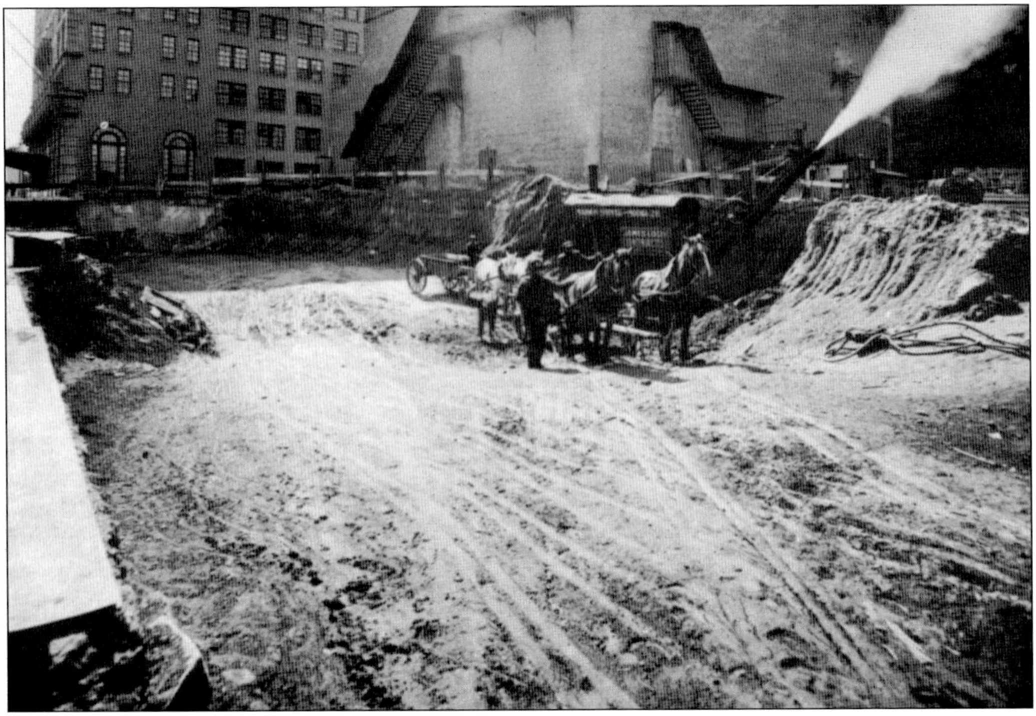

The DuPont Building on Market Street was under construction in 1917. The playhouse is at the right. This part of the construction extended the building to Orange Street. (Courtesy personal collection.)

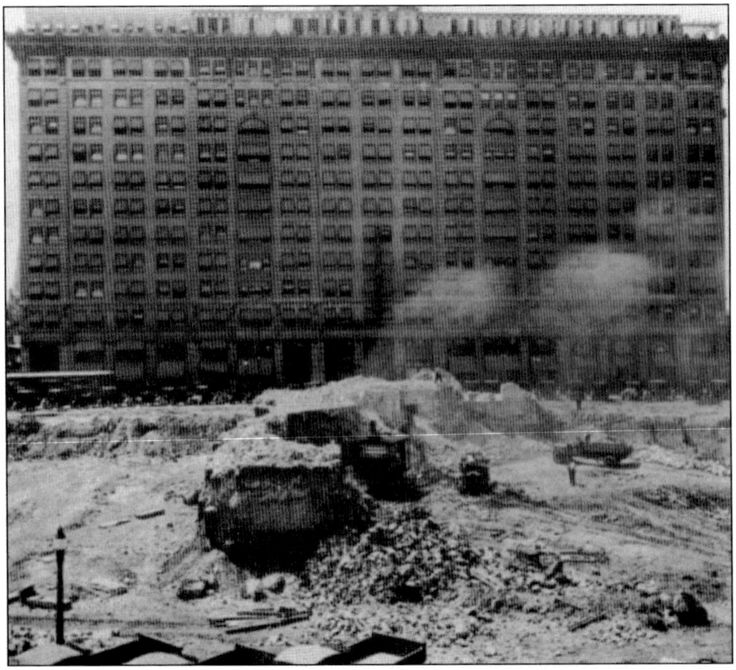

This is Rodney Square while it was under construction in 1920. The square was completed the following year. (Courtesy personal collection.)

This aerial view of the north part of Market Street and King Street was taken in 1940. The DuPont Building dominates the skyline. (Courtesy personal collection.)

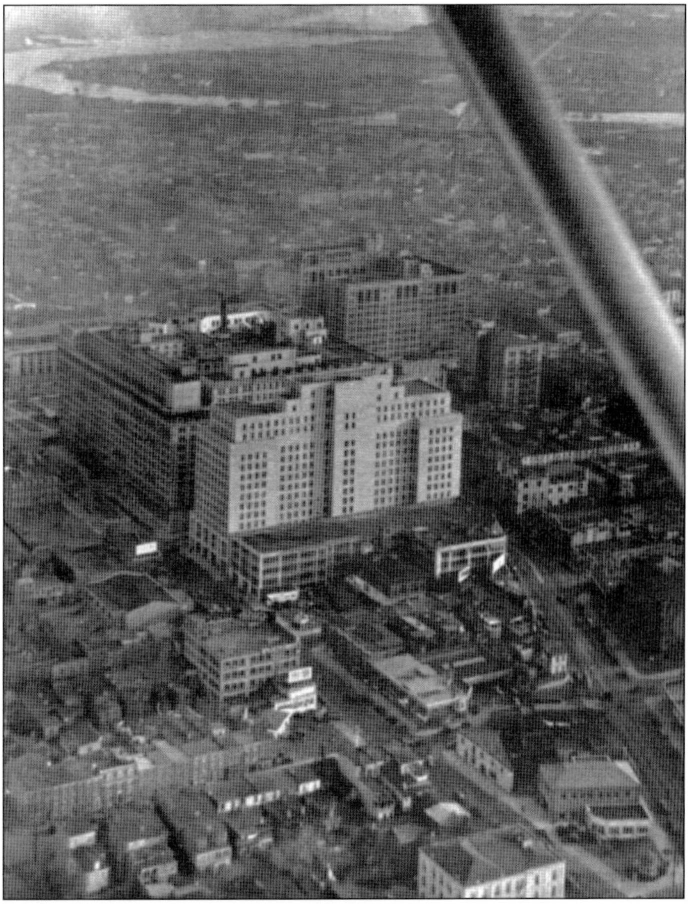

This postcard from the 1940s shows Rodney Square and the Delaware Trust Company Building, constructed in 1921 in the Classic Revival style. The Market Street facade is reminiscent of ancient Roman buildings. William DuPont, president of the Delaware Trust Company in the 1930s, had a secret exit out of his office and was known to often sneak out in the middle of the day to go duck hunting. (Courtesy personal collection.)

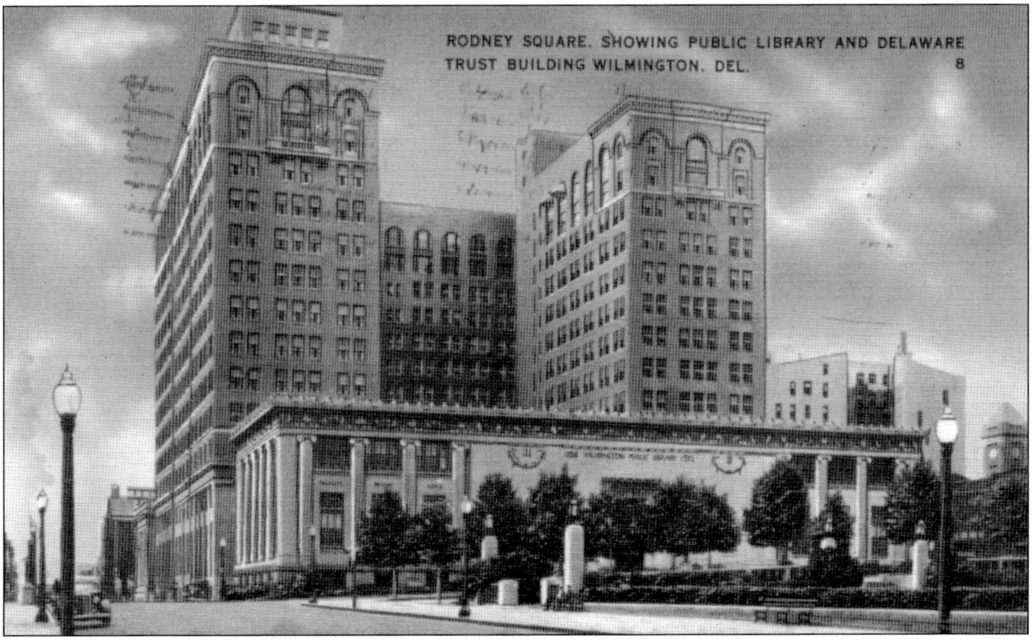

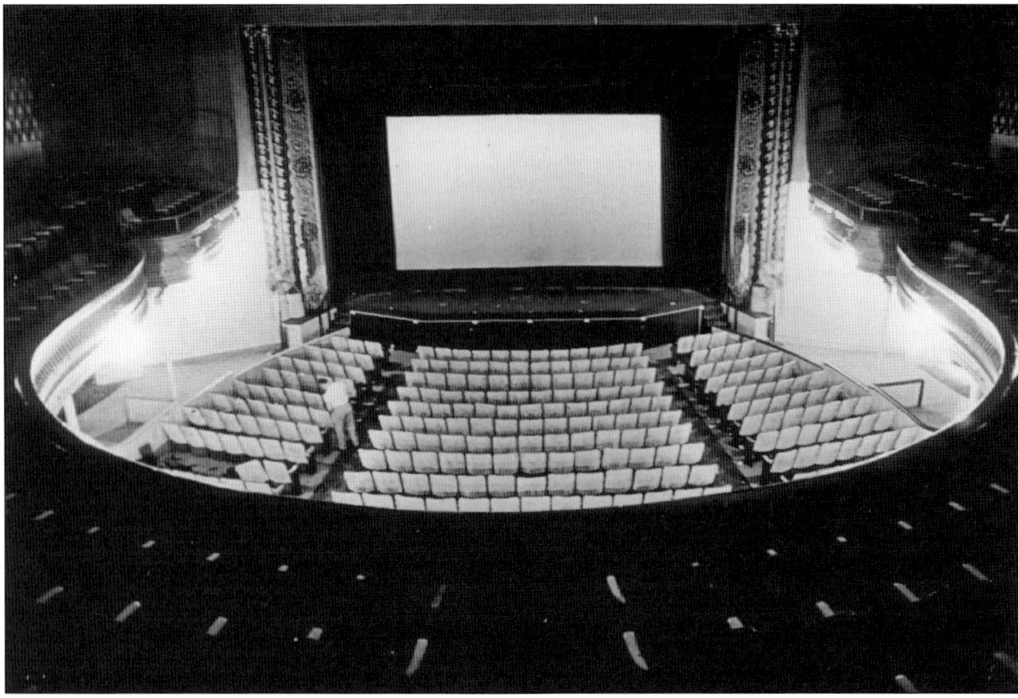

The Delaware Grand Lodge became a theater and hosted Victorian melodramas, minstrel shows, burlesque, and vaudeville. Among the performers on this stage were Ethel Barrymore, "Buffalo Bill" Cody, and John Philip Sousa. It was used as a movie theater from 1930 to 1967, and it was later the home of the Delaware Symphony Orchestra. (Courtesy National Register of Historic Places, National Park Service.)

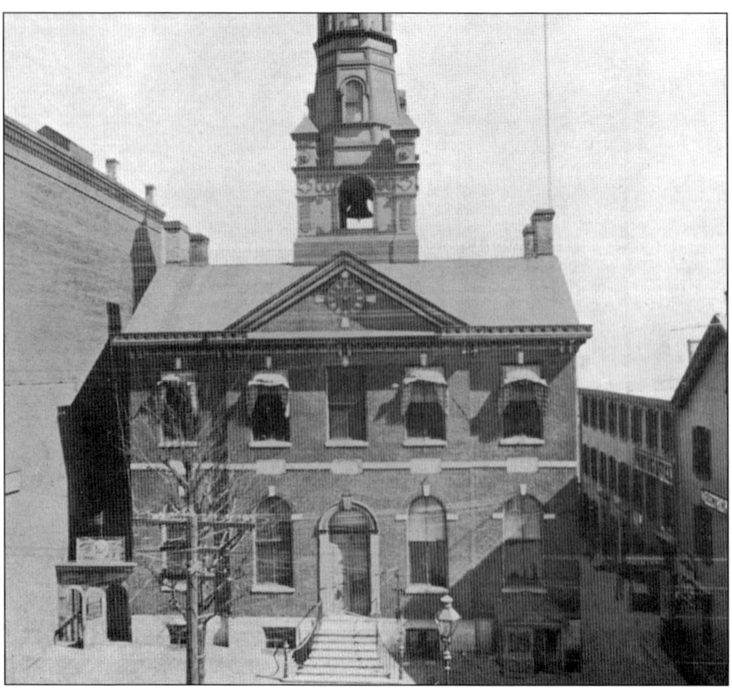

This photograph is of the old city hall, built in 1798 and shown here in 1902. After the new city hall was constructed, this building was turned over to the Historical Society of Delaware, and it is still used as the society's headquarters. (Courtesy personal collection.)

This imposing structure was the old Wilmington City courthouse, pictured in 1902. It has been replaced by a more modern structure. (Courtesy personal collection.)

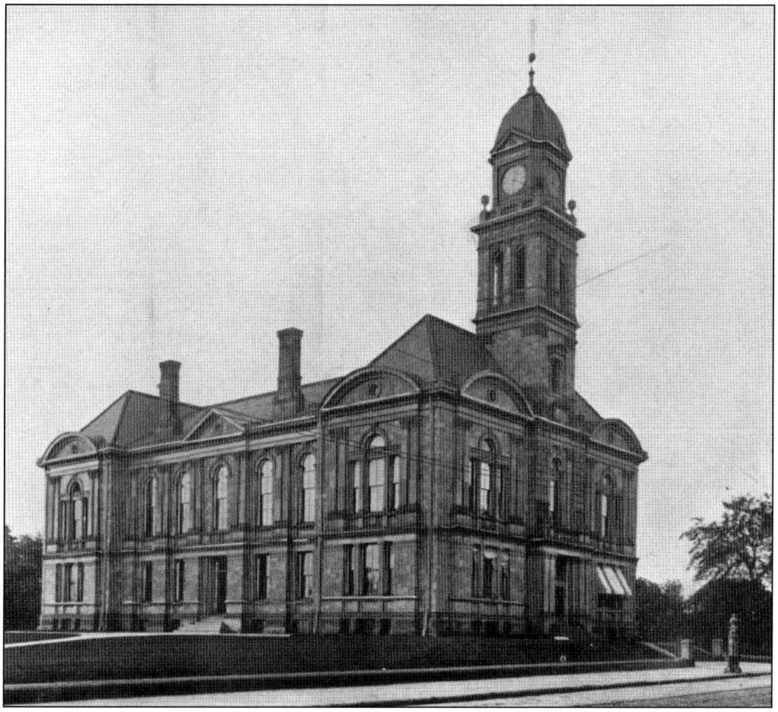

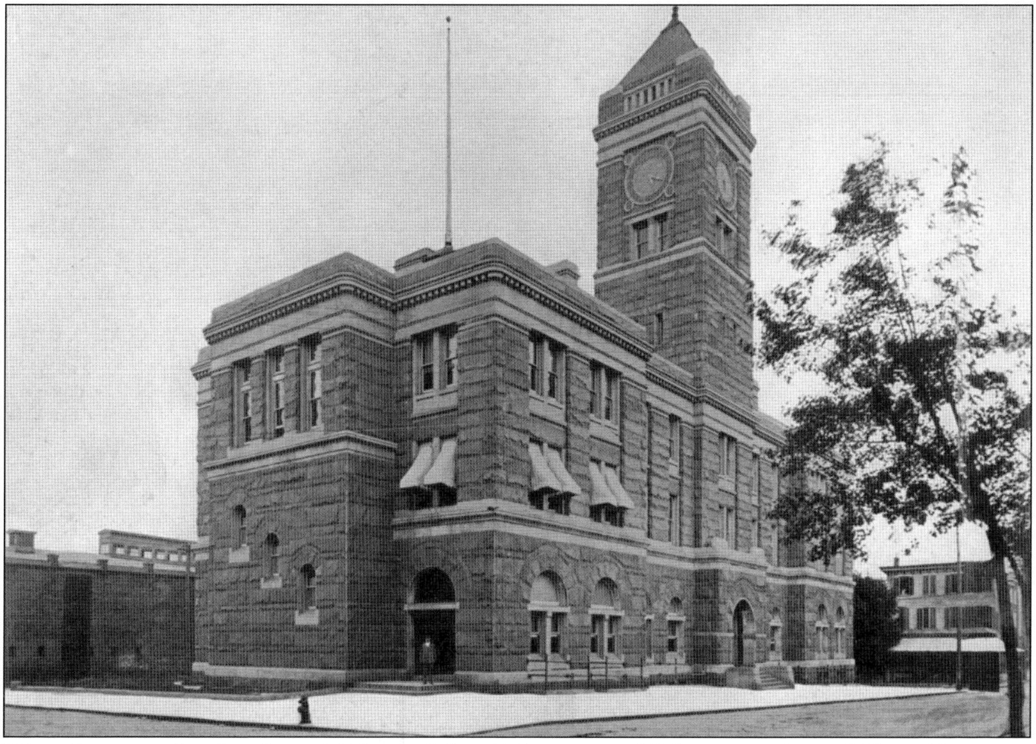

This photograph, also from 1902, is of the 19th-century Wilmington Post Office. (Courtesy personal collection.)

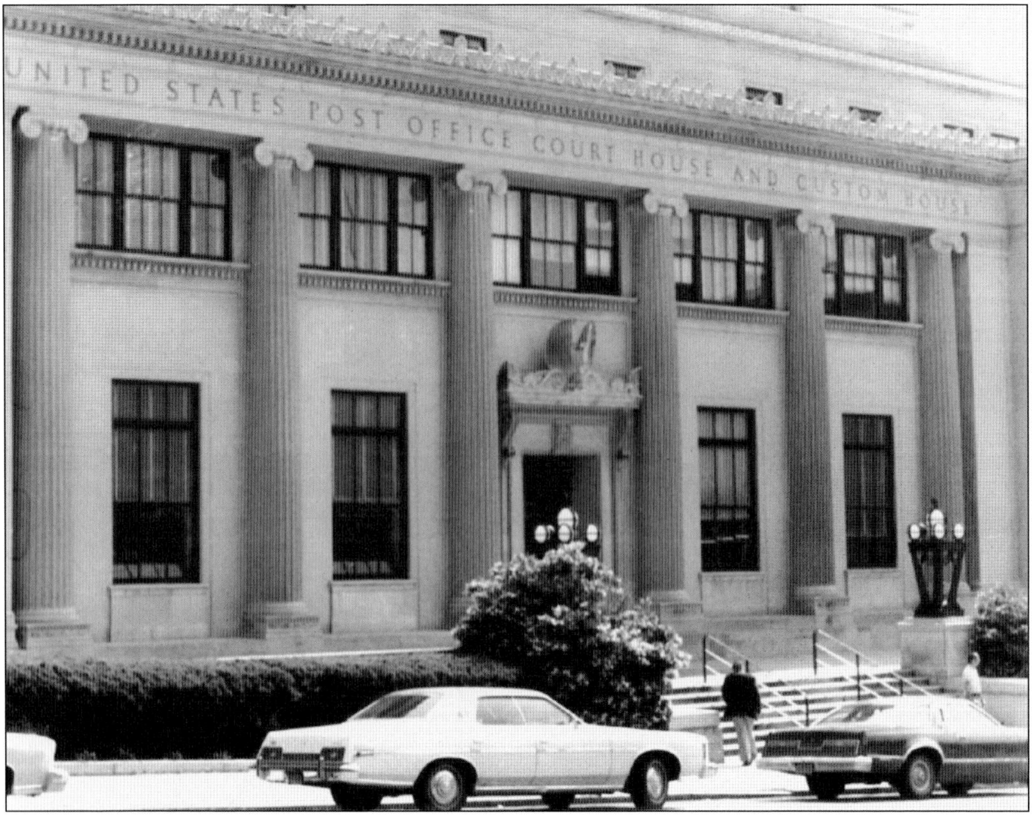

The new city hall, at Eleventh and Market Streets, also operated as the post office and customs house. It was designed by Irwin & Leighton between 1933 and 1935, and construction was completed in 1937. It is in the Classical Revival style. It is a three-story, cut-stone structure with six large stone pillars across the main entrance. The gross building area is 104,669 square feet. (Courtesy National Register of Historic Places, National Park Service.)

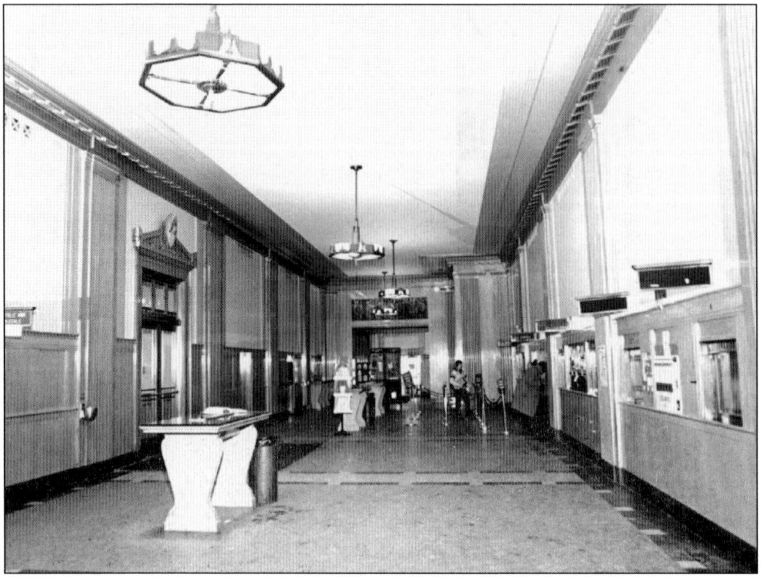

The lobby of city hall was decorated in richly carved woods, tiled floors, and chandelier lighting. It now serves as Wilmington Trust headquarters. (Courtesy National Register of Historic Places, National Park Service.)

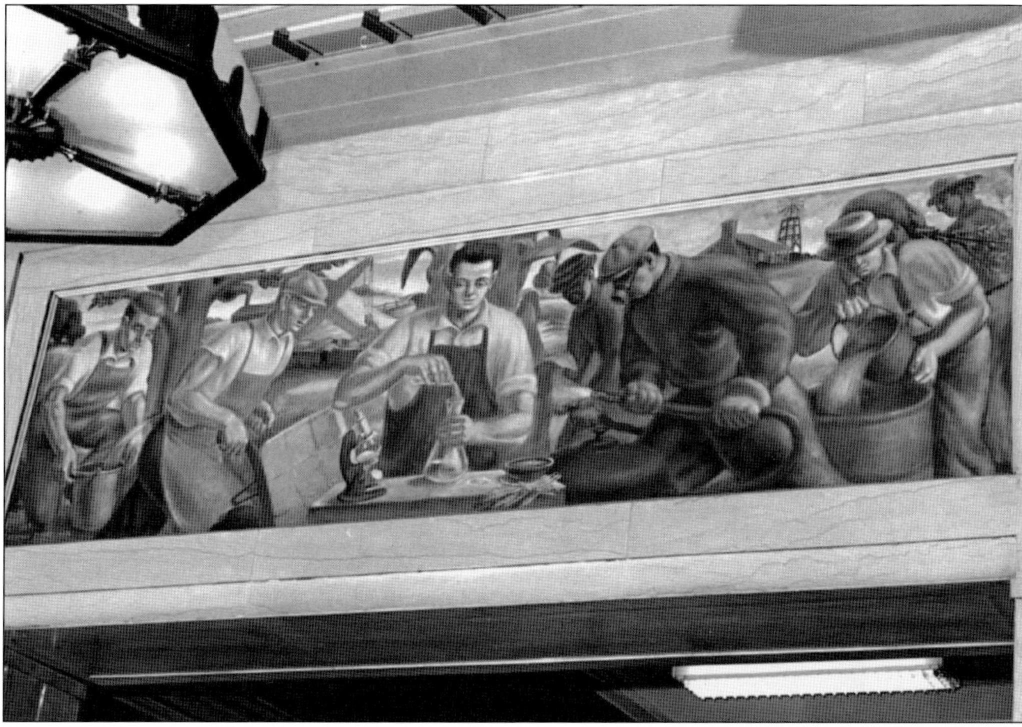

The courthouse was decorated with murals painted by artists under contract with the Works Progress Administration during the Depression. These are two murals that flank either side of the lobby. They pay homage to the fact that Wilmington was the center of the chemical industry at the time. (Both, courtesy National Register of Historic places, National Park Service.)

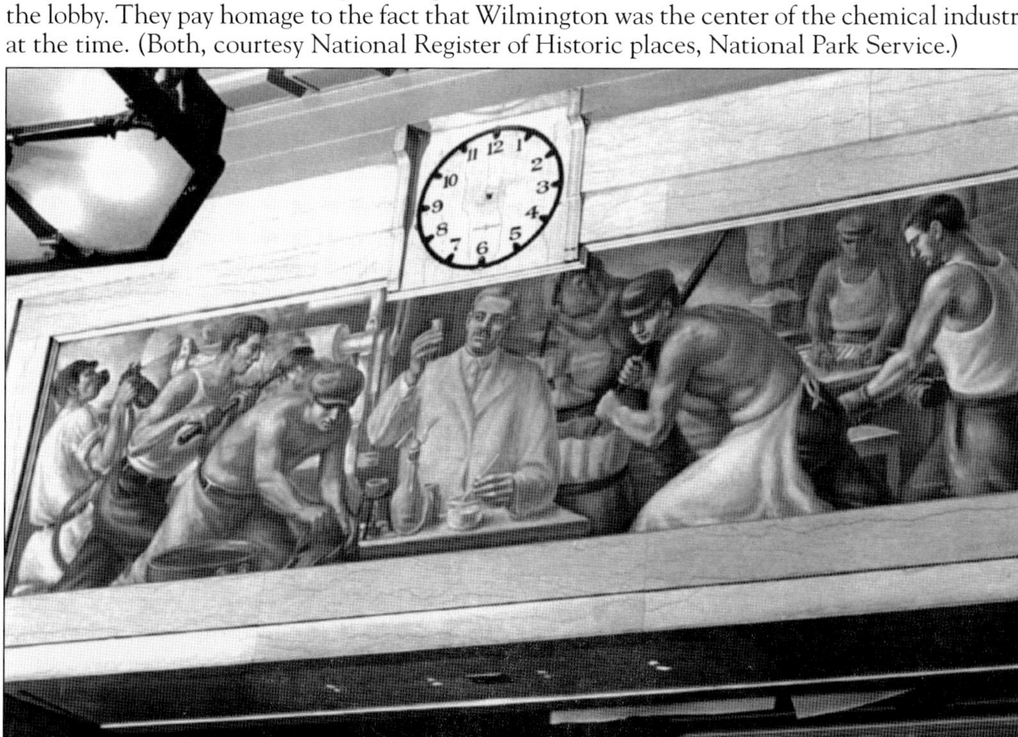

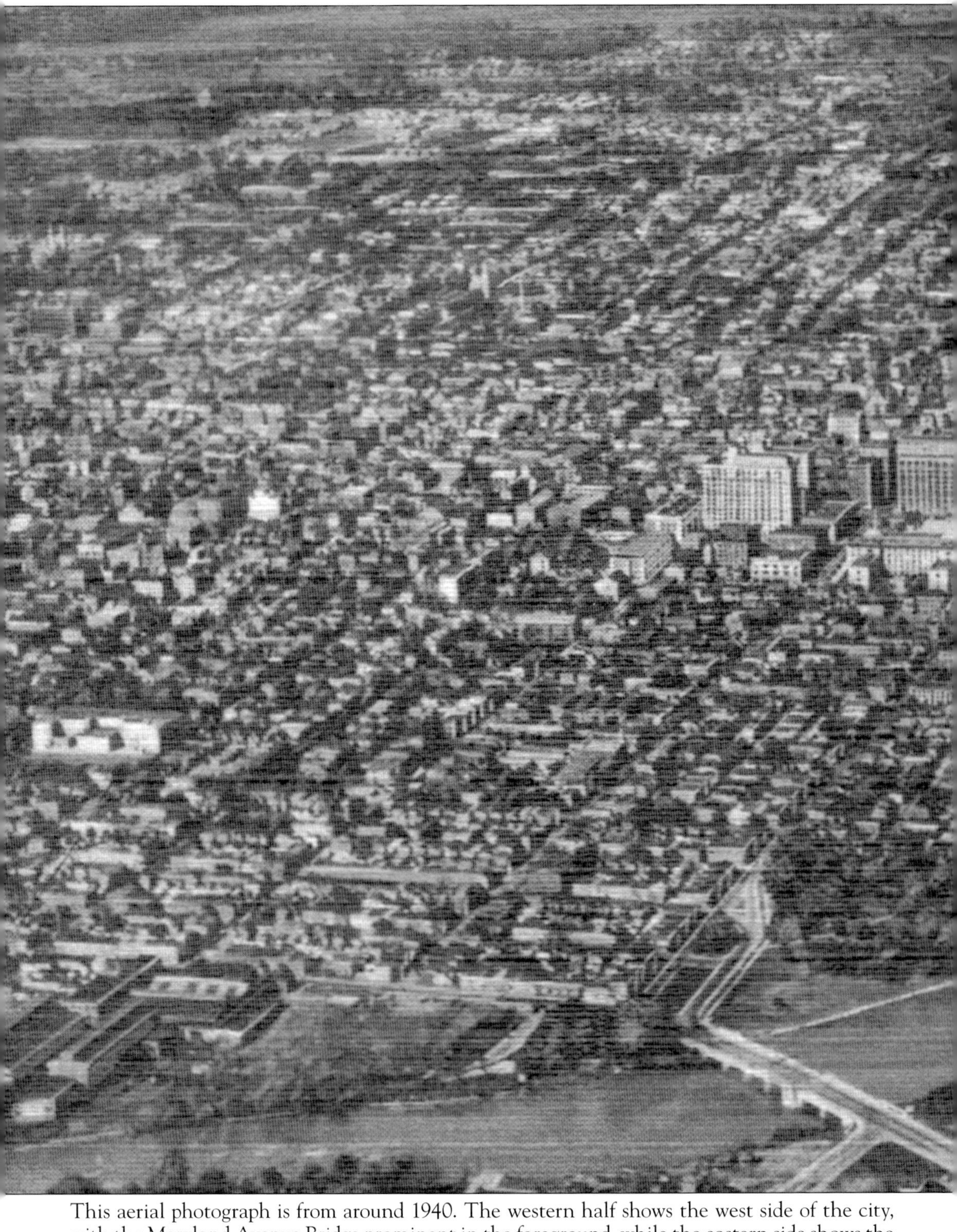

This aerial photograph is from around 1940. The western half shows the west side of the city, with the Maryland Avenue Bridge prominent in the foreground, while the eastern side shows the

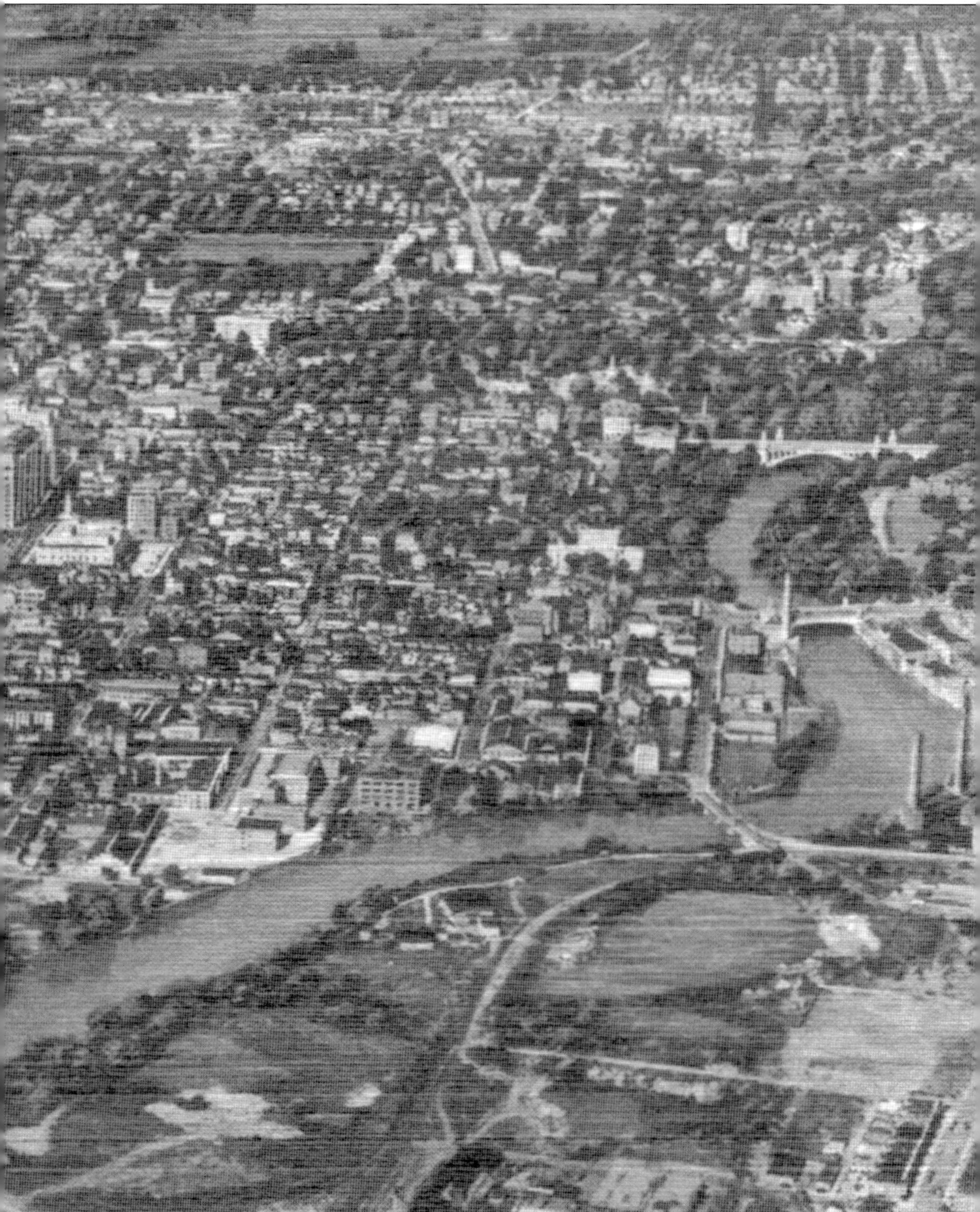

DuPont Highway, Market Street, and Washington Street Bridges spanning the Christina River. (Courtesy personal collection.)

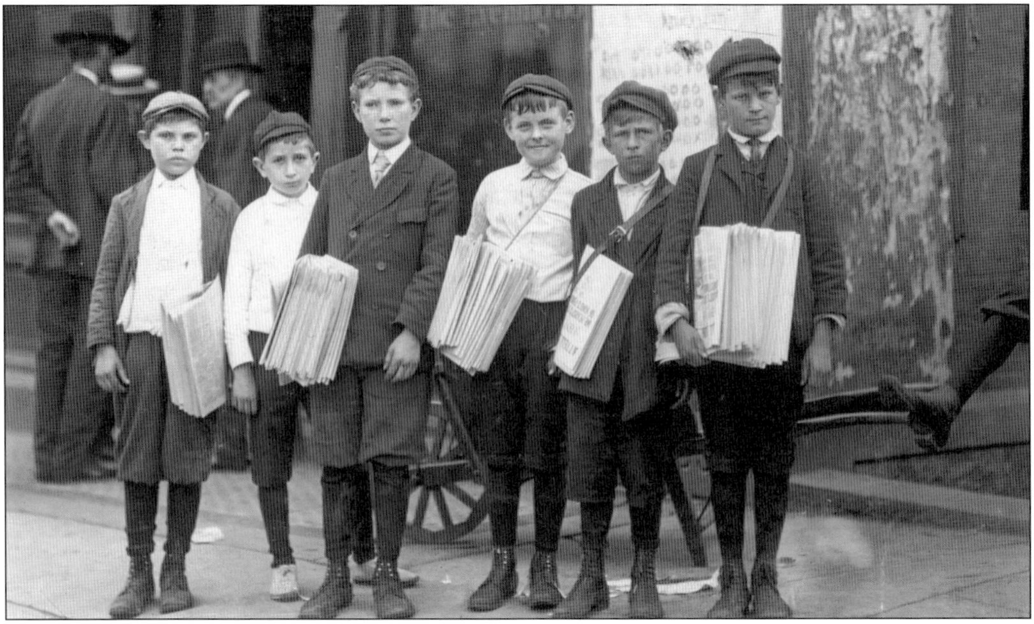

From 1908 to 1912, photographer Lewis Hine documented the condition of child laborers in America, part of the social change that resulted in child labor laws. He visited Wilmington in 1910, shooting a number of photographs of children in working conditions. (Both, courtesy Library of Congress.)

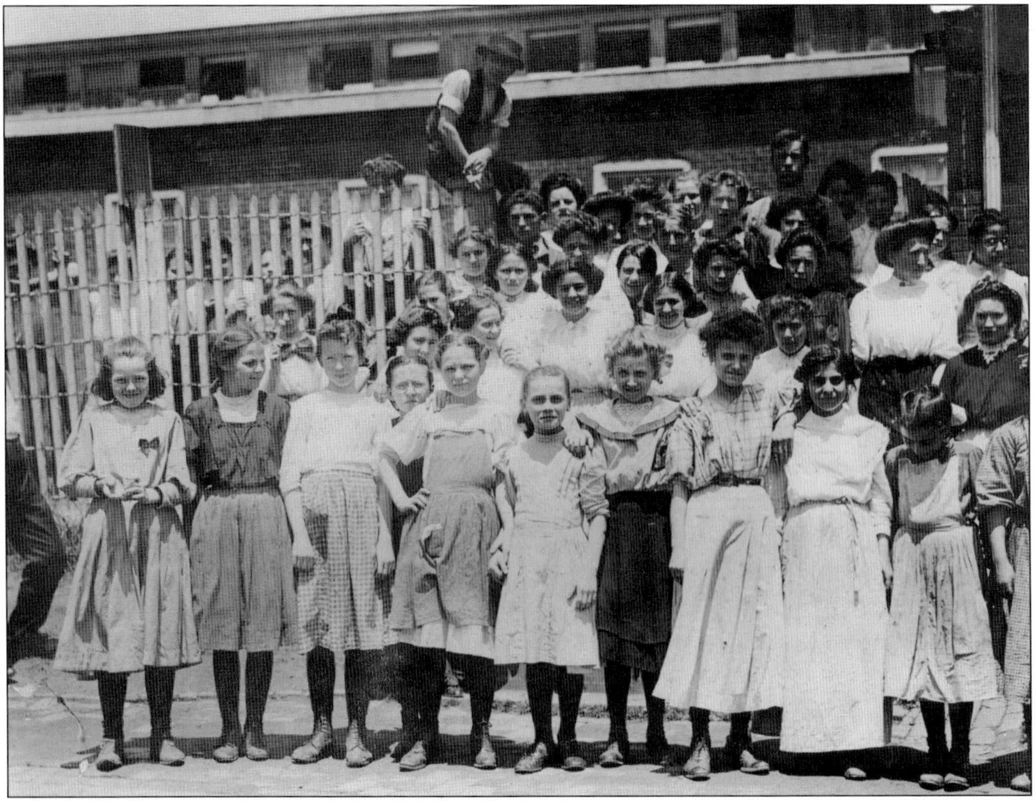

Another of Hines's photographs captured this peanut vendor in Wilmington. (Courtesy Library of Congress.)

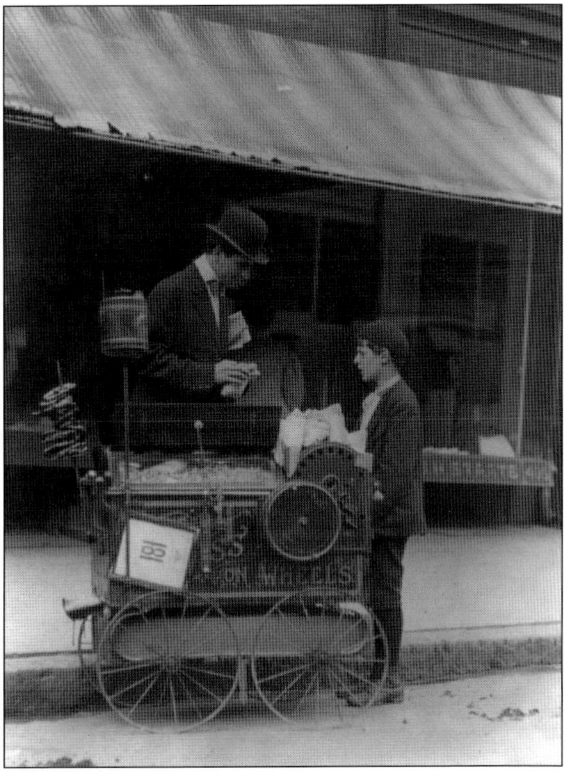

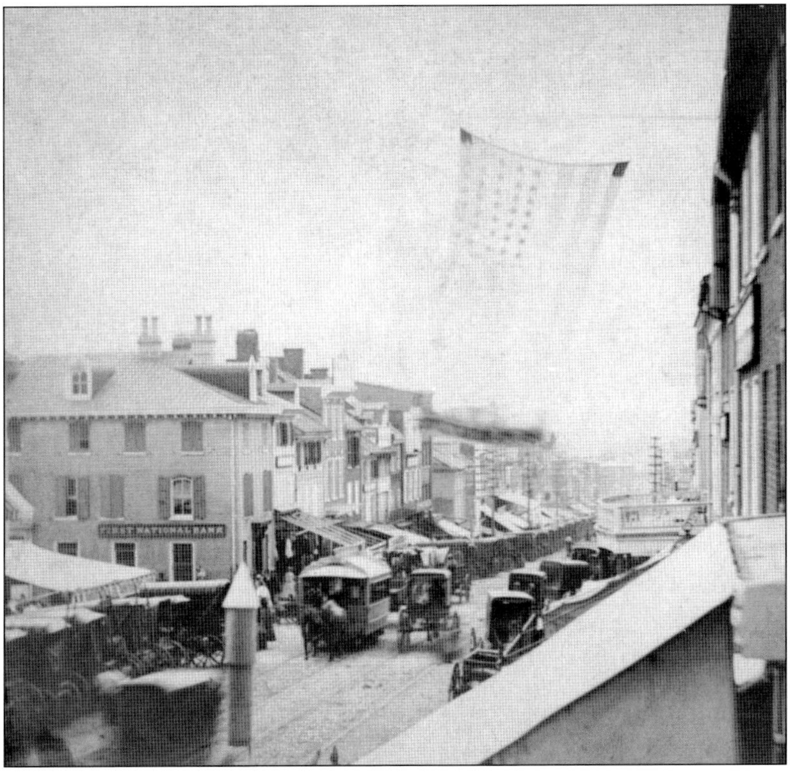

This stereoscopic view of Market Street dates to the late 19th century and shows the hustle and bustle of the city. It includes attached commercial and commercial/residential structures dating from the mid-18th to the early 20th century. Stereoscopic viewers gave people a 3-D view of the subject. (Courtesy National Register of Historic Places, National Park Service.)

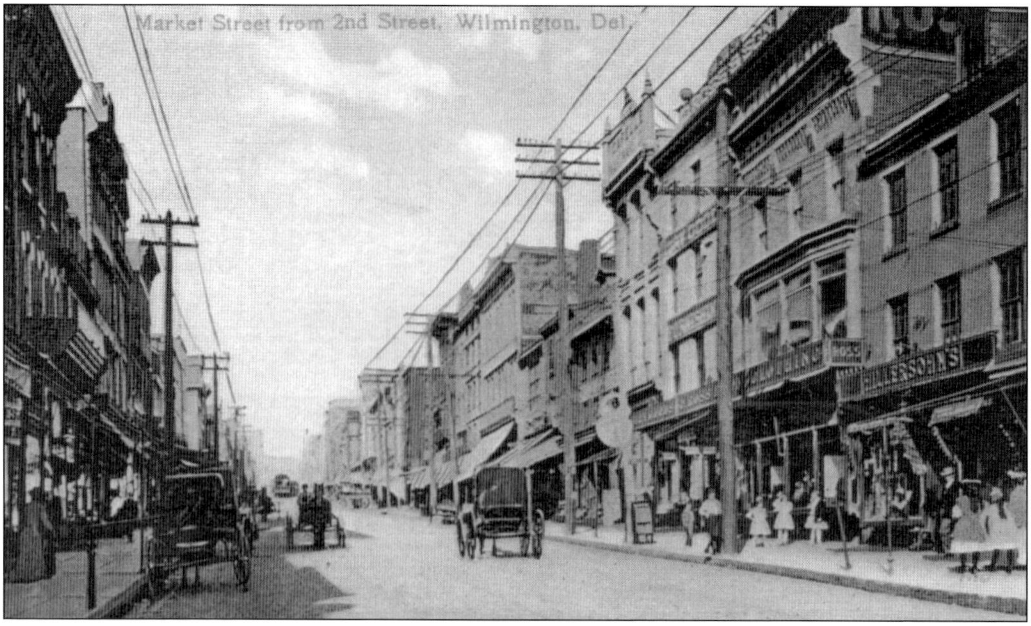

The southern end of Market Street becomes a busy mercantile strip, with rows and rows of closely gathered shops. It went into disarray in the 1970s but has since become revitalized and converted into a walkable brick strip lined with shops and outdoor bistros. The buildings reflect a variety of popular architectural styles, including Classical Revival, Greek Revival, Federal, and Art Deco. This postcard dates to the 1890s. (Courtesy personal collection.)

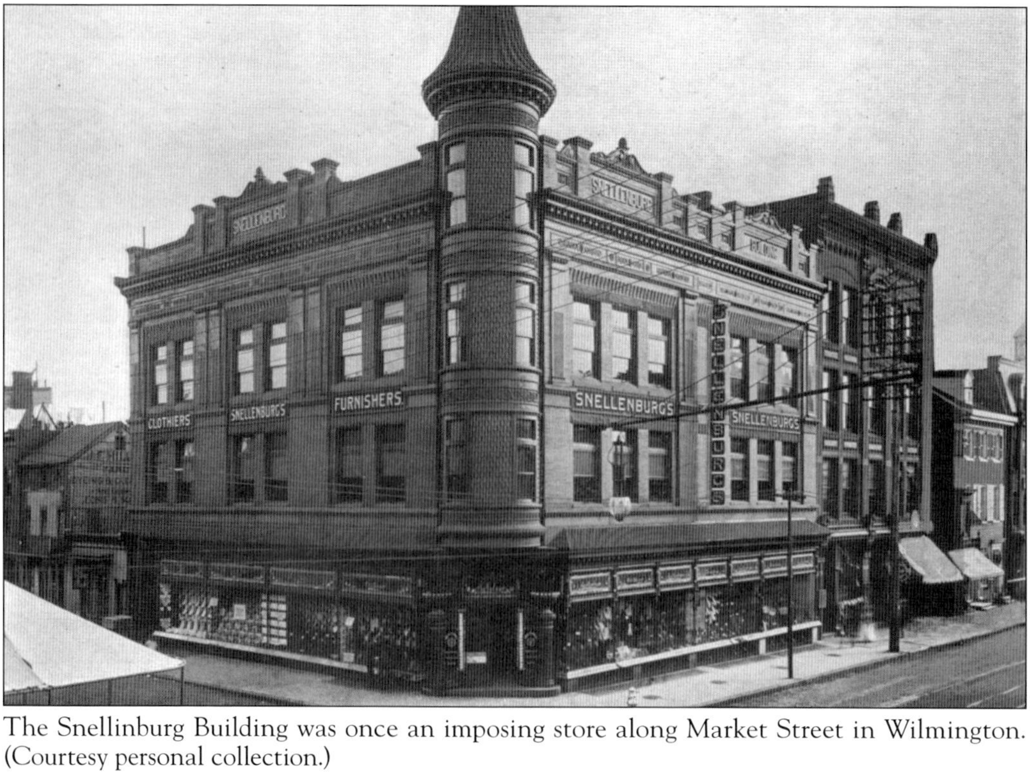

The Snellinburg Building was once an imposing store along Market Street in Wilmington. (Courtesy personal collection.)

The Robelen Piano Company Building on Market Street, as seen in 1902, offered pianos, organs, repairs, and sheet music to the community. (Courtesy personal collection.)

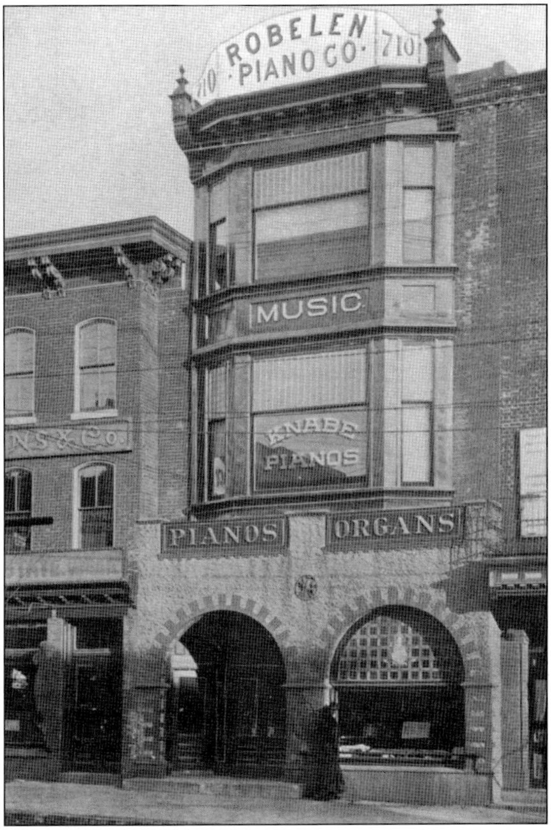

Also from 1902, this image shows that the E.L Peacock Company provided carpets, furniture, and bedding in its massive store on King Street. (Courtesy personal collection.)

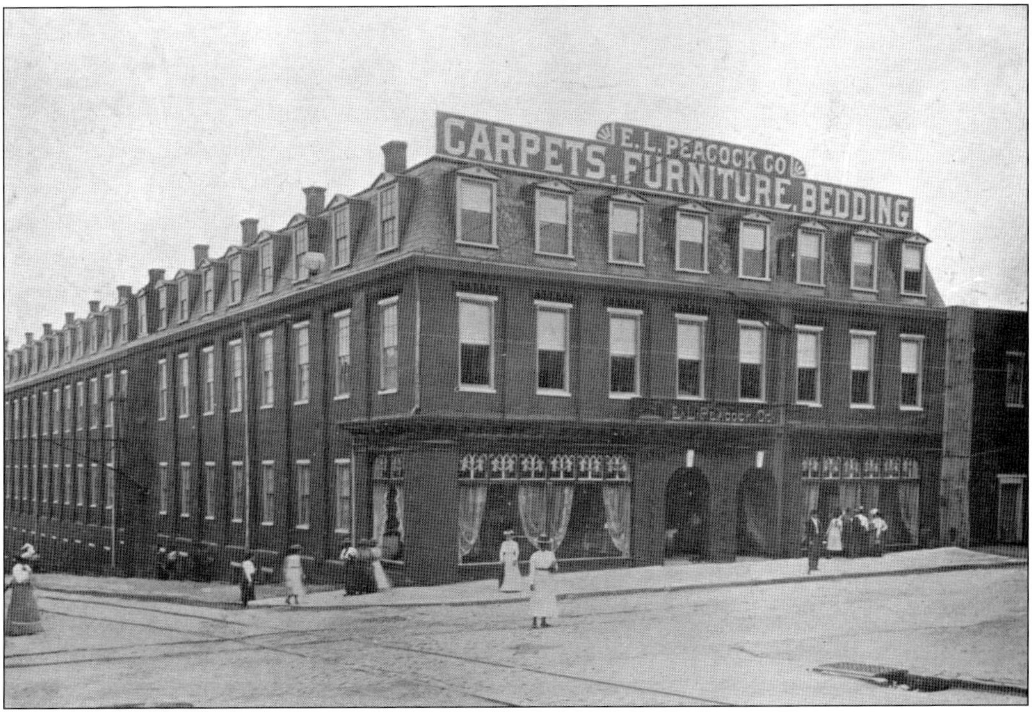

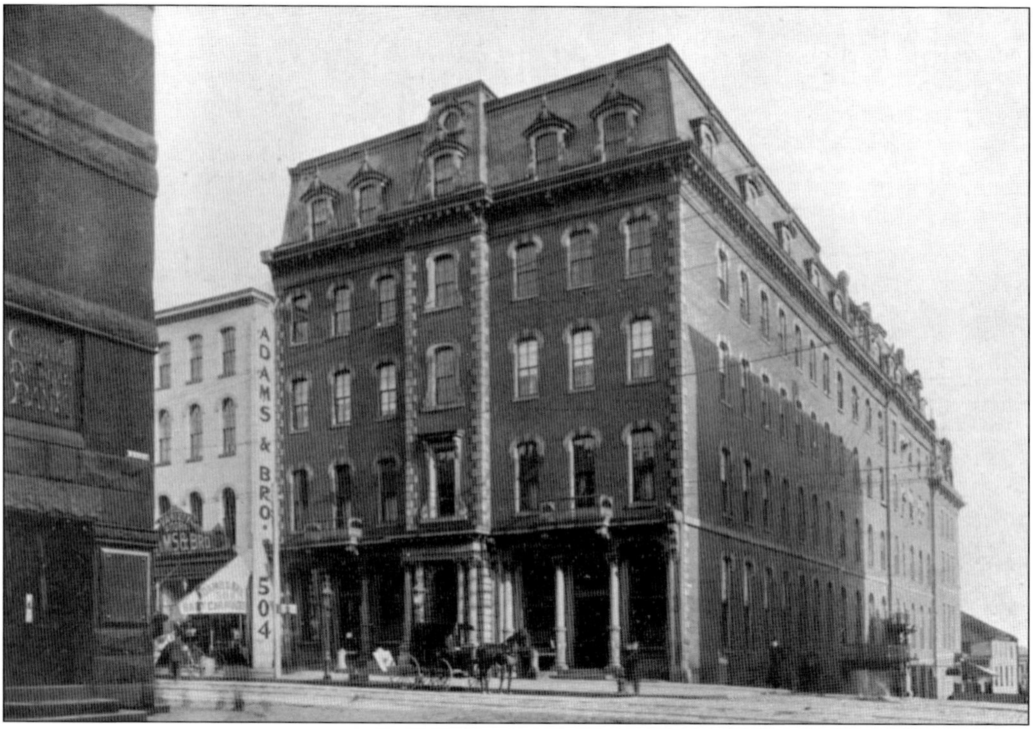

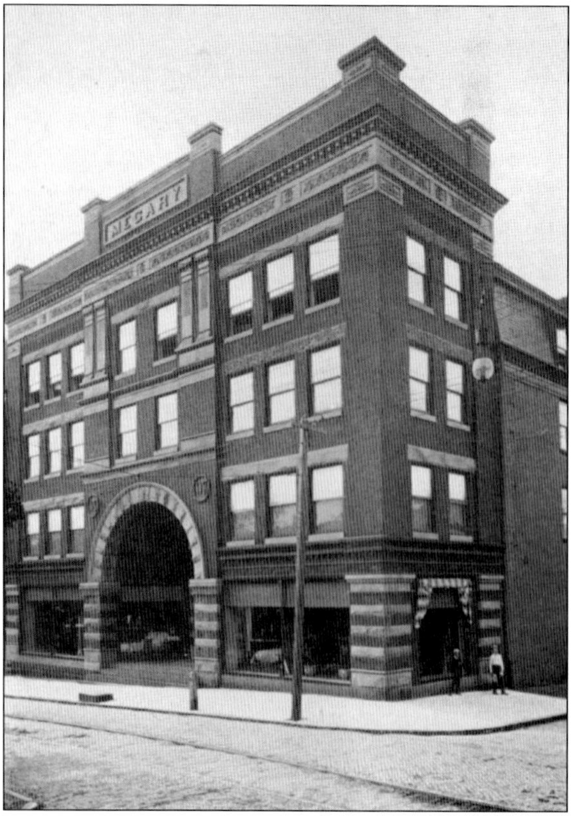

The Clayton House was located at Fifth and Market Streets. It contained stores on the first floor and offices on the other four. (Courtesy personal collection.)

McGary's Furniture Store was located at Sixth and Tatnall Streets and was built with his name on it. (Courtesy personal collection.)

The Equitable Building stood at Ninth and Market Streets and was the home of the Equitable Insurance Company. (Courtesy personal collection.)

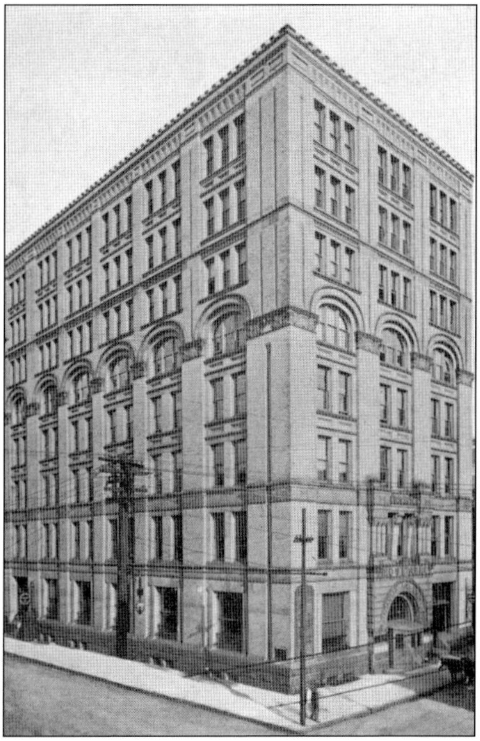

The Diamond State Telephone Company opened a new headquarters at Ninth and Tatnall Streets in July 1928. (Courtesy personal collection.)

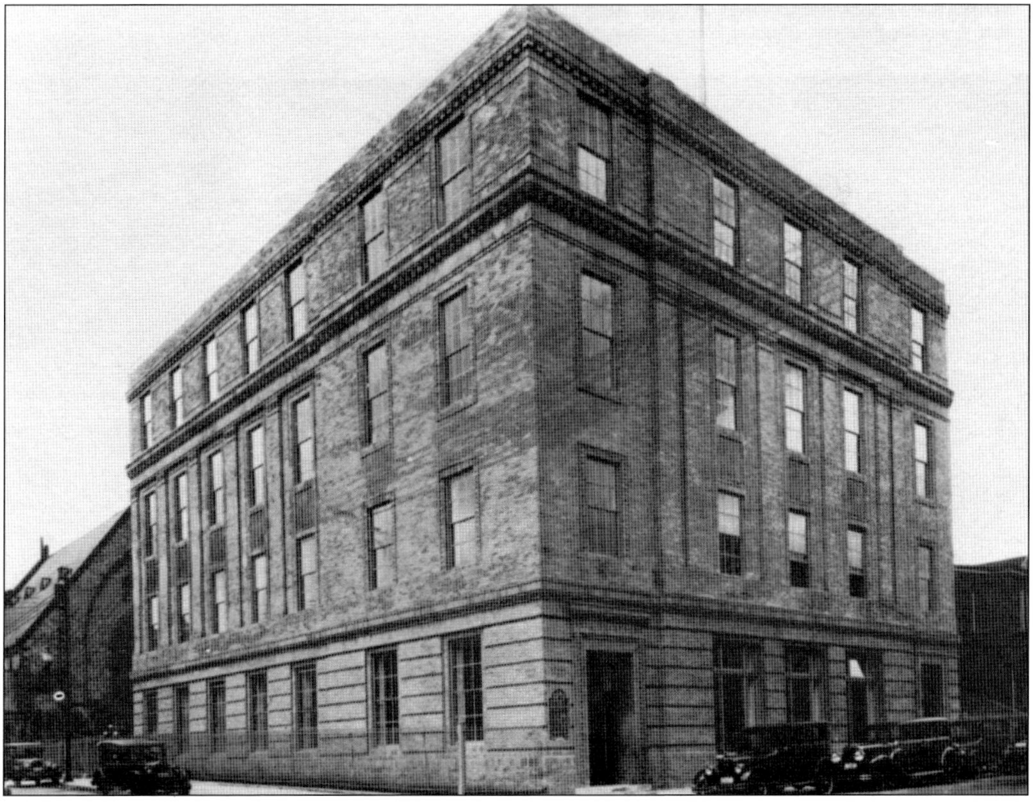

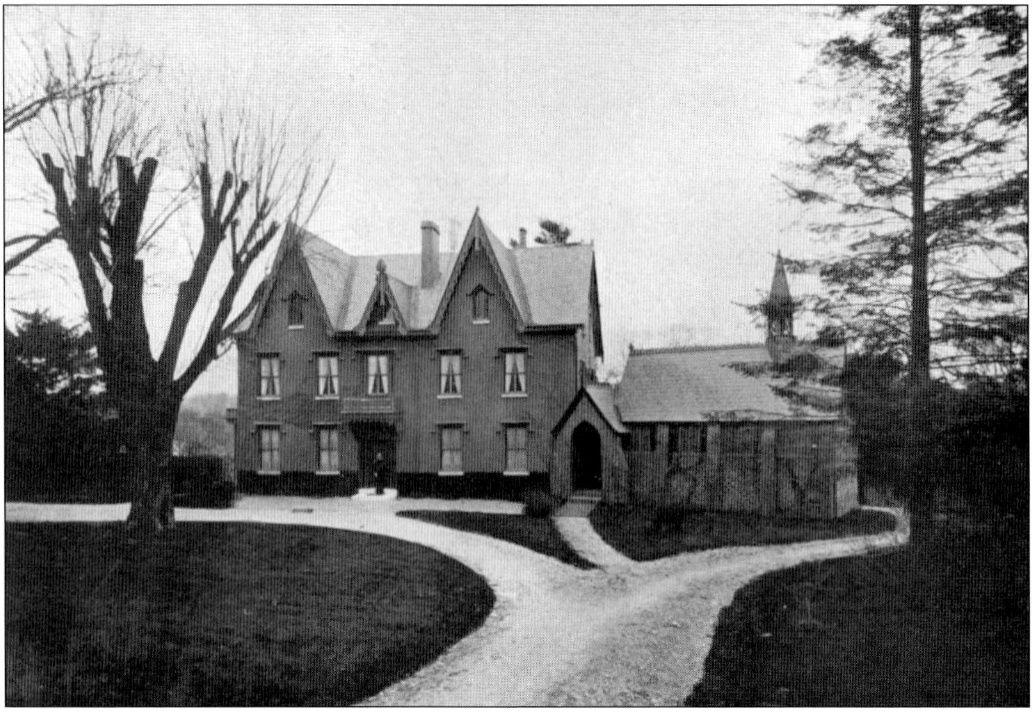

The homes around Victorian Wilmington were as lavish as the businesses. Bishopstead at Fourteenth and Orange Streets, shown here in 1902, was the residence of Bishop Coleman. (Courtesy personal collection.)

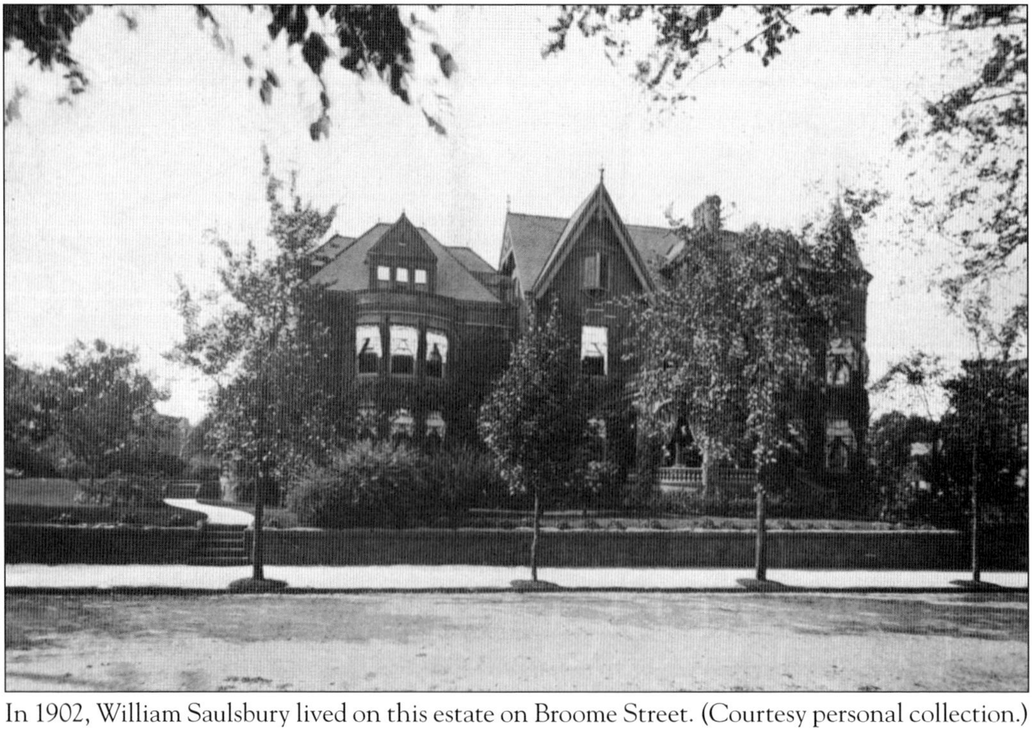

In 1902, William Saulsbury lived on this estate on Broome Street. (Courtesy personal collection.)

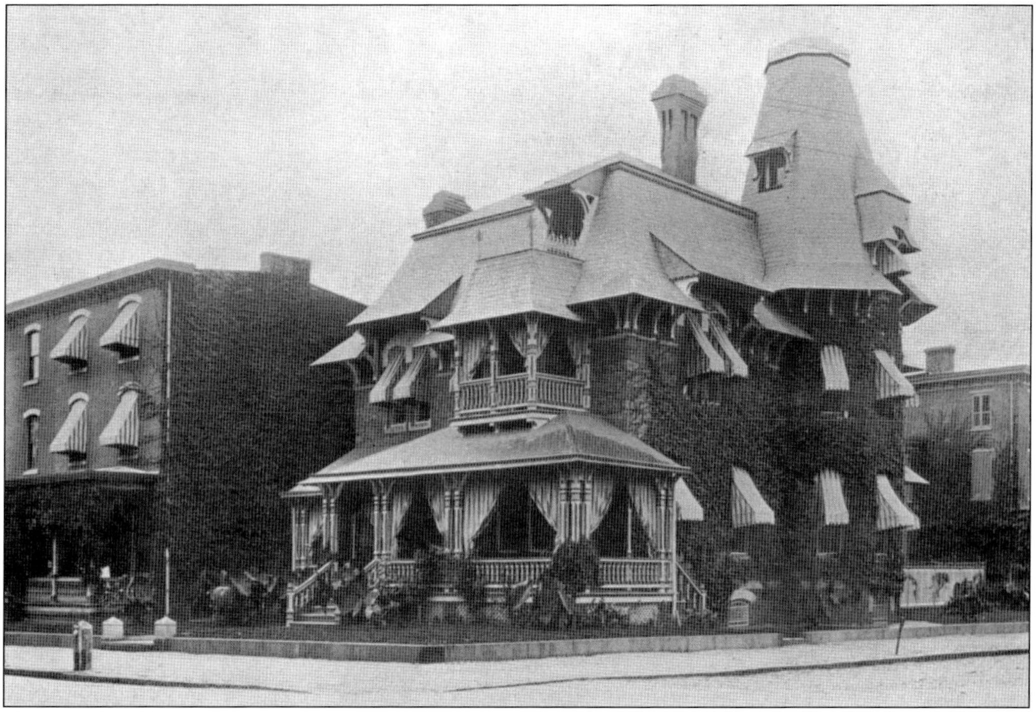

In the same year, Richard Patzowsky lived in a colorful and unique house on the corner of Eleventh and Jefferson Streets. (Courtesy personal collection.)

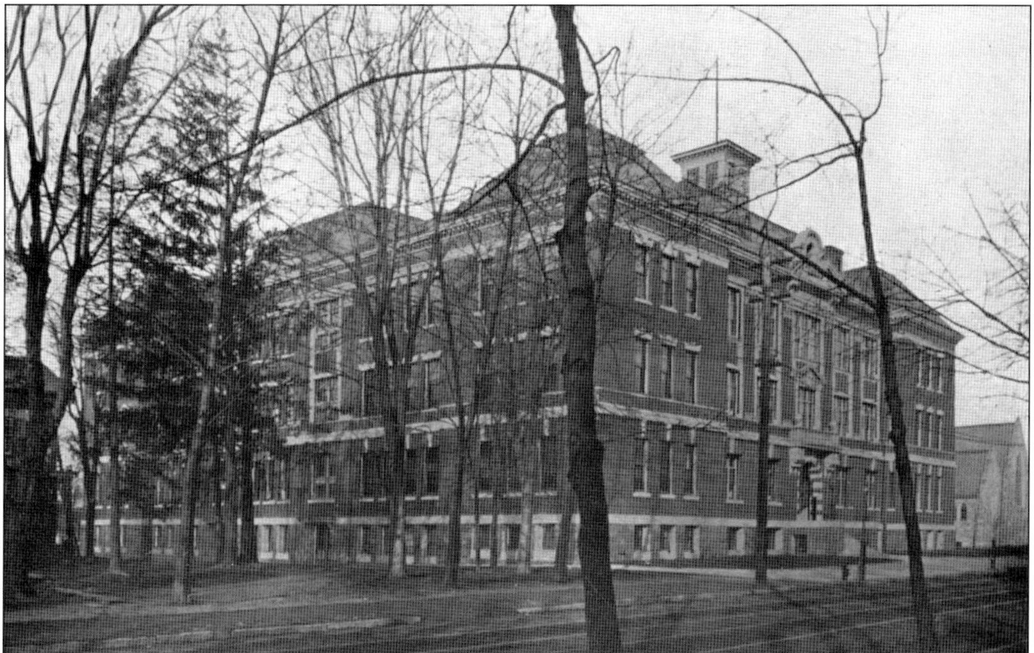

The growth of Wilmington also brought an influx of children. The Wilmington High School was built in 1900 on Delaware Avenue, replacing an earlier one on Eighth Street. (Courtesy personal collection.)

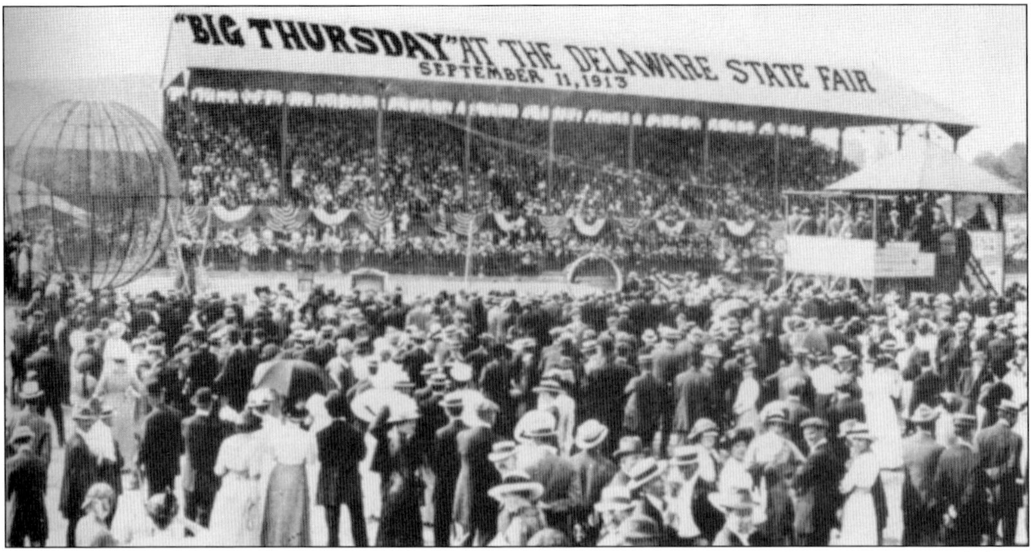

Wilmington was also the center of entertainment. The state fair was held at Wawaset Park long before it was moved down state to Harrington. (Courtesy personal collection.)

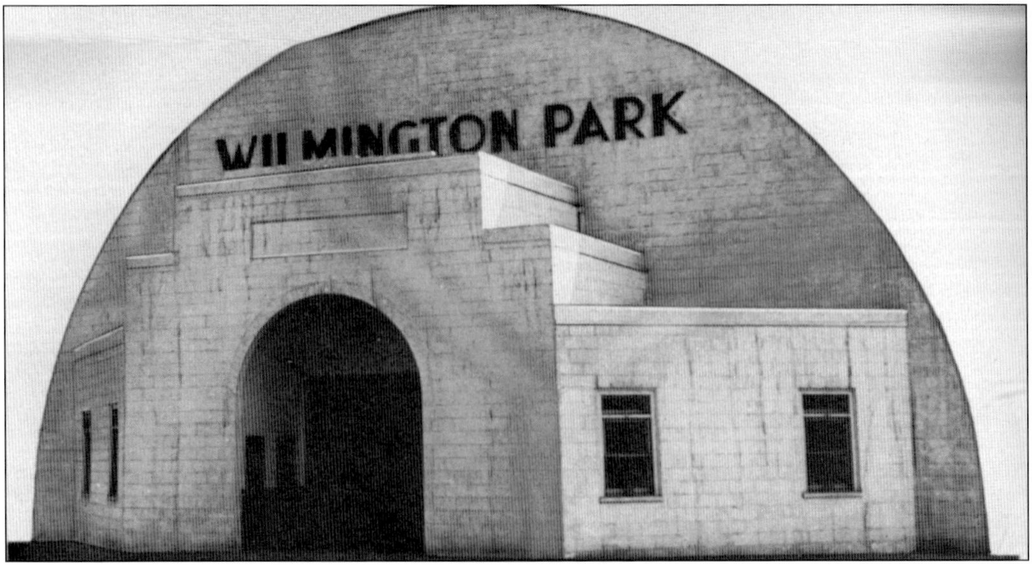

Wilmington Park was the home of the original Blue Rocks, a minor-league team of the Phillies through which some of the 1950 Whiz Kids got their starts. (Courtesy personal collection.)

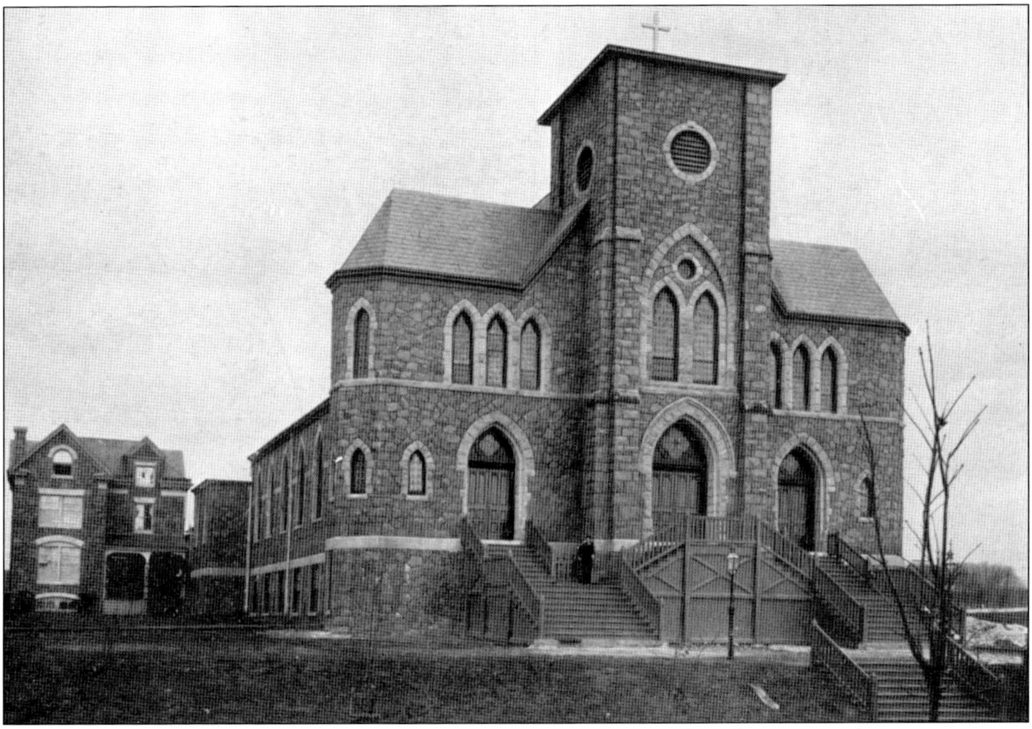

The churches around town were equally impressive. St. Ann's Church was at Gilpin Avenue and Union Street. (Courtesy personal collection.)

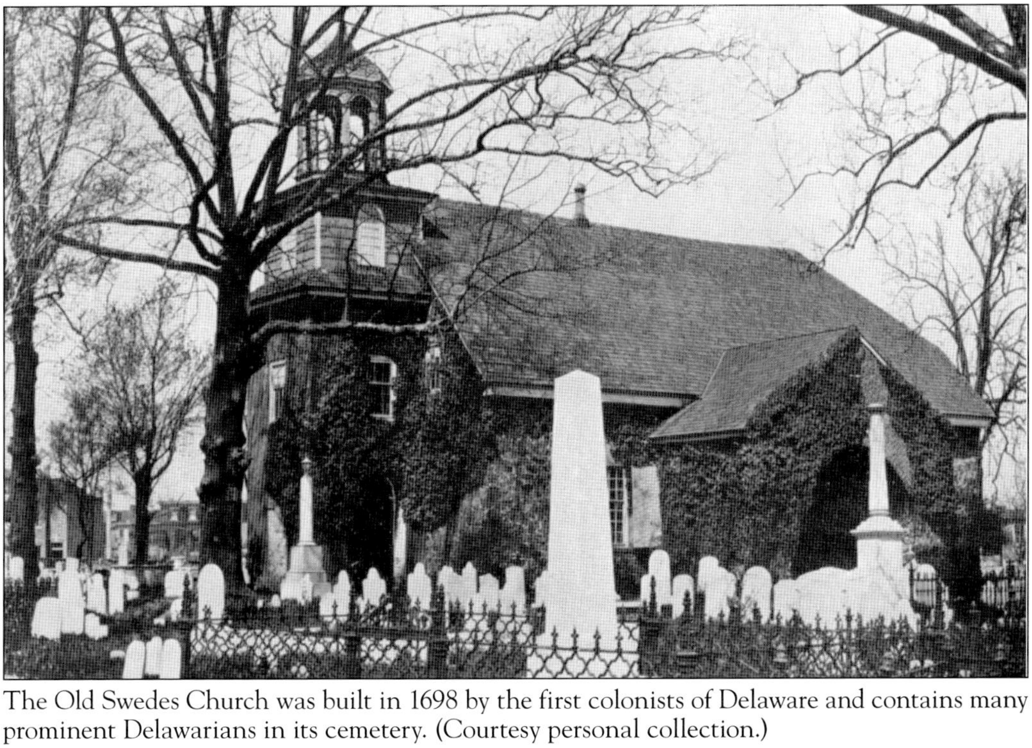

The Old Swedes Church was built in 1698 by the first colonists of Delaware and contains many prominent Delawarians in its cemetery. (Courtesy personal collection.)

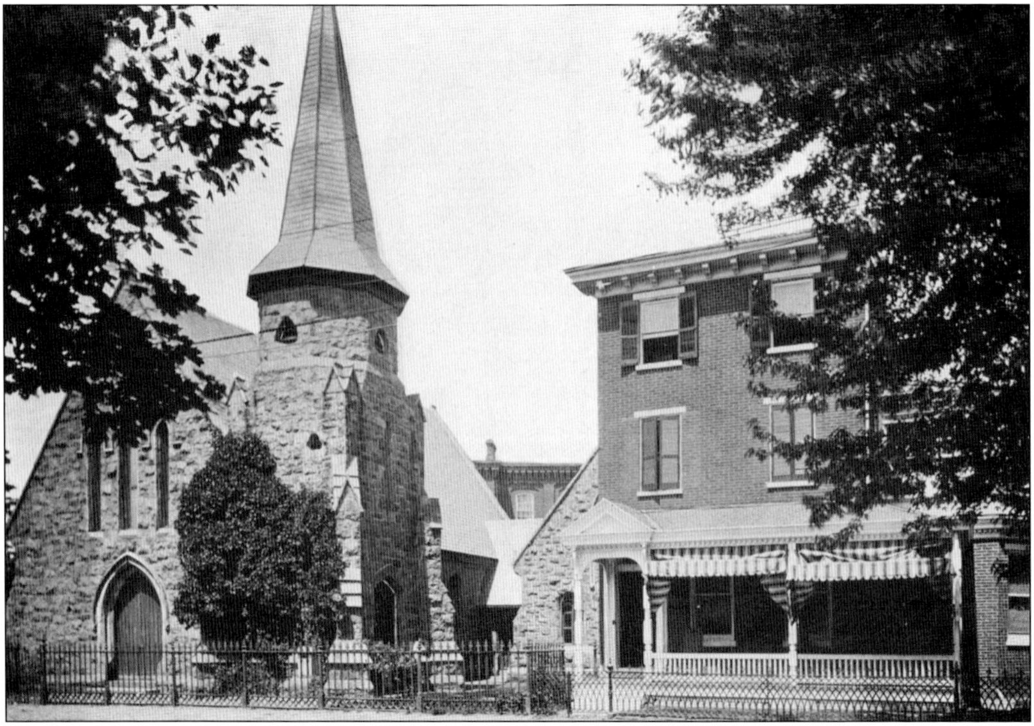

The New Jerusalem Church and Manse stood at Delaware Avenue and Washington Streets. (Courtesy personal collection.)

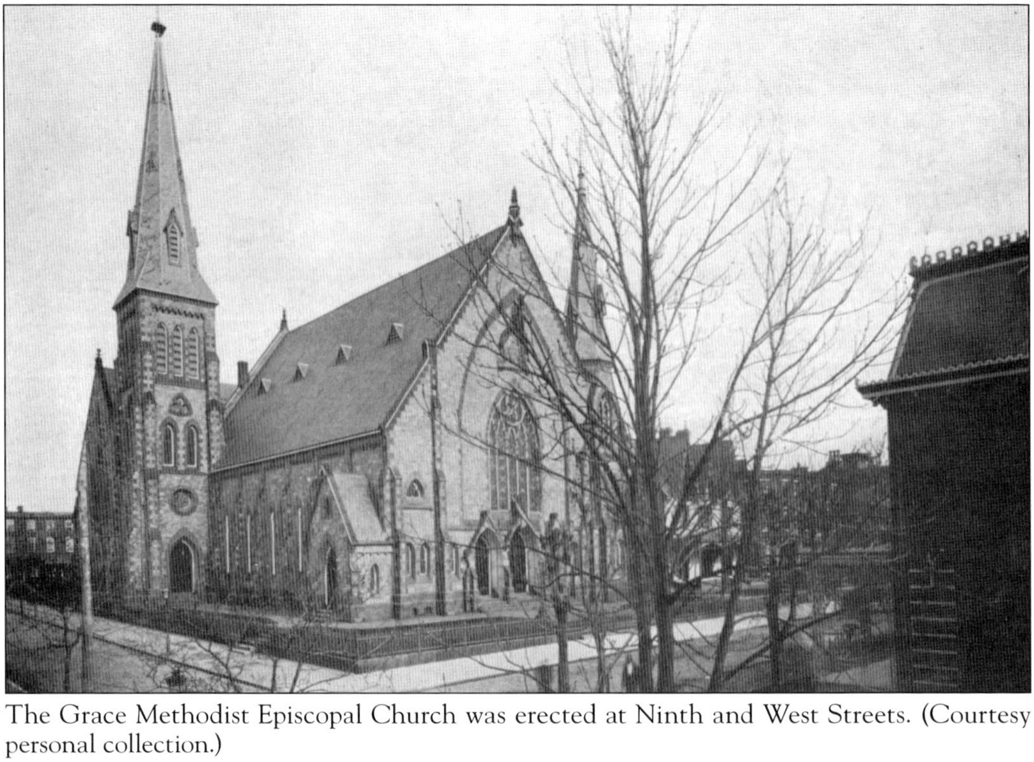

The Grace Methodist Episcopal Church was erected at Ninth and West Streets. (Courtesy personal collection.)

The old Customs House at 516 North King Street was a Greek Revival structure built in 1855 by Emmi B. Young. It was the first permanent customs house in Delaware, although it was shared by the Federal Court and US Post Office until 1897. It also served as the induction center during the Korean and Vietnam Wars. (Courtesy Historic American Building Survey, Library of Congress.)

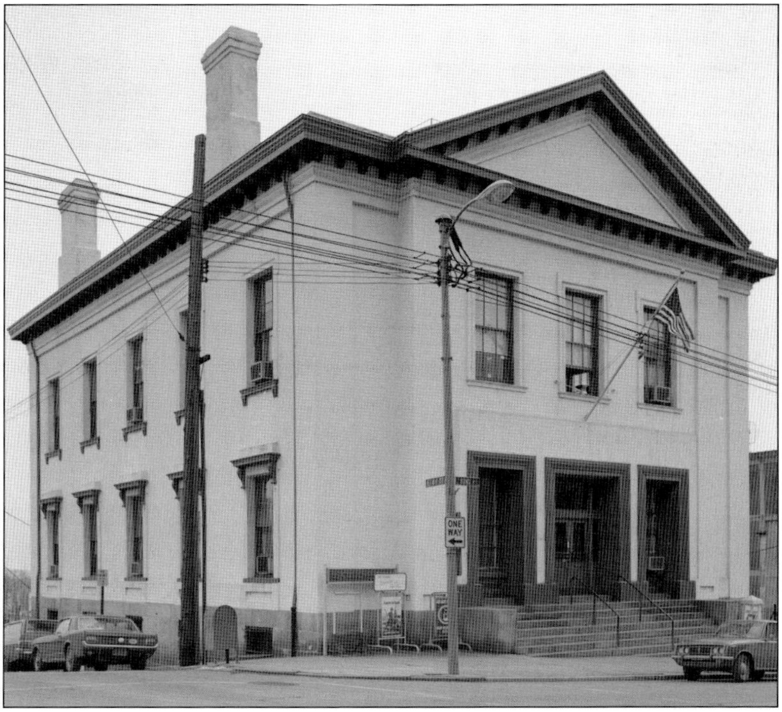

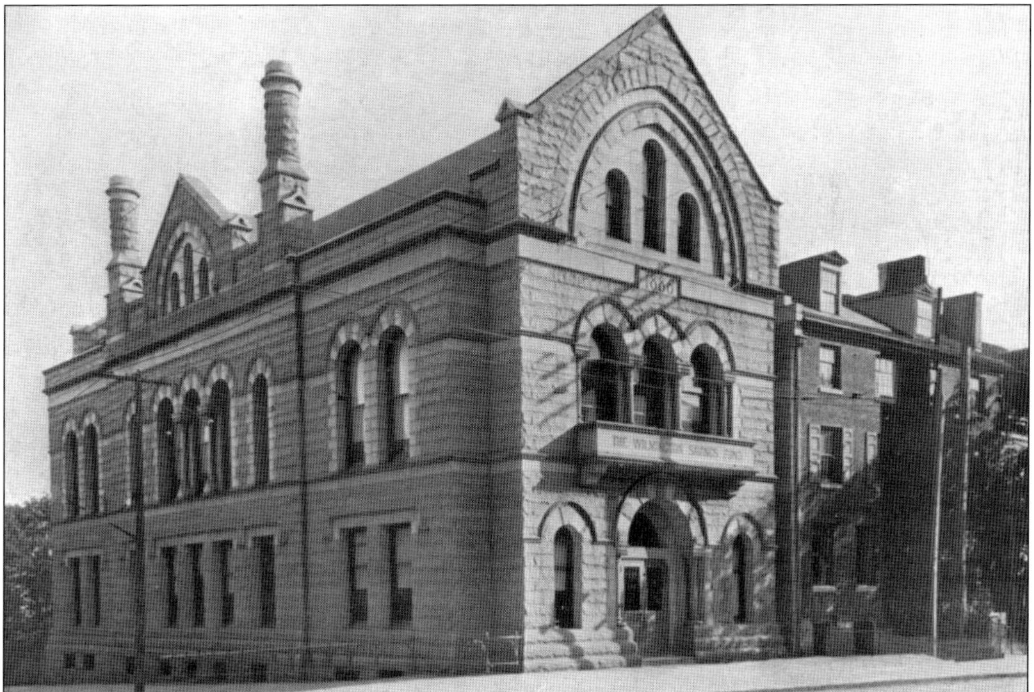

The first branch of the Wilmington Savings Fund Society, shown here in 1902, was located on Tenth and Market Streets. The bank spread statewide as the suburban population later grew. (Courtesy personal collection.)

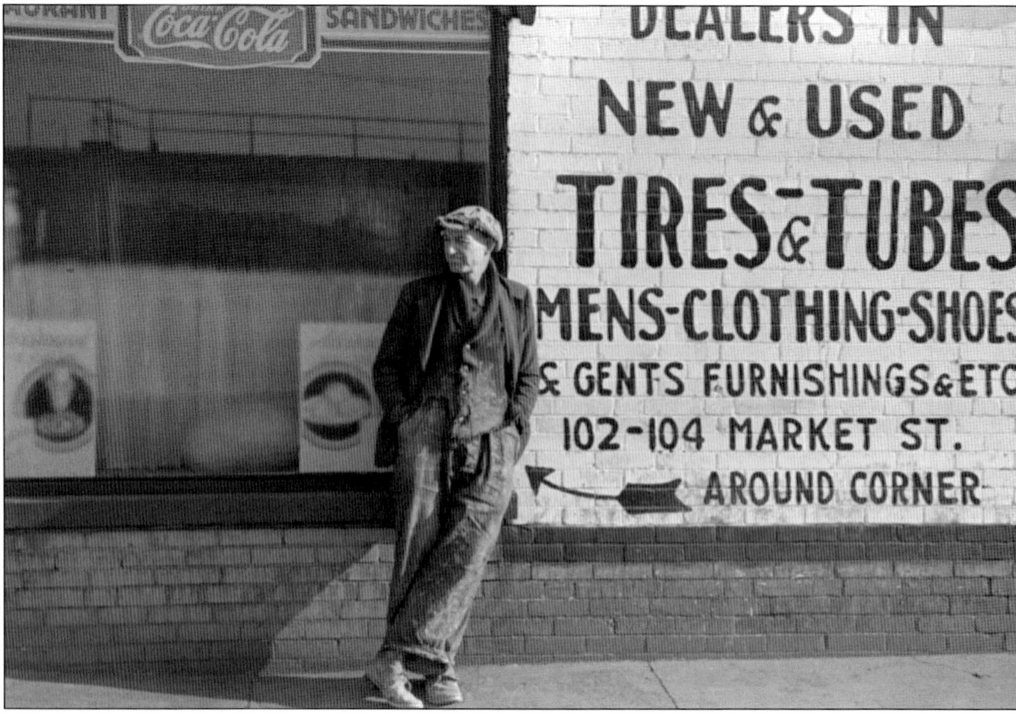

This man was lounging idly when his photograph was taken during the Depression. Like elsewhere in America, jobs were scarce in Wilmington. (Courtesy Library of Congress.)

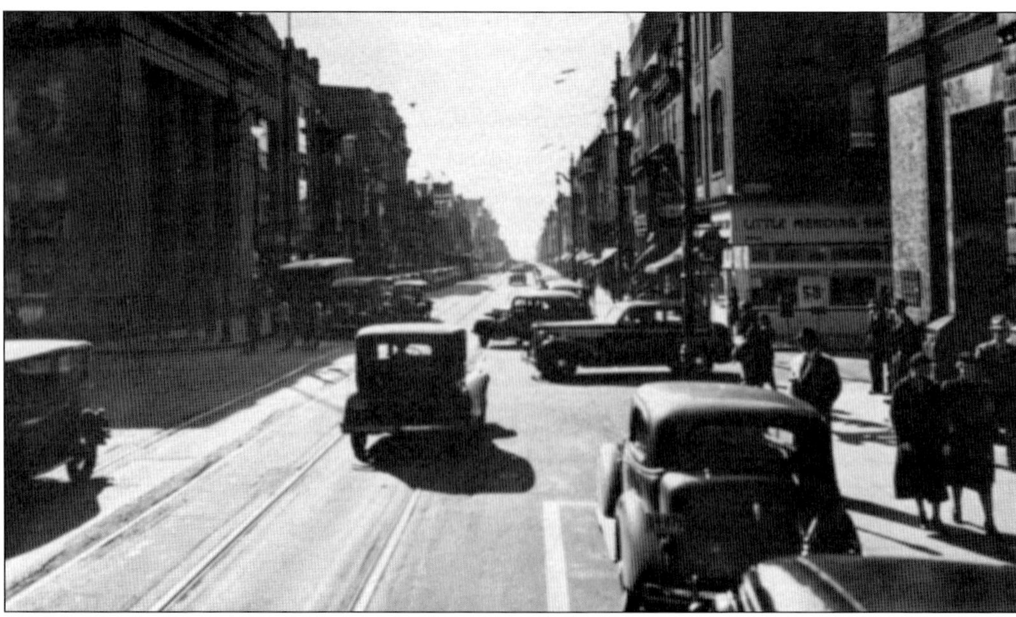

In an effort to raise revenue and control parking, the City of Wilmington added parking meters along Market Street in 1937. (Courtesy personal collection.)

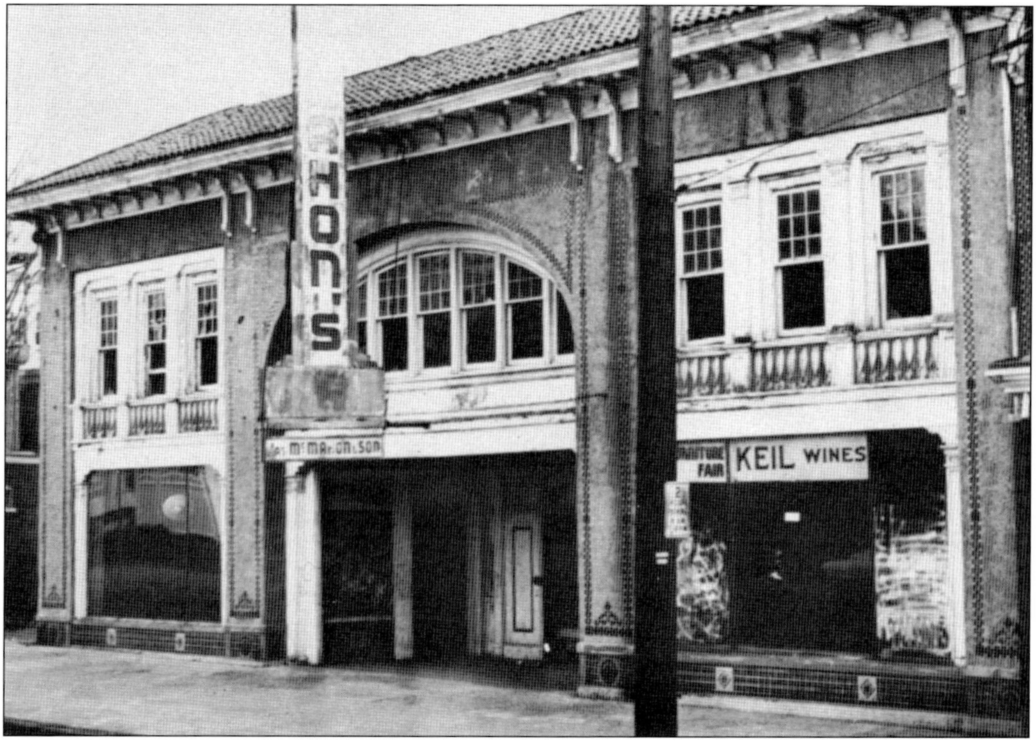

The auditorium on Eleventh Street near Madison Street was originally used for boxing and other sporting matches and later hosted jazz concerts and the first flower show. It became the McMahon Furniture Store and was demolished around 1957. (Courtesy personal collection.)

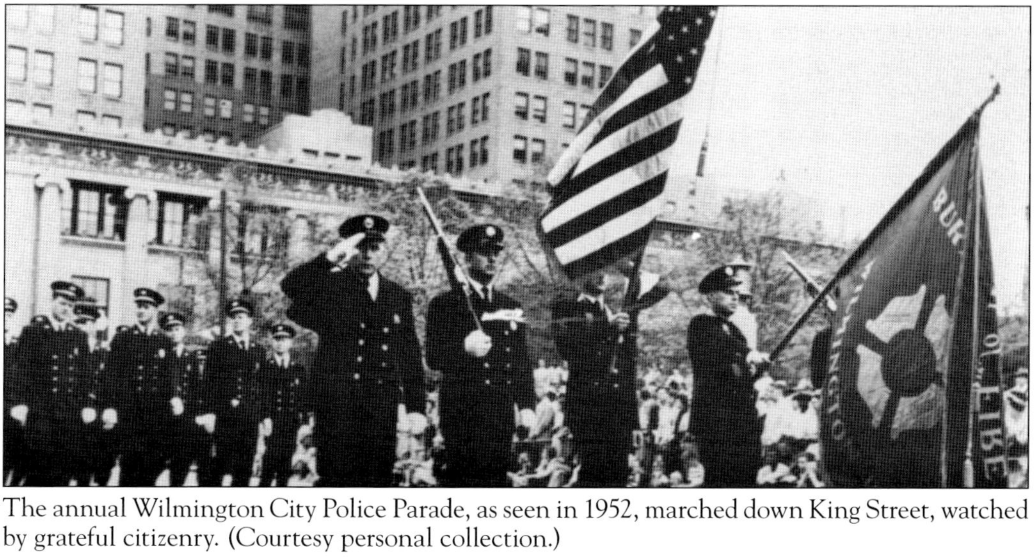

The annual Wilmington City Police Parade, as seen in 1952, marched down King Street, watched by grateful citizenry. (Courtesy personal collection.)

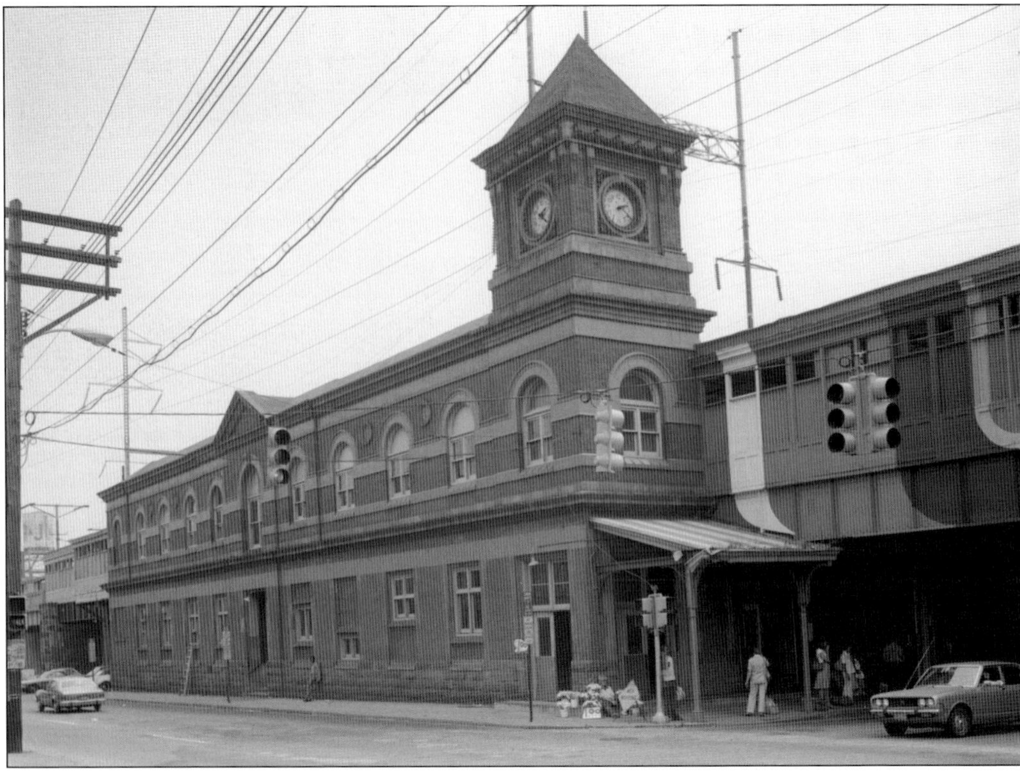

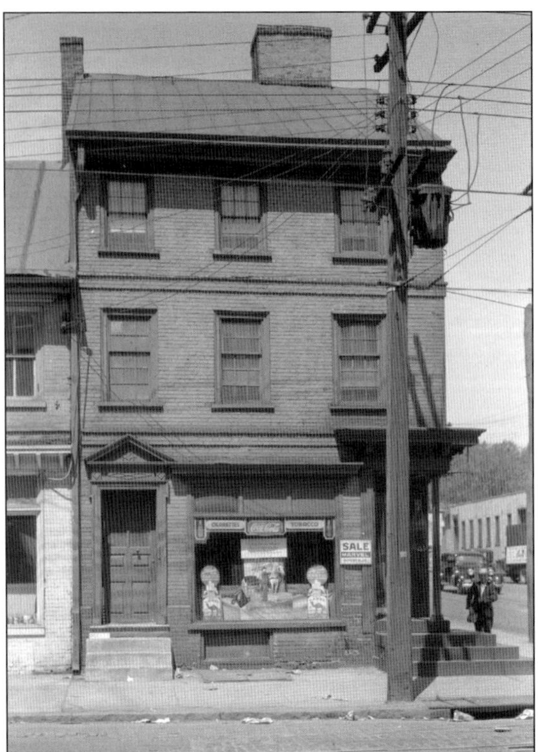

Just east of where the Old Post Road along Market Street turns west is the Joseph R. Biden Railroad Station. It was built in 1907 for $300,000 by the Pennsylvania Railroad. It was designed by renowned architect Frank Furness, who also designed the adjacent Pennsylvania Railroad Building. This 1976 photograph shows the original structure, but the Pennsylvania Railroad Building has been renovated as of 2014. (Courtesy National Register of Historic Places, National Park Service.)

During the 18th and early 19th centuries, Front Street was a lower-class neighborhood that largely catered to seafarers and others in the shipping crafts. One of the prominent members of the community was Captain Mendenhall. The Mendenhall House, shown in this late-19th-century photograph, was demolished during the construction of Martin Luther King Boulevard. (Courtesy National Register of Historic Places, National Park Service.)

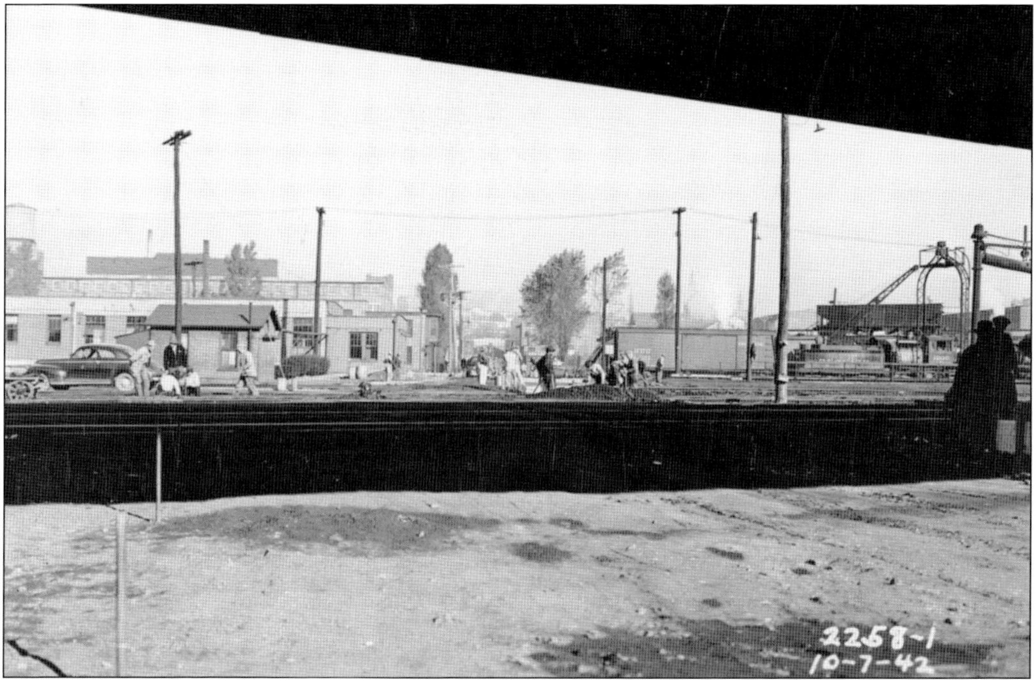

The Wilmington & Northern Railroad was one of hundreds of regional rail lines that would eventually be bought up and consolidated by the Pennsylvania Railroad. Its shops were just east of Maryland Avenue in Wilmington. (Courtesy Historic American Building Survey, Library of Congress.)

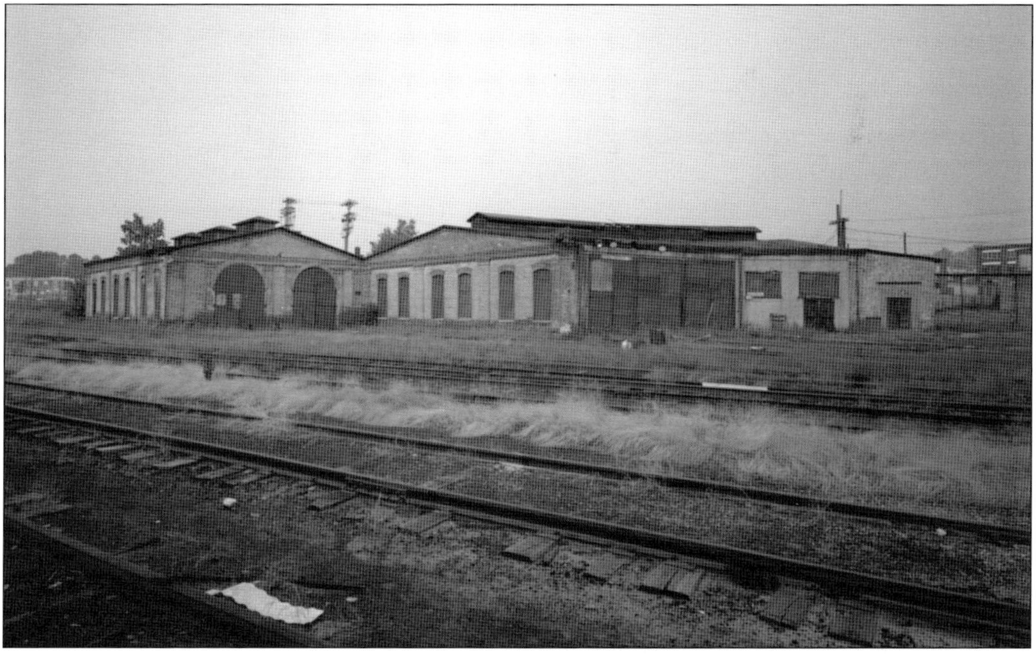

This photograph from the 1950s shows all that was left of the Wilmington & Northern shops after the railroad had been discontinued. The area has been transformed into an entertainment complex with an IMAX theater. (Courtesy Historic American Building Survey, Library of Congress.)

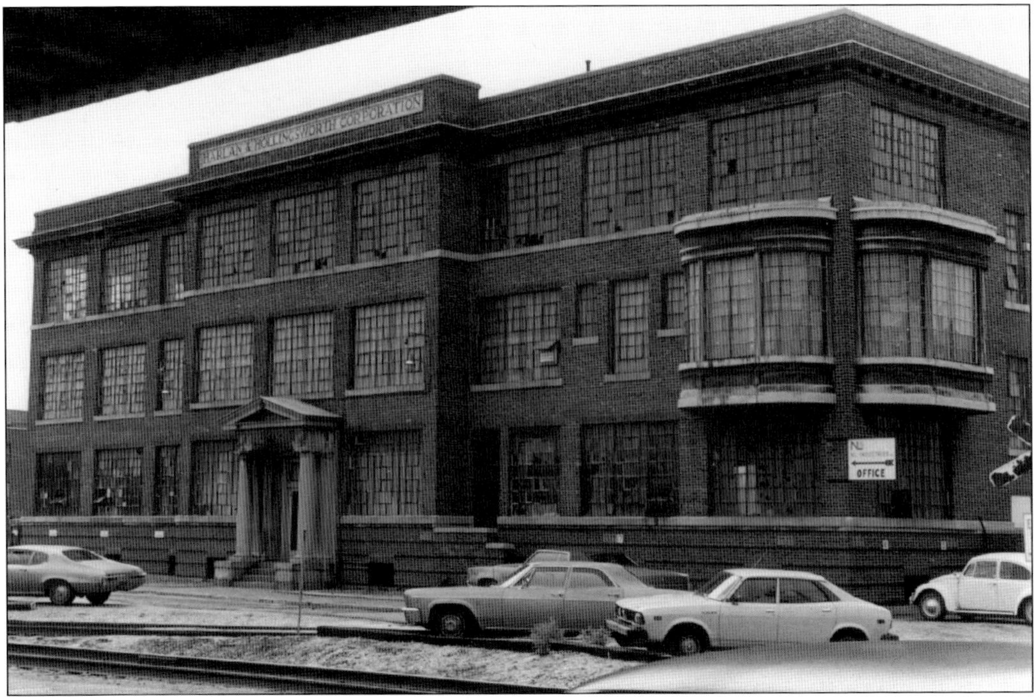

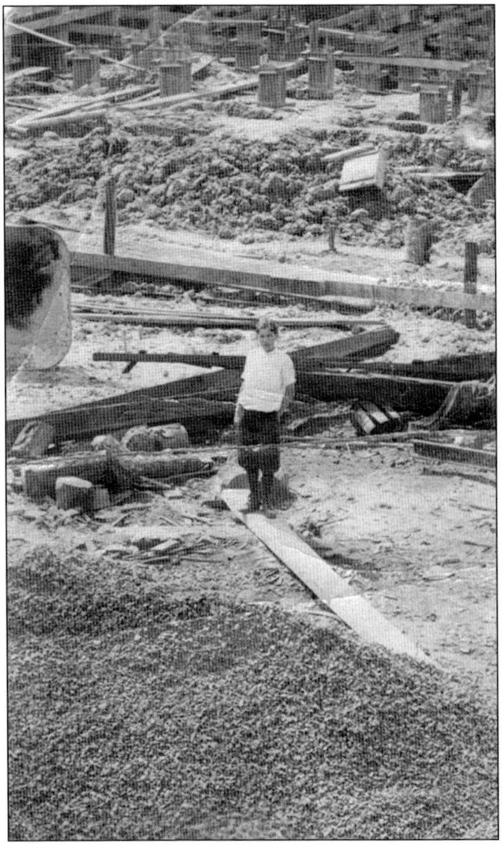

One of the most important industries of late-19th-century Wilmington was exemplified in the shipyard of Harlan and Hollingsworth. (Courtesy National Register of Historic Places, National Park Service.)

A child, John B. Ray, stands in the Harlan and Hollingsworth shipyard about 1920. (Courtesy personal collection.)

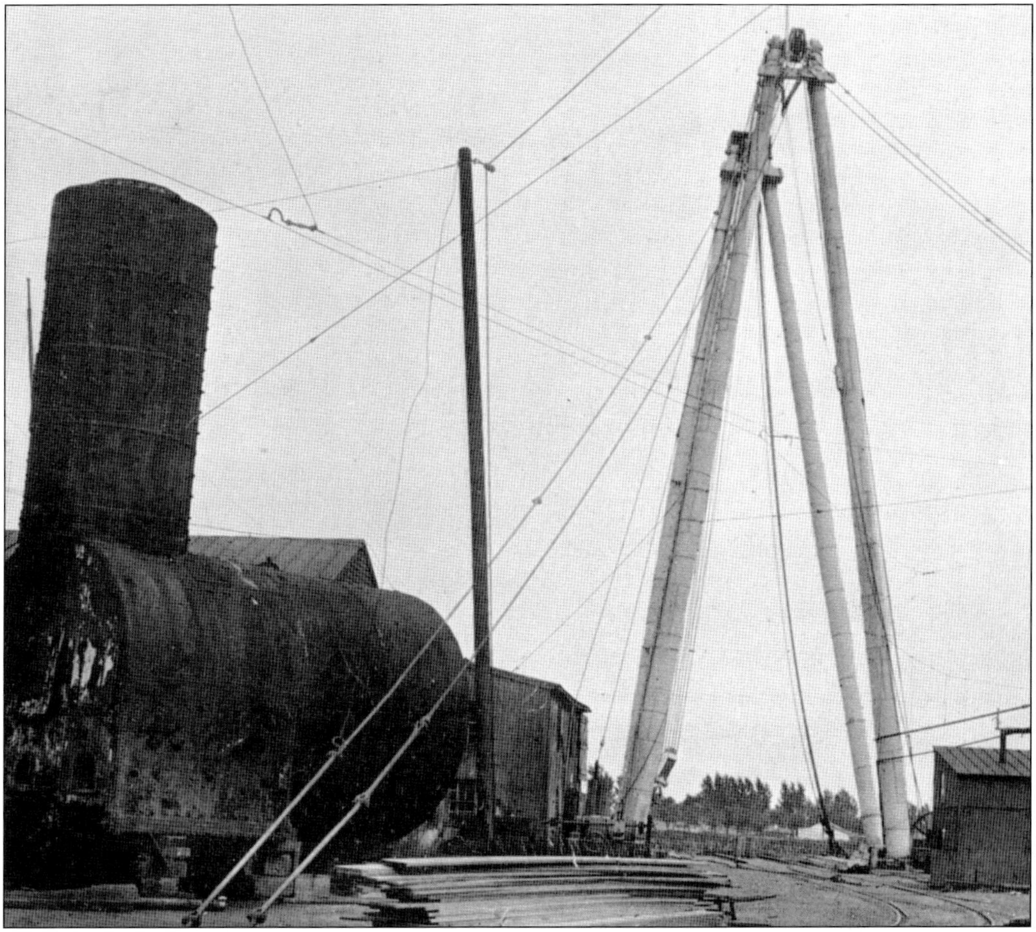

The masts at Harlan and Hollingsworth, shown above, were used in the shipbuilding process. At right, a ship sits in its berth during construction. (Both, courtesy National Register of Historic Places, National Park Service.)

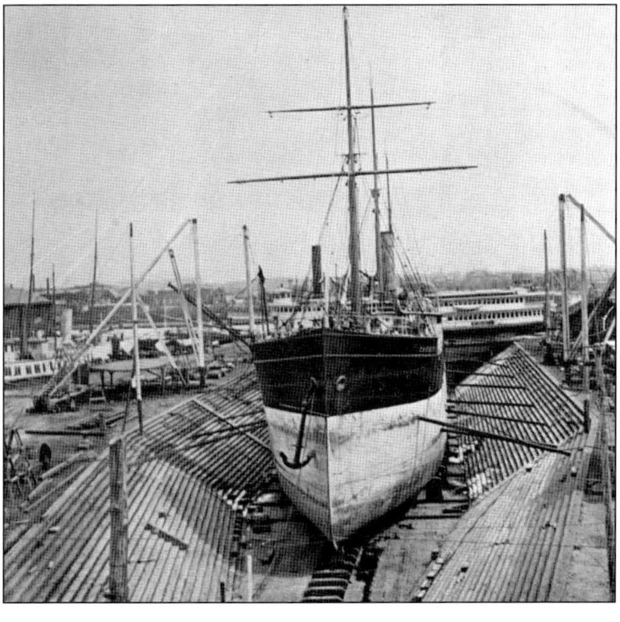

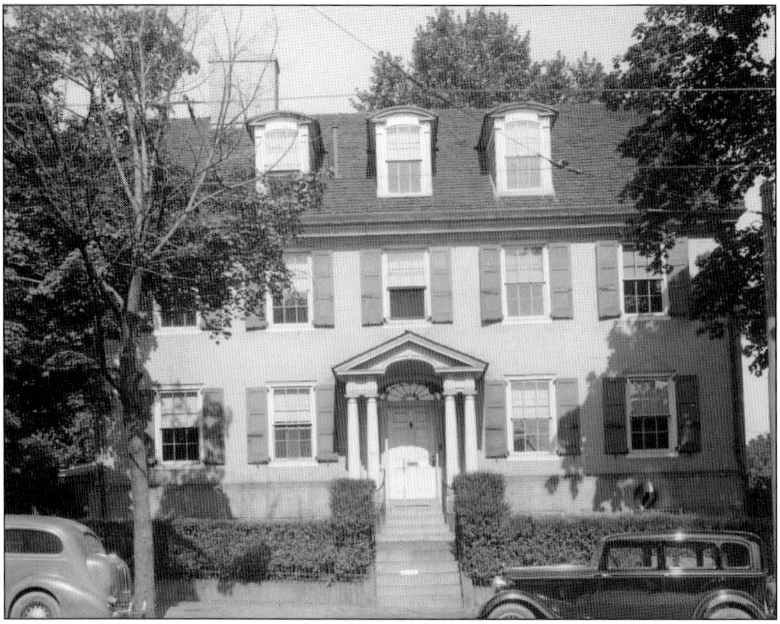

The Banning House at 809 South Broom Street is the former home of one of the city's developers, James Latimer Banning. Banning Park on Maryland Avenue is named after him. (Courtesy Historic American Building Survey, Library of Congress.)

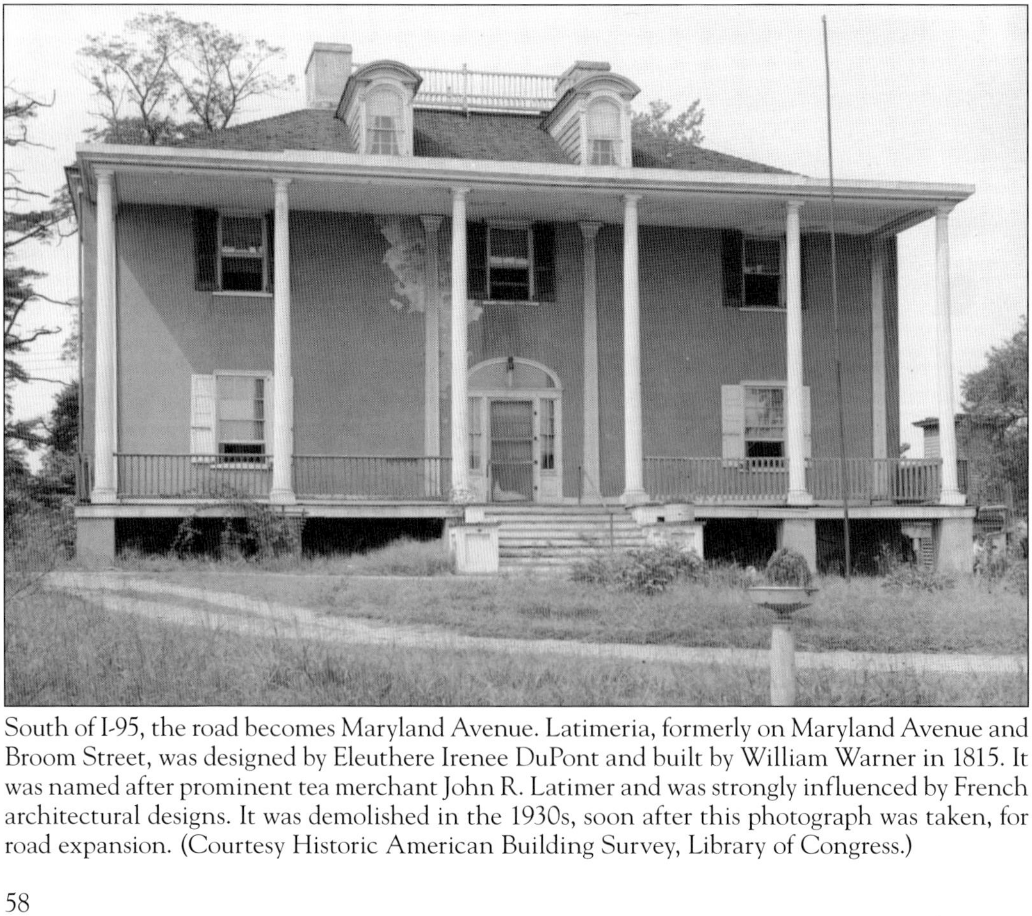

South of I-95, the road becomes Maryland Avenue. Latimeria, formerly on Maryland Avenue and Broom Street, was designed by Eleuthere Irenee DuPont and built by William Warner in 1815. It was named after prominent tea merchant John R. Latimer and was strongly influenced by French architectural designs. It was demolished in the 1930s, soon after this photograph was taken, for road expansion. (Courtesy Historic American Building Survey, Library of Congress.)

Four

Richardson Park

Richardson Park was one of the first suburban communities in Delaware. South of Wilmington, the King's Highway is known today as Maryland Avenue. Just outside the city limits is Richardson Park, the first suburban community outside Wilmington. It was popular at its height because a trolley line ran to this point, allowing families to work in Wilmington but live out in the suburbs.

The area was first settled by a John Richardson, who established a mill seat there in 1687. His large family included his son John Richardson II, who built the Woodstock House, now in Banning Park. Numerous other Richardson descendants were in the area, including Richard Richardson, who built a mill in 1785, which was operated by the family until 1890, and John Richardson, who lived in a brick house in the area. Another mill was operated in the area by Samuel Canby. After the mills were no longer profitable, the area was sold to investors for residential development.

At the turn of the 20th century, the land was divided into building lots as one of the first suburban communities out of Wilmington. It was accessible to the city by Maryland Avenue and also to the Dupont and Hercules factories via DuPont Road. It began to be serviced by a trolley line in 1910, with the trolley going from Five Points in Richardson Park to Wilmington in 10 minutes.

As Richardson Park matured, it became a suburban neighborhood itself, with shops and restaurants and churches and schools. Other neighborhoods soon sprang up between Richardson Park and Newport, including Elmhurst, dominated by cottages and bungalows, and Woodcrest, with small, one-story brick homes.

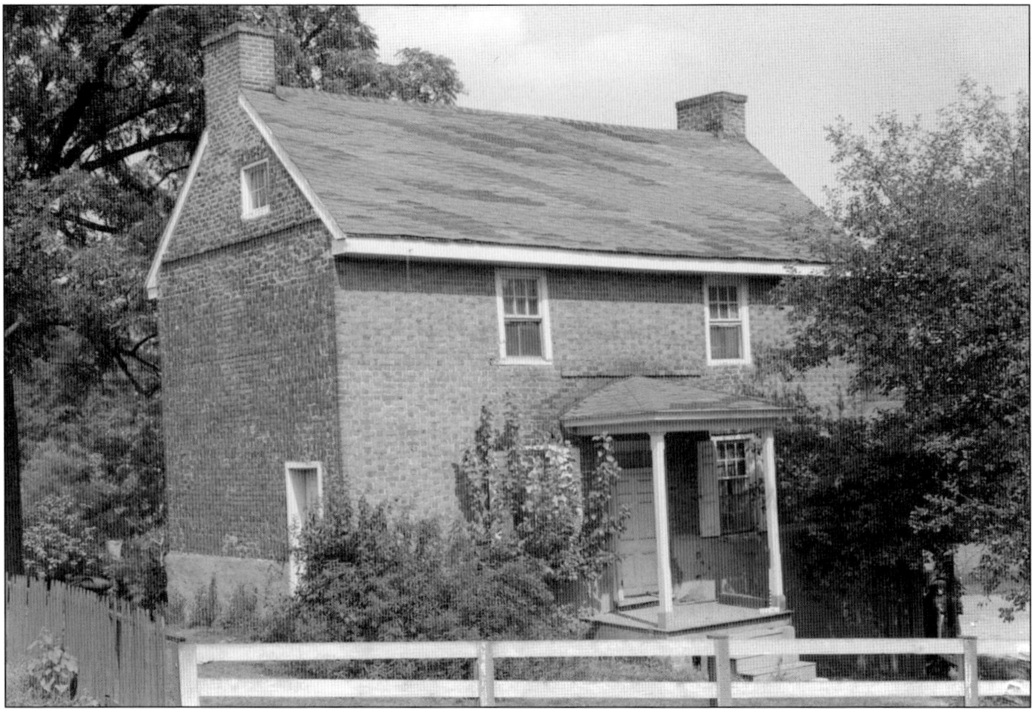

John Richardson, whose family the neighborhood was named after, lived in this farmhouse in the 18th century. (Courtesy Historic American Building Survey, Library of Congress.)

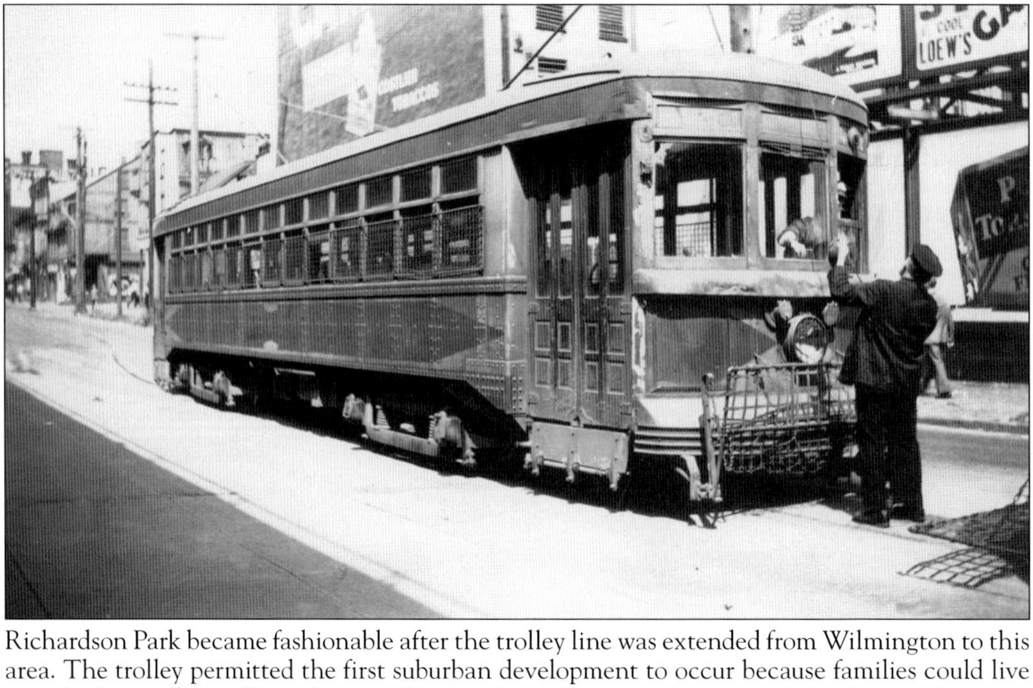

Richardson Park became fashionable after the trolley line was extended from Wilmington to this area. The trolley permitted the first suburban development to occur because families could live outside the city but still get there easily to work or shop. (Courtesy personal collection.)

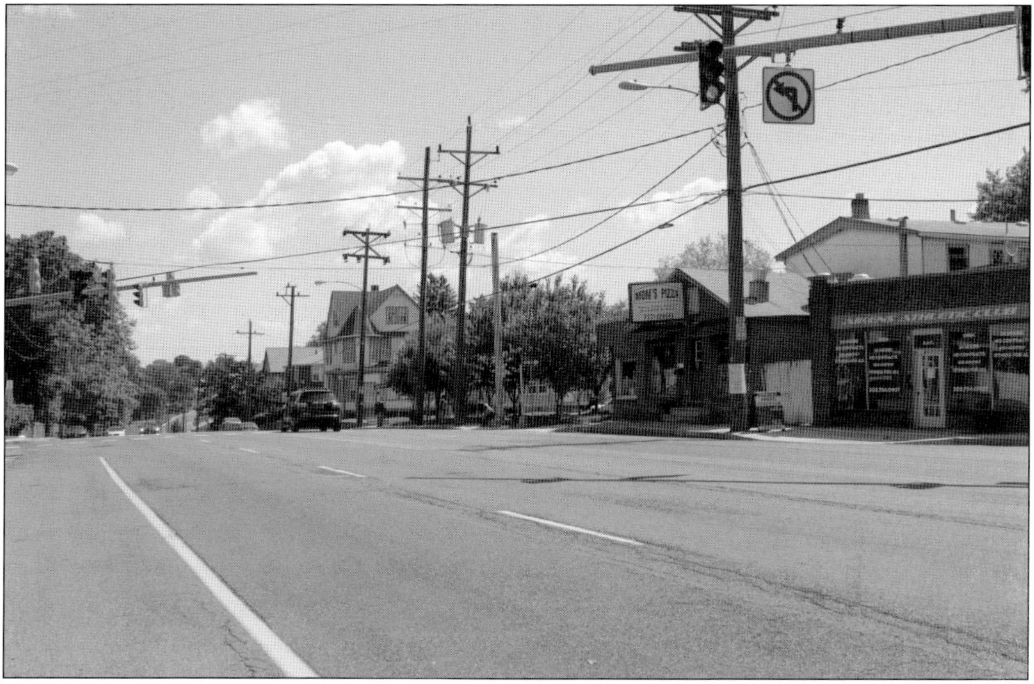

The center of Richardson Park is Five Points, where Maryland Avenue intersects DuPont Road. In the 1950s, a photography studio was located in this building. (Courtesy personal collection.)

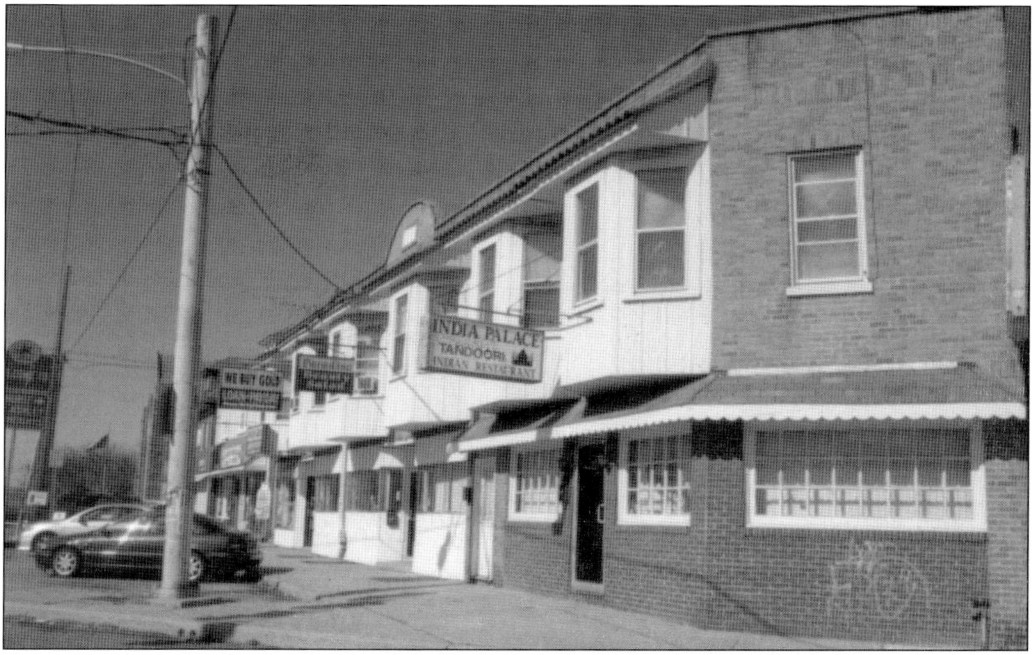

One of the earliest suburban strip malls was built at Five Points in the 1940s. The individual stores have changed hands many times, pointing to the changing demographics of the Richardson Park area. (Courtesy personal collection.)

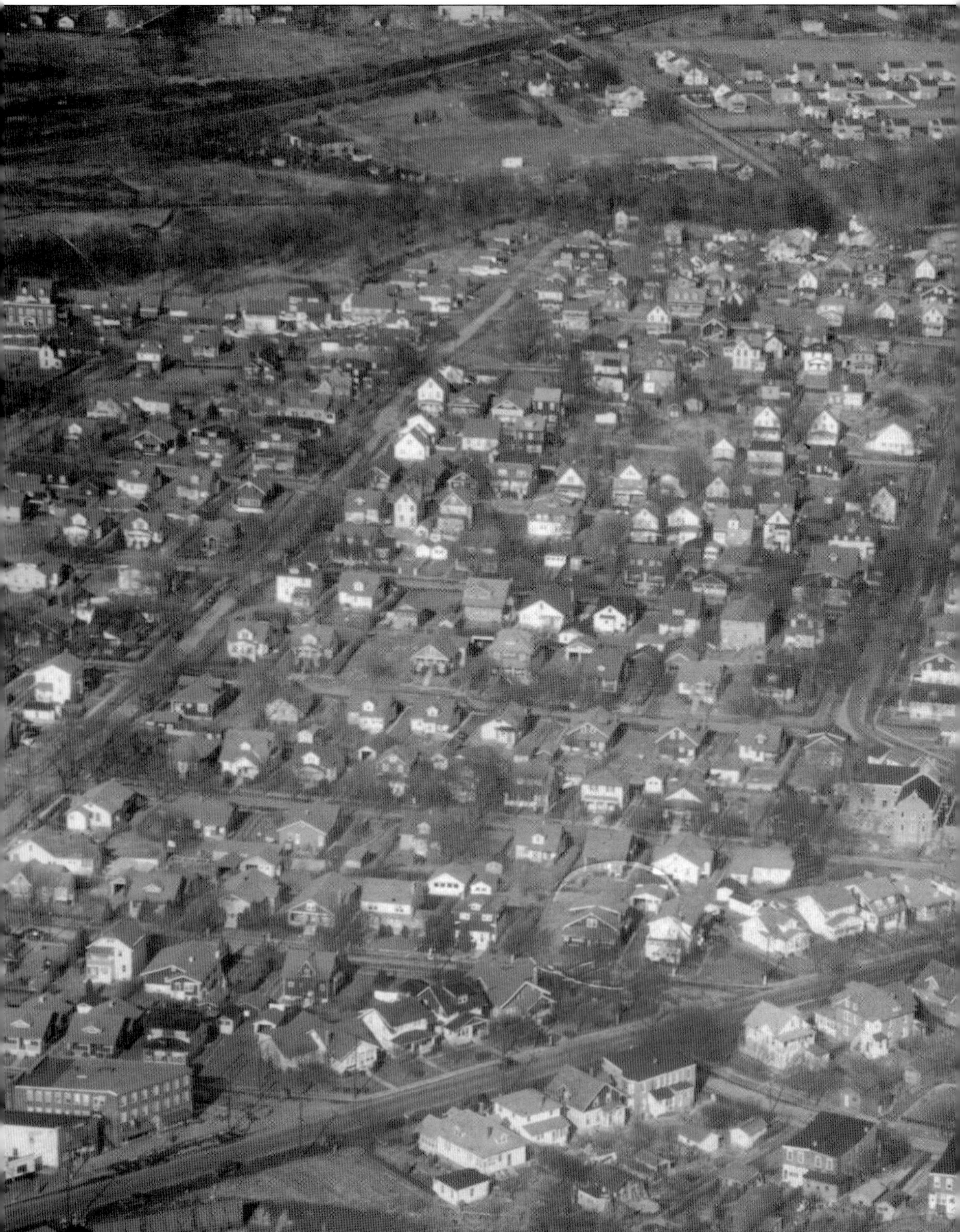

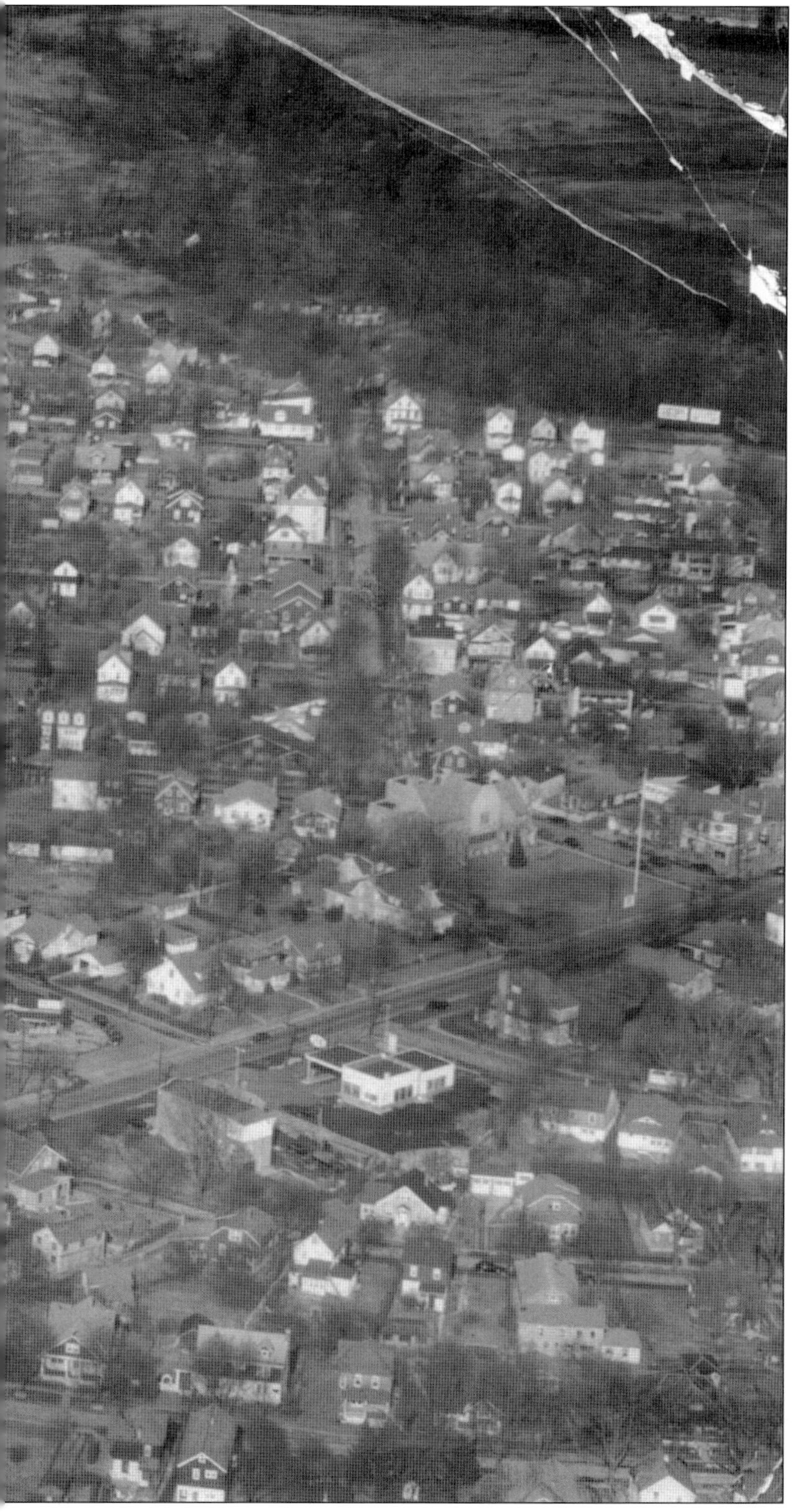

Just to the south of Richardson Park is the neighborhood of Elmhurst, built in the 1930s. Elmhurst homes, mostly bungalows and cottages, are more modest than those in Richardson Park. It became a favorite of blue-collar workingmen from the nearby General Motors assembly plant. This aerial photograph from about 1950 shows the Elmhurst neighborhood from Boxwood Road to Summit Avenue. The eastern half of this photograph is Richardson Park, from Matthies Avenue to Five Points. Maryland Avenue is at the bottom of the photograph. Five Points was the intersection of Maryland Avenue, Matthies Avenue, and North and South DuPont Roads. Canby Park is located in the upper right corner. (Courtesy personal collection.)

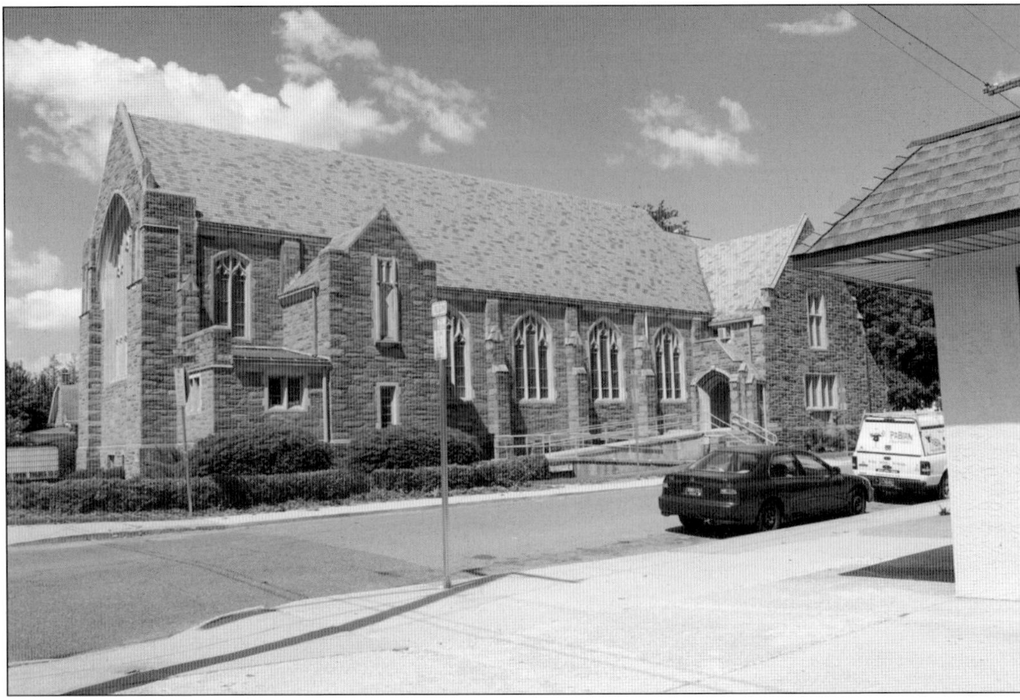

The Richardson Park Methodist Church was built in 1925. Originally, members met under trees at Belmont Avenue and DuPont Road and then built a modest church on Glenrich Avenue in 1908. The current church was enlarged in 1950 and renovated recently. (Courtesy personal collection.)

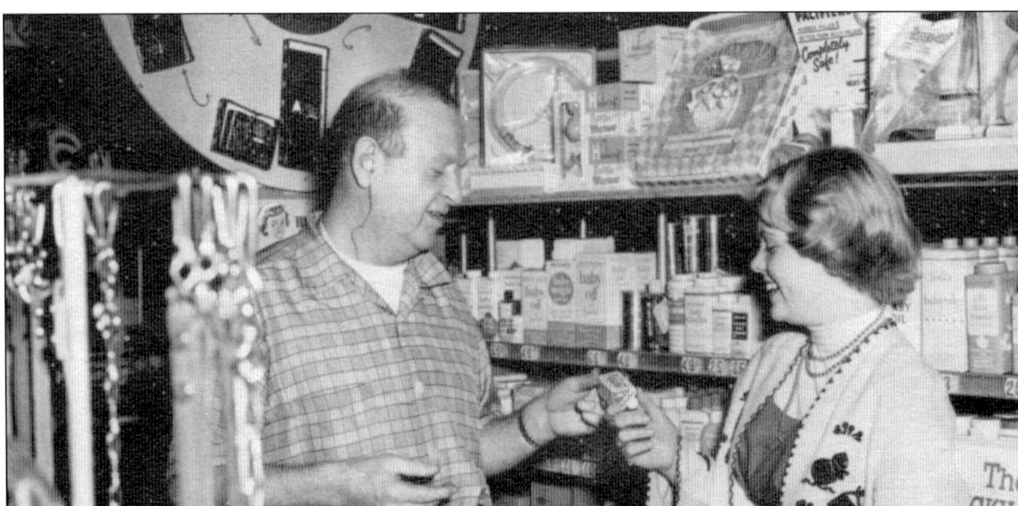

Starr's Pharmacy was an important business to the community in the 1950s. Located on the corner of Matthies Avenue and Maryland Avenue, the business was destroyed in a fire and never recovered. (Courtesy Conrad High School Yearbook, 1955, personal collection.)

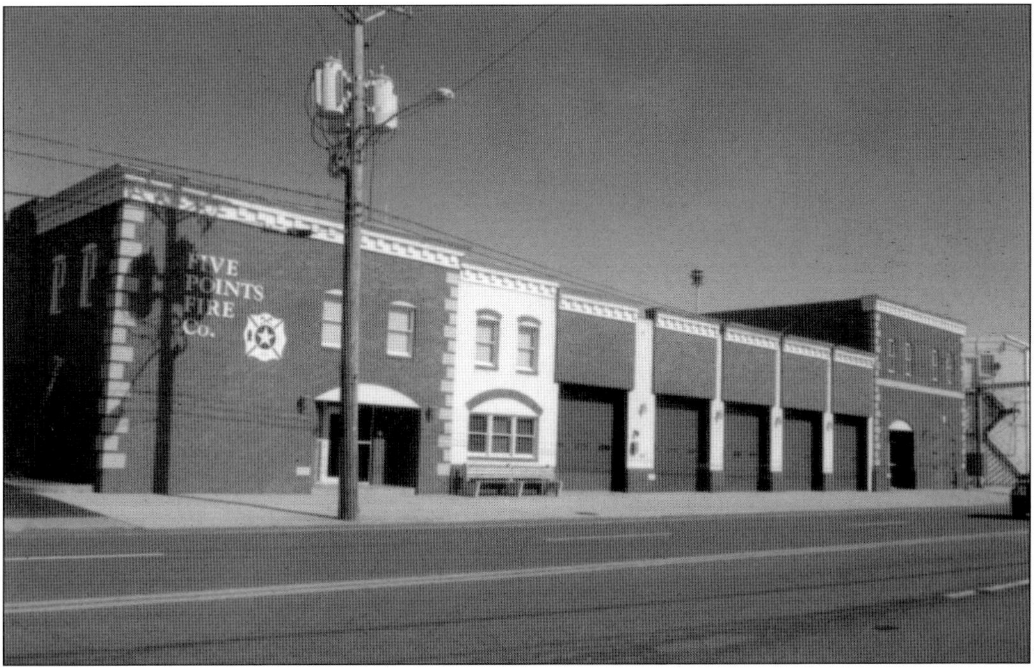

A little farther south on Maryland Avenue, the Five Points Fire Company has been serving the area since 1921. The original firehouse was on Eureka Street, but in 1952, the fire company had outgrown the location and purchased the five-bay Hastings Garage and Chevrolet. (Courtesy personal collection.)

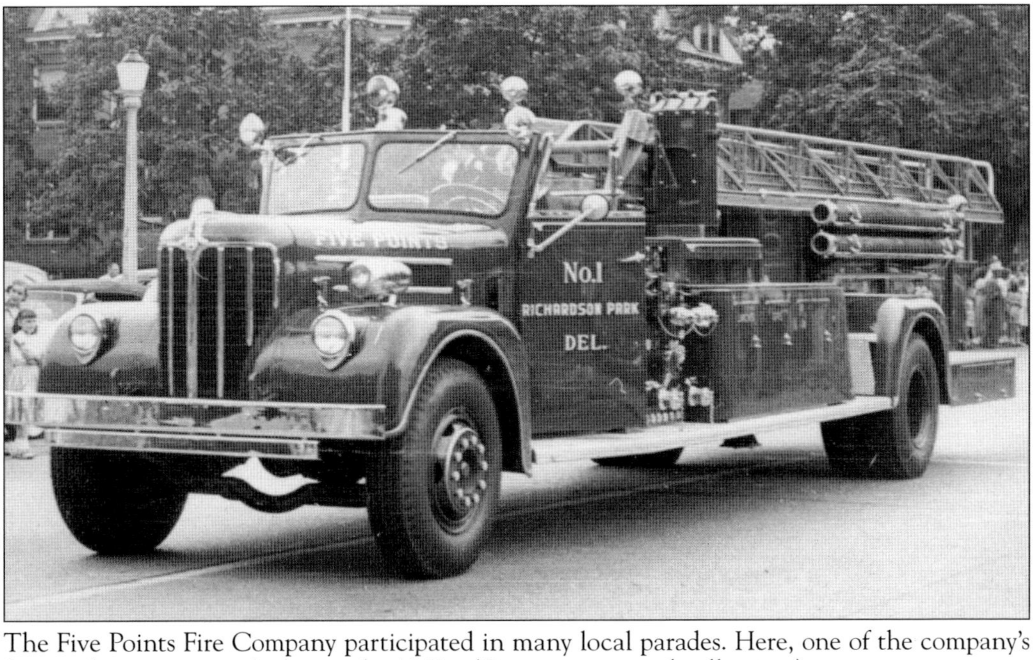

The Five Points Fire Company participated in many local parades. Here, one of the company's fire trucks joins a parade during the 1960s. (Courtesy personal collection.)

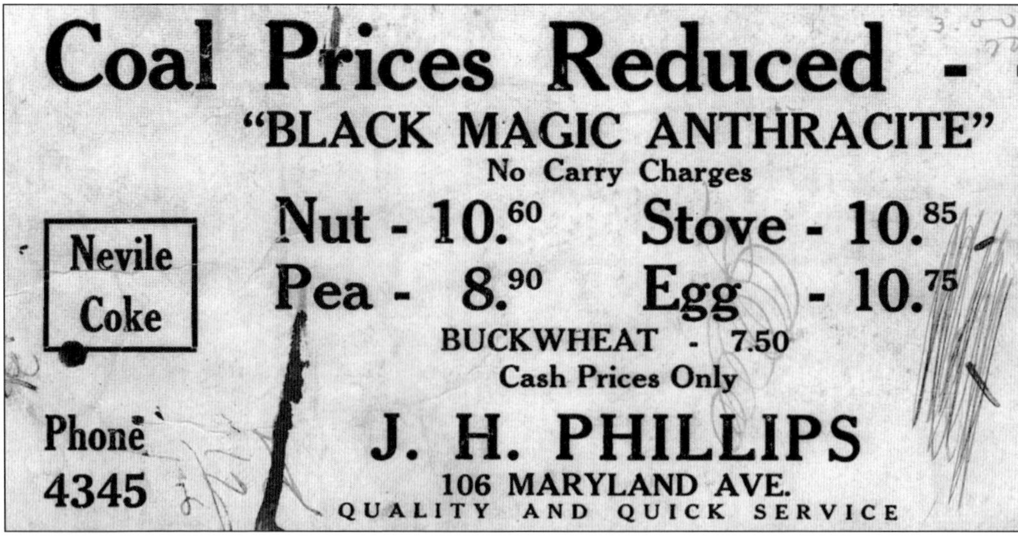

The Philips Coal Company on Maryland Avenue delivered coal on contract. Residents in the area had coal chutes that led to bins in the basement, where they could stoke their furnaces. (Courtesy personal collection.)

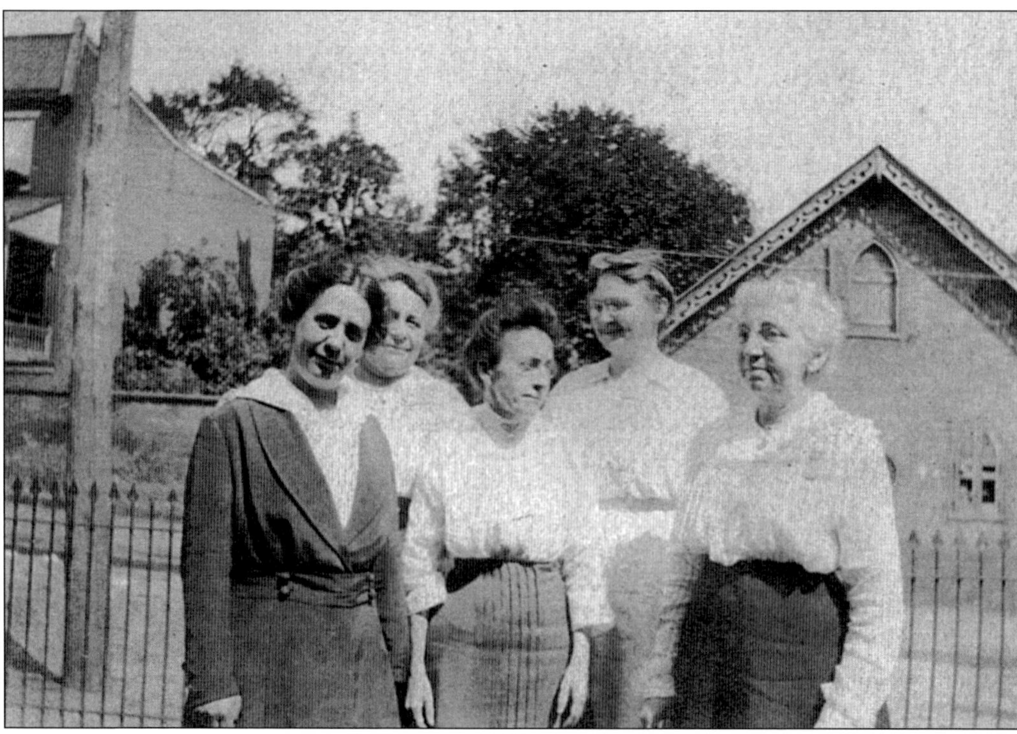
This photograph dates to the 1940s and shows the teachers of School No. 4, an elementary school in Richardson Park. The author's grandmother Elizabeth Reese Baumgardt is on the right. (Courtesy personal collection.)

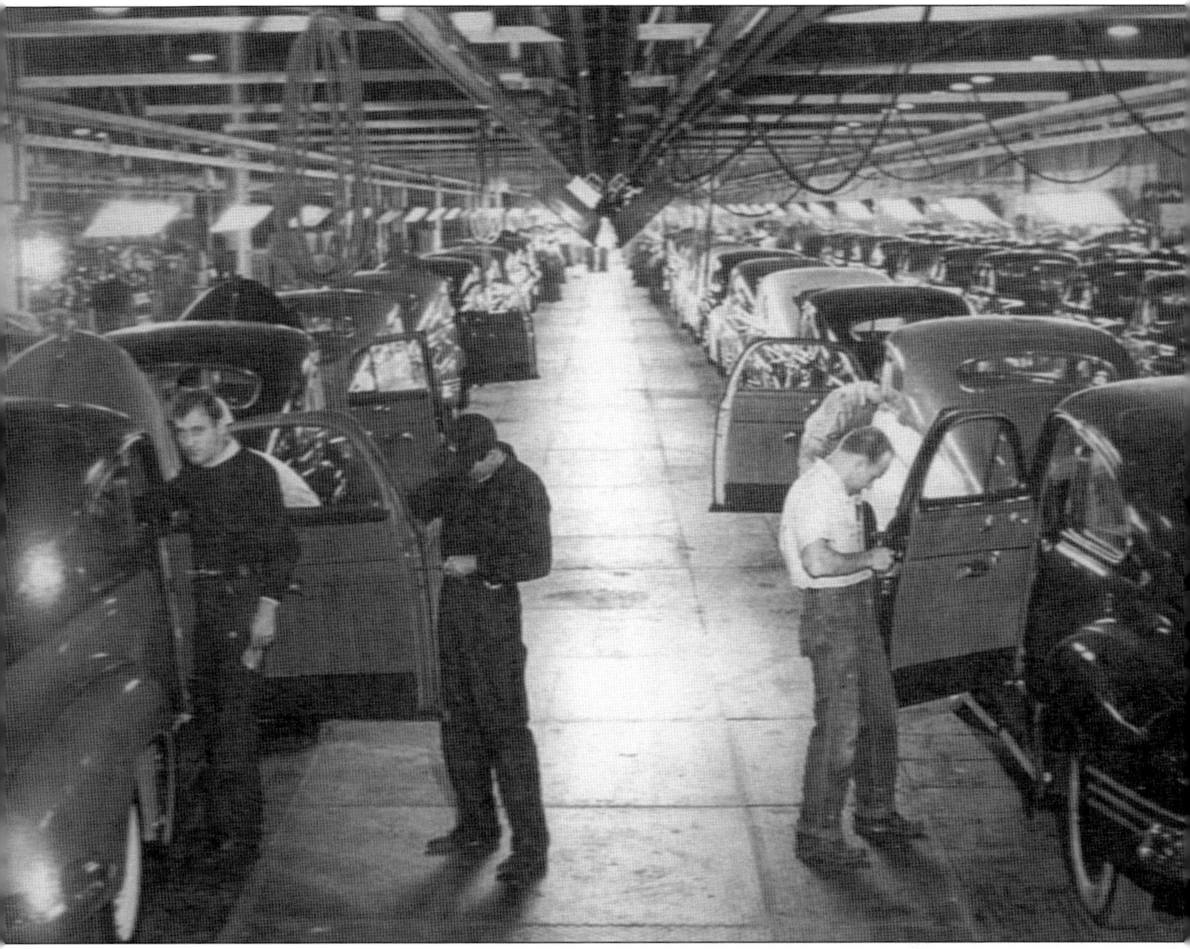

The Elmhurst neighborhood, just south of Richardson Park, was a more blue-collar community. Many of the residents worked in the General Motors Plant on Boxwood Road, just to the north of Elmhurst. This photograph shows the GM Plant assembly line in 1947. The General Motors Wilmington Assembly Plant operated from 1947 to 2009. (Courtesy personal collection.)

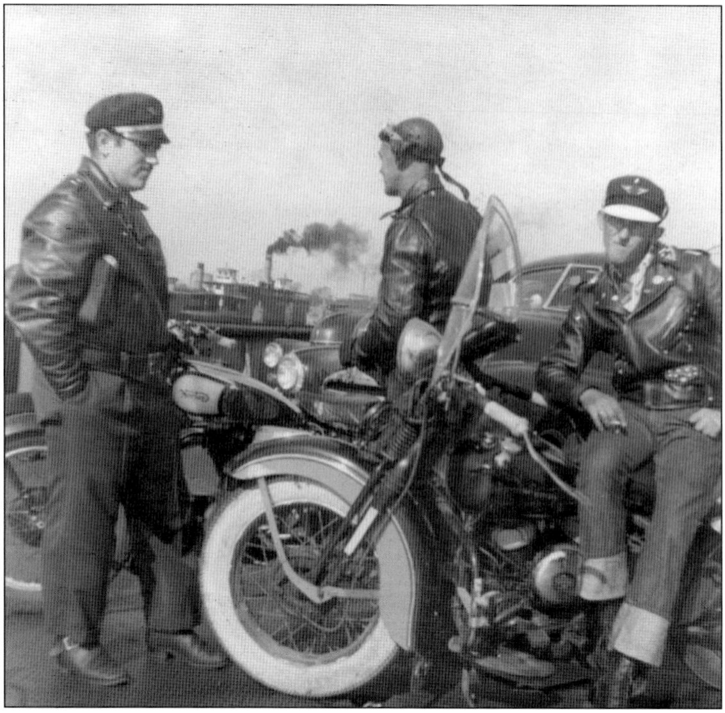

After James Dean and Marlon Brando introduced the world to motorcycles, bikers dominated the Richardson Park scene in the 1950s. The Motor Knights Motorcycle Club was based at 1300 Third Street in Wilmington. At left, the man on the right of this photograph is the author's father, William "Billy" Baumgardt, around 1954. (Courtesy personal collection.)

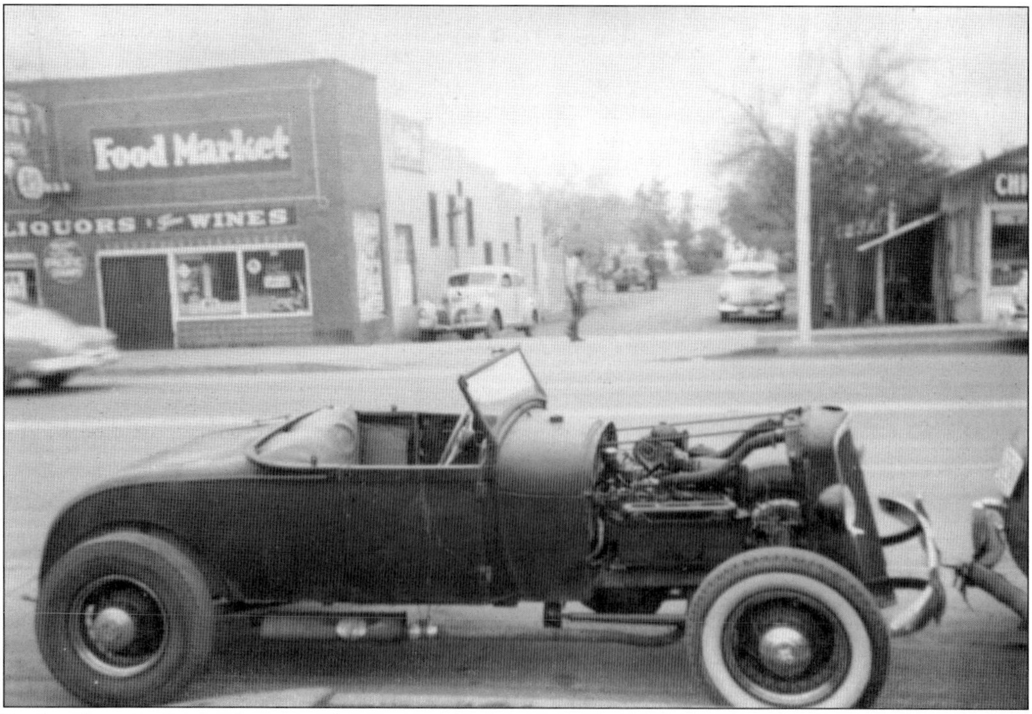

Richardson Park also became the center of activity for youths who emulated James Dean during the birth of the hot rod and motorcycle craze of the 1950s. Four-lane Maryland Avenue was well suited for racing up and down the avenue. This photograph shows one of the hot rods along Maryland Avenue. (Courtesy Personal Collection.)

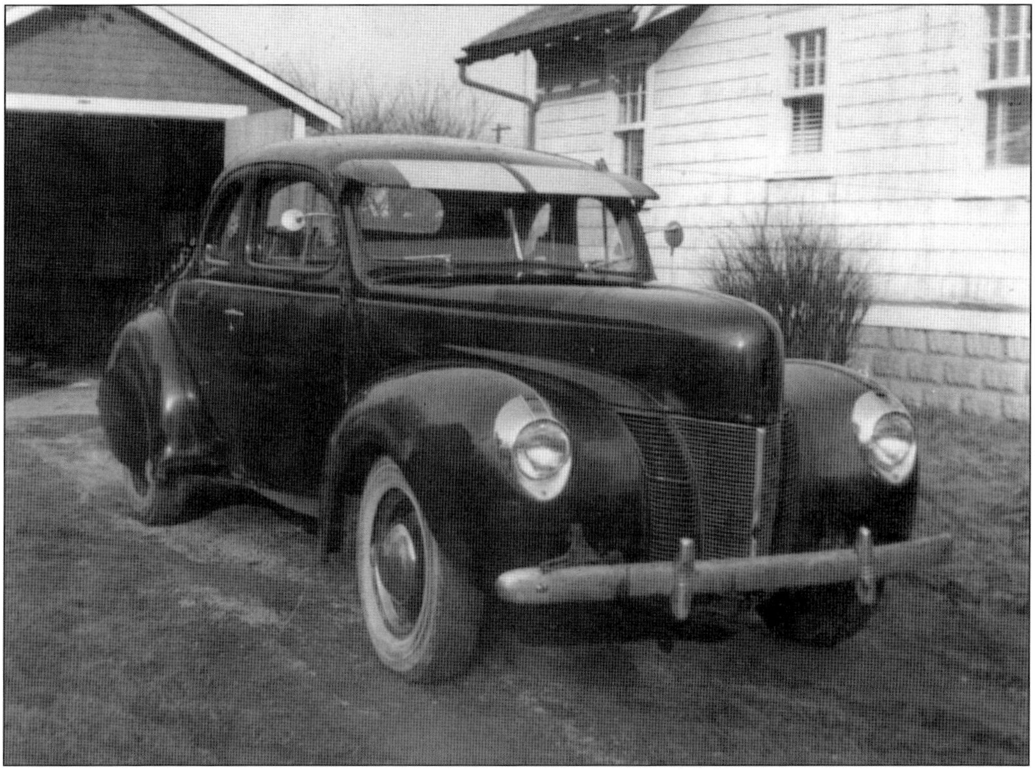

In addition to a fascination with motorcycles, the author's father also had a lifelong passion for automobiles. This was his 1940 Custom Ford, in Bill Baumgardt's driveway on Lake Street in Elmhurst. (Courtesy personal collection.)

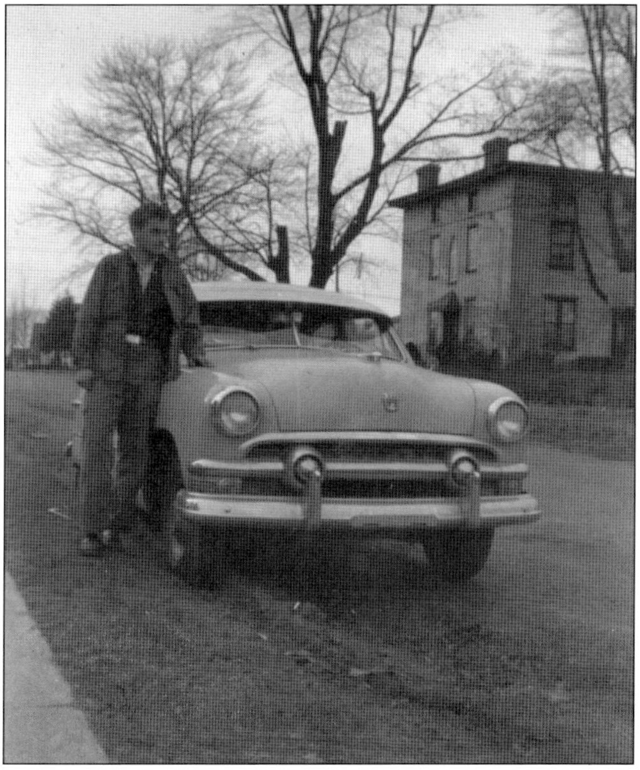

A local Elmhurst friend of Bill Baumgardt, Bob Hoffman, is pictured with his souped-up car in the 1950s in Richardson Park. He later moved to a farm near Glasgow where he raised his family, but he stayed a close friend the rest of his life. (Courtesy personal collection.)

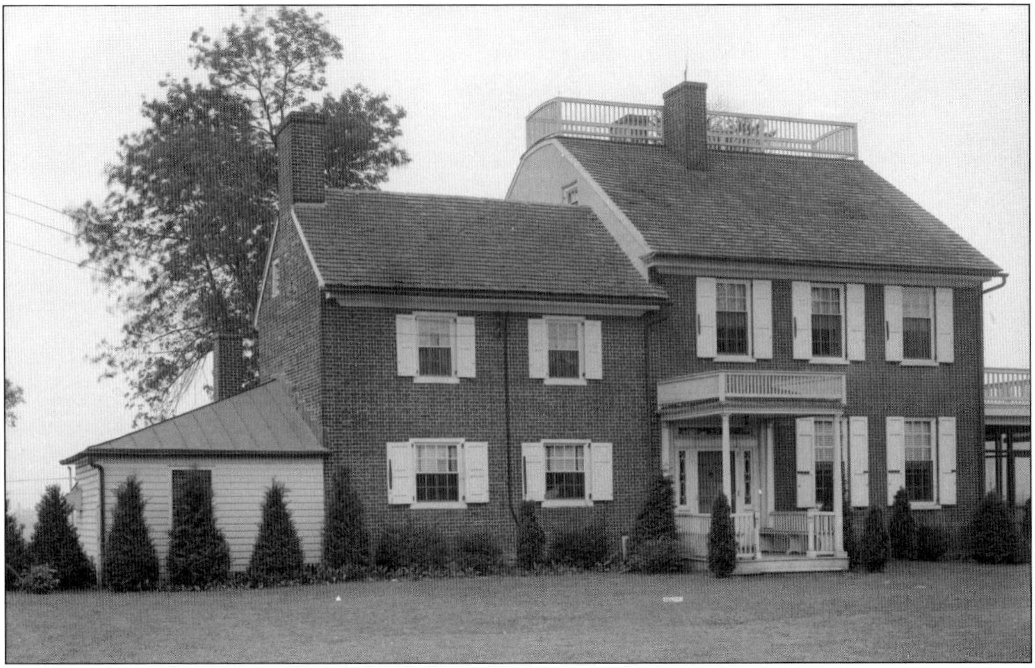

Woodstock, an 18th-century farmhouse in Banning Park, was once the center of a large farm on Boxwood Road, but it is now surrounded by Banning Park. (Courtesy National Register of Historic Places, National Park Service.)

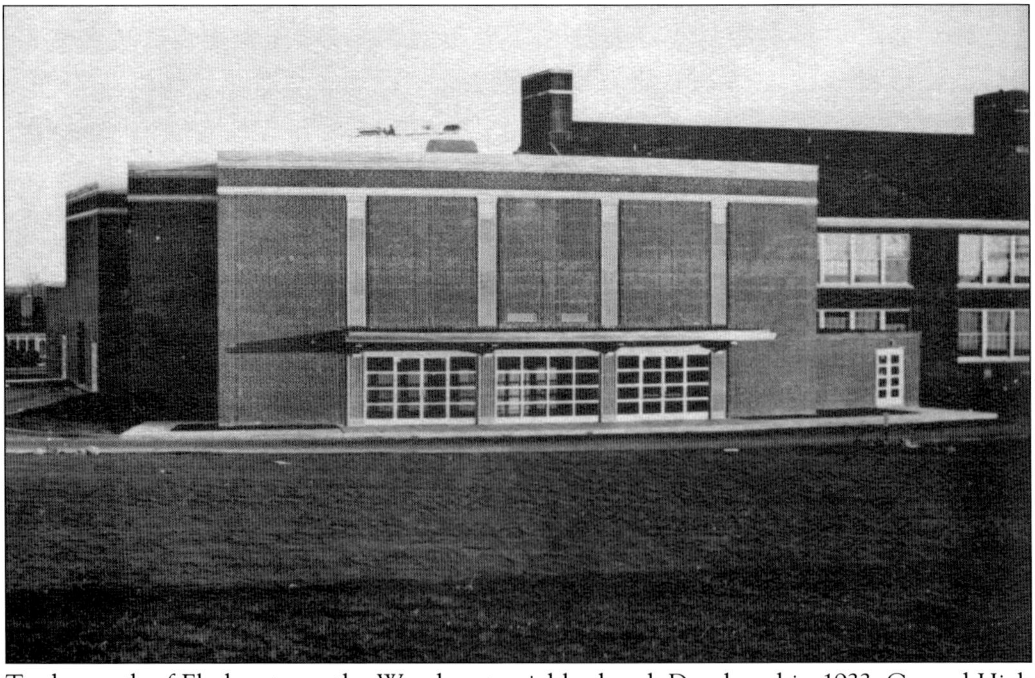

To the south of Elmhurst was the Woodcrest neighborhood. Developed in 1933, Conrad High School opened in September 1935. It was named after prominent judge and educator Henry C. Conrad (1852–1930). This photograph is dated to 1955, before the school was modified. (Courtesy Conrad High School Yearbook, 1955, personal collection.)

The youths in Richardson Park and Elmhurst attended one of the first suburban schools built in Delaware, Conrad High School. It has since been turned into a special school for science education. This program is from one of the earliest Conrad school productions, in 1937. (Courtesy personal collection.)

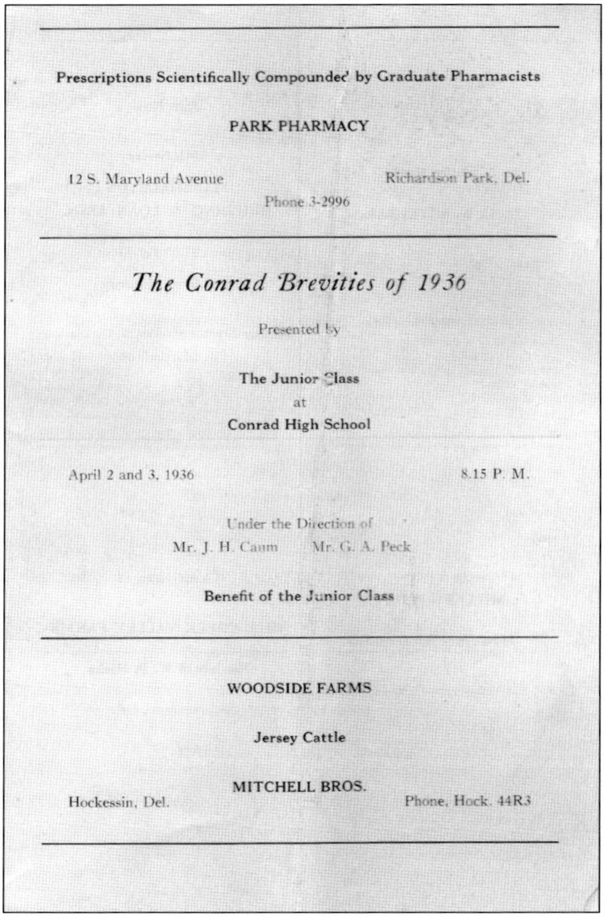

Prescriptions Scientifically Compounded by Graduate Pharmacists

PARK PHARMACY

12 S. Maryland Avenue Richardson Park, Del.
Phone 3-2996

The Conrad Brevities of 1936

Presented by

The Junior Class
at
Conrad High School

April 2 and 3, 1936 8.15 P. M.

Under the Direction of
Mr. J. H. Caum Mr. G. A. Peck

Benefit of the Junior Class

WOODSIDE FARMS

Jersey Cattle

MITCHELL BROS.
Hockessin, Del. Phone, Hock. 44R3

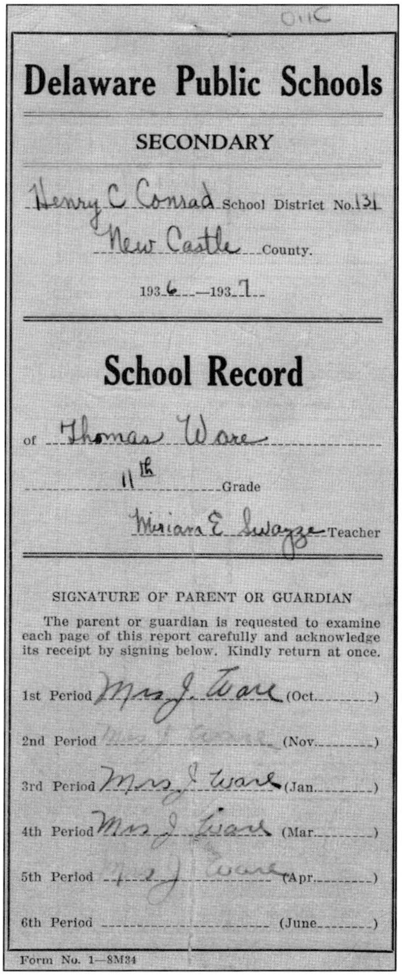

Delaware Public Schools

SECONDARY

Henry C Conrad School District No. 131
New Castle County.

1936—1937

School Record

of Thomas Ware

11th Grade

Miriam E. Swayze Teacher

SIGNATURE OF PARENT OR GUARDIAN

The parent or guardian is requested to examine each page of this report carefully and acknowledge its receipt by signing below. Kindly return at once.

1st Period Mrs J. Ware (Oct.____)

2nd Period (Nov.____)

3rd Period Mrs J. Ware (Jan.____)

4th Period Mrs J. Ware (Mar.____)

5th Period Mrs J. Ware (Apr.____)

6th Period (June____)

Form No. 1—8M34

Pictured here is a report card from the 1936–1937 class of Conrad High School. (Courtesy personal collection.)

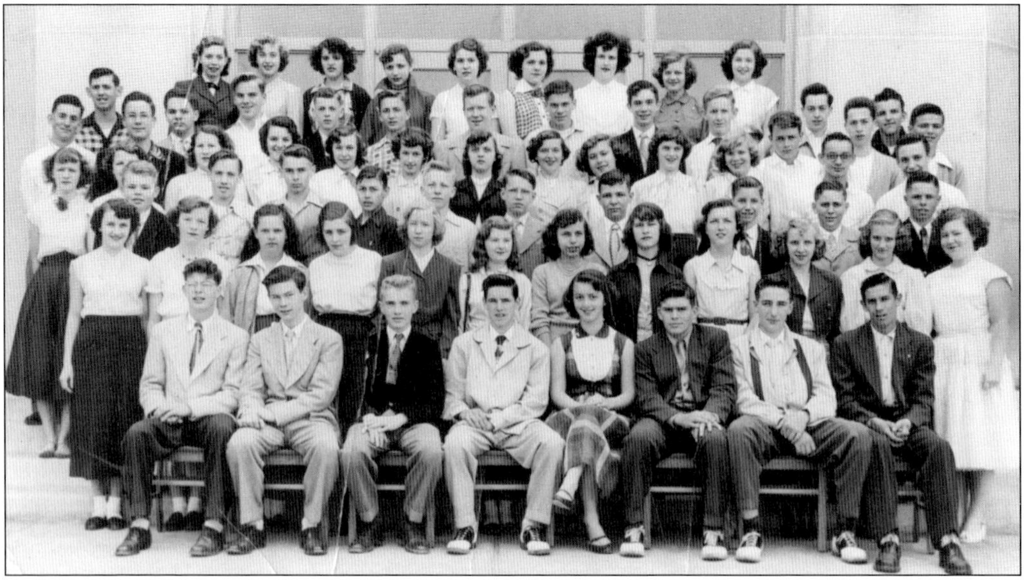

This is the graduating class of Conrad High School in 1955. The author's mother, Barbara Anne Davis, is in the second row, fifth from the left. (Courtesy personal collection.)

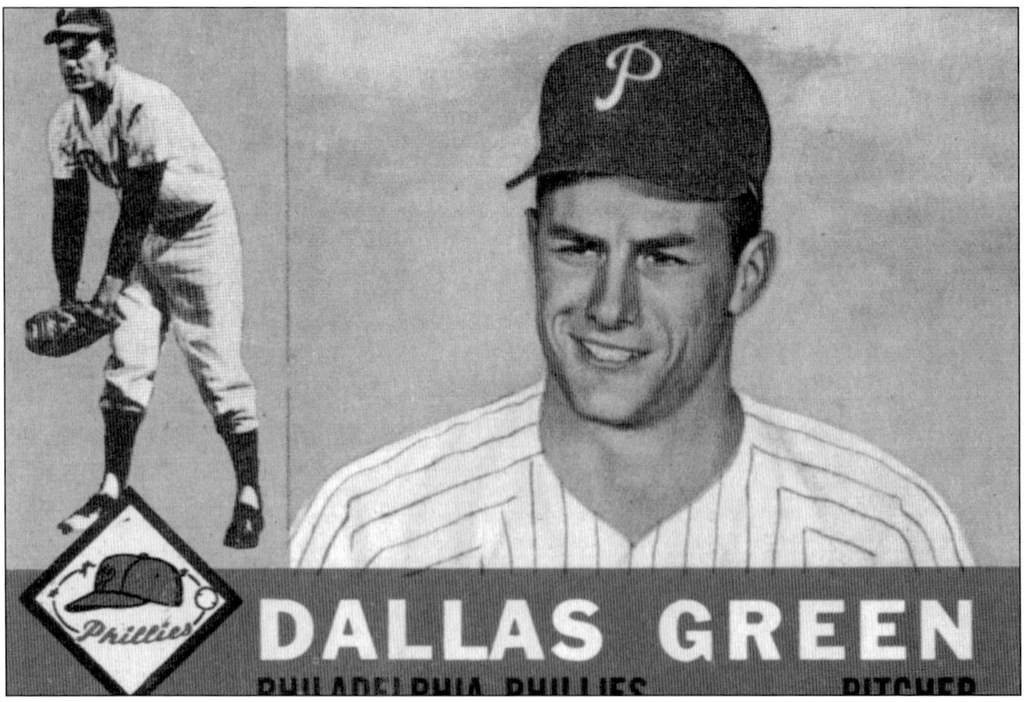

A better-known alumni of Conrad High, Dallas Green, became a star pitcher for the Phillies from 1960 to 1967 and later returned as manager of the team from 1979 to 1981, leading the team to the World Series in 1980. He has been inducted into the Delaware Sports Hall of Fame and the Philadelphia Wall of Fame in Citizens Bank Park in Philadelphia. (Courtesy personal collection.)

Five

Newport

The town of Newport was first settled by the Dutch in 1641, but in 1731, John Justis purchased 100 acres of farmland and laid out a town he called Newport-Ayre. Justis saw the area's potential as a commercial crossroads and a port. The town dropped "Ayre" from the name in 1793 when it was naming the new post office there.

Newport became a center of commerce in the early 19th century, as Conestoga wagons transported farm products from as far away as Lancaster County, Pennsylvania, to Newport's Landocks on the Christina River, where the supplies were loaded on ships bound for Boston, New York, and Philadelphia. The town's important role in trade ebbed as new roads favored the larger town of Wilmington and the railroad reached the area in 1837.

Newport incorporated in 1873 and became a manufacturing center, boasting chemical works, a glue factory, and ironworks in 1900. Henrik J. Krebs, founder of Krebs Pigments and Chemical Company, built a plant in town in 1908. The facility was purchased by E.I. DuPont de Nemours and Company in 1929 and later sold to Ciba-Geigy in 1984.

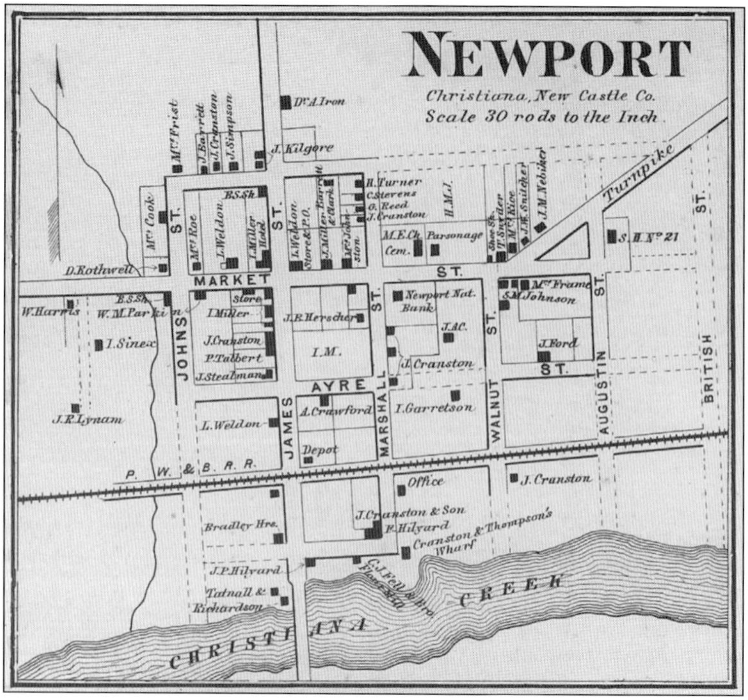

In Beer's atlas map of Newport from 1868, many of the historic homes are shown with the names of their original owners. With the exception of Basin Road, much of the town is uncharged. (Courtesy personal collection.)

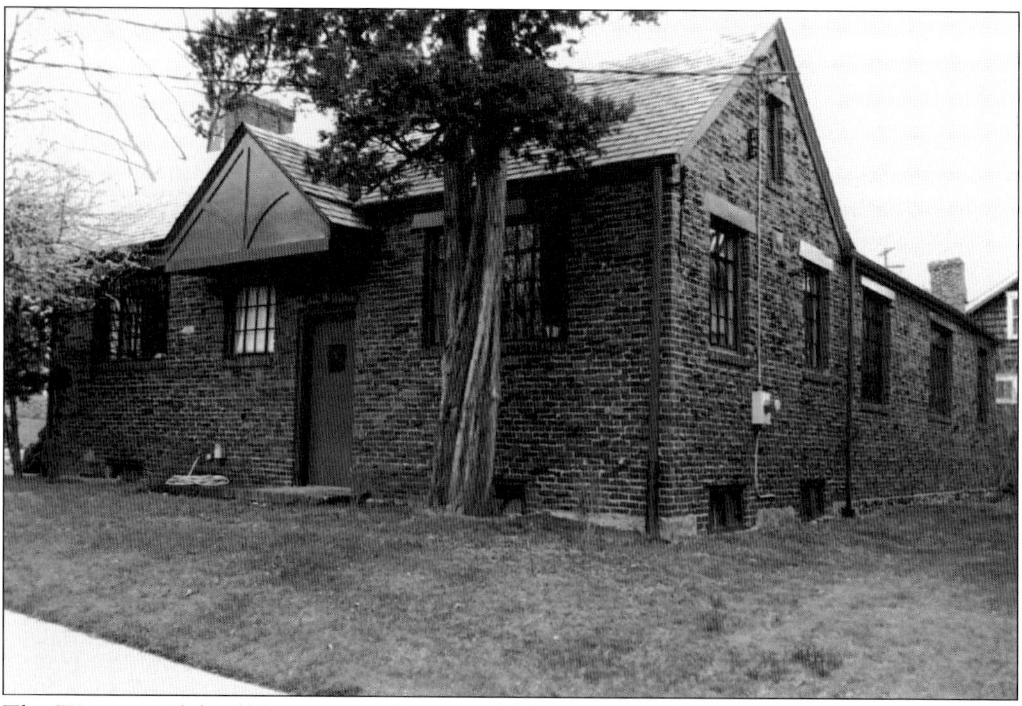

The Woman's Club of Newport is a historic clubhouse. It was built in 1934 and is a one-story, T-plan structure in the Tudor Revival style. It has a gable roofed main block with a broad wing extend to the rear, resulting in the T-configuration. The roof of the wing is slightly higher than that of the front section and terminates in a "jerkinhead" gable. (Courtesy National Register of Historic Places.)

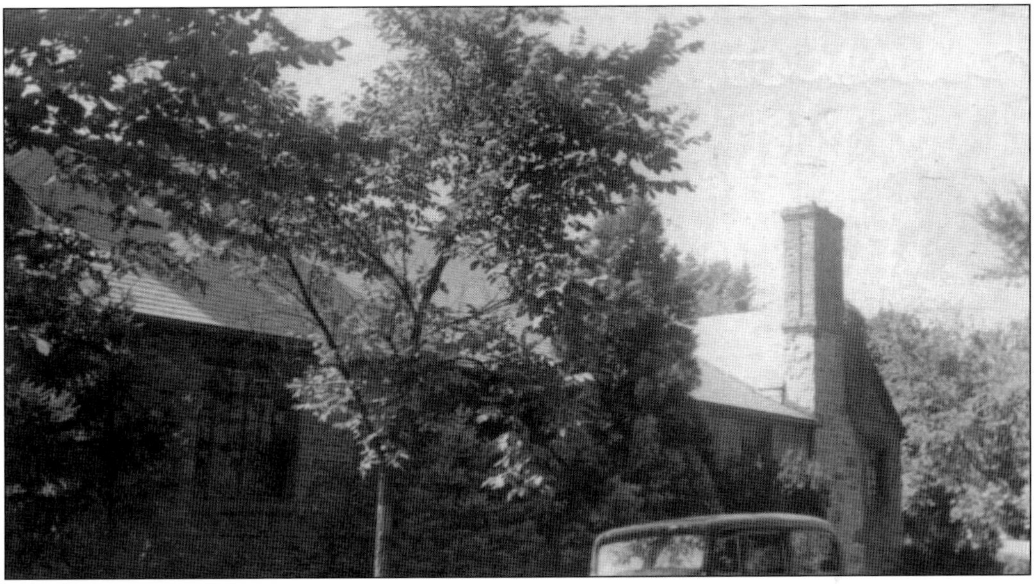

The Woman's Club also operated as the Concordia Church during the 1940s. This photograph, dating to World War II, was taken by a serviceman from Minnesota stationed in Delaware. Originally built for the Woman's Club of Newport, the clubhouse was sold to the Town of Newport for use as a town hall in 1976. (Courtesy personal collection.)

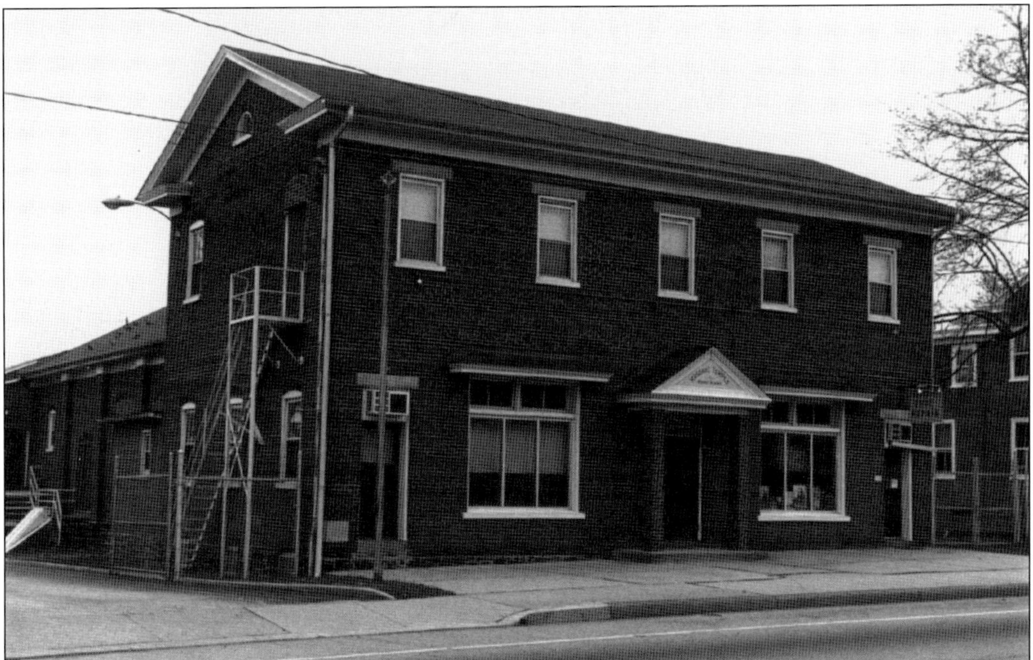

The Newport Masonic Hall, Armstrong Lodge No. 26, at 112–114 East Market Street in Newport is a two-story, five-bay brick building constructed in 1913. A large addition was built in 1958. The building is in a Colonial Revival style, with two commercial spaces on the first floor and a lodge room and auditorium on the second. It was listed in the National Register of Historic Places in 1993. (Courtesy National Register of Historic Places, National Park Service.)

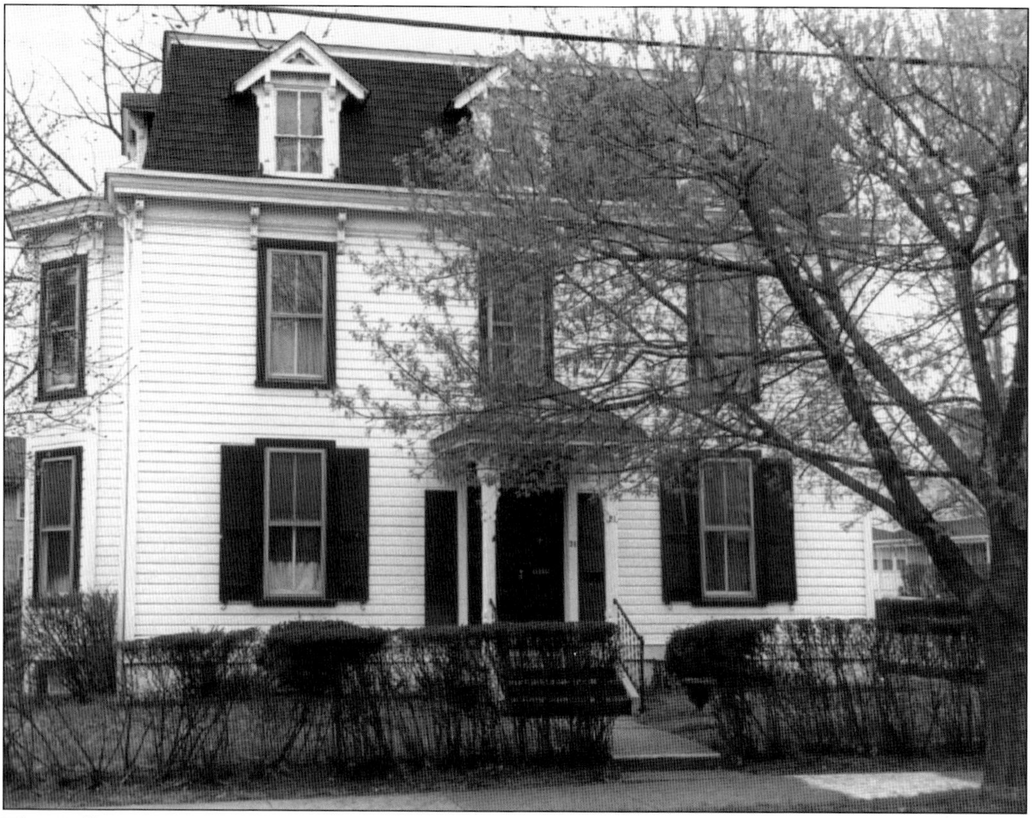

The Collison House at 21 North Walnut Street in Newport is a fine example of architecture. Built in 1885, it is a two-and-a-half-story, three-bay frame dwelling with a mansard roof in the Second Empire style. (Courtesy National Register of Historic Places, National Park Service.)

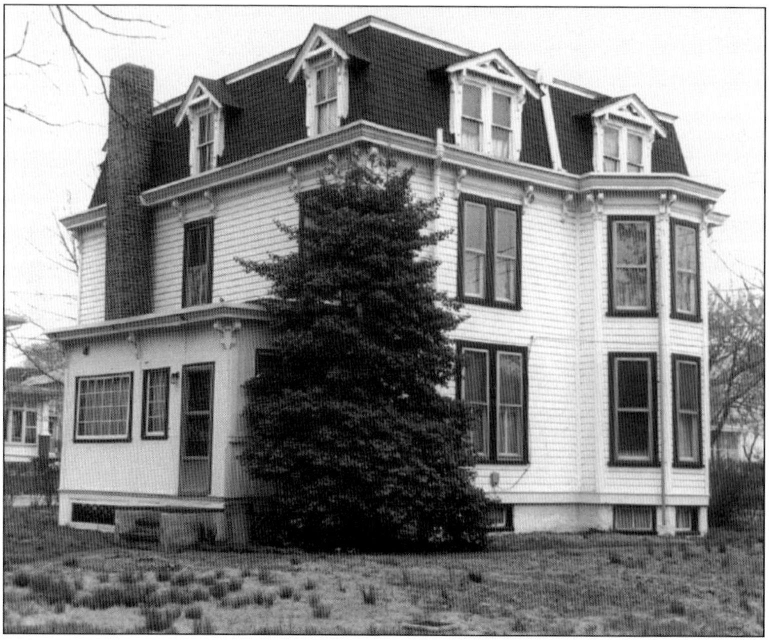

Here is another view of the architecturally significant Collison House. The mansard roof has broad gable dormers and a two-story projecting bay. It was added to the National Register in 1993. (Courtesy National Register of Historic Places, National Park Service.)

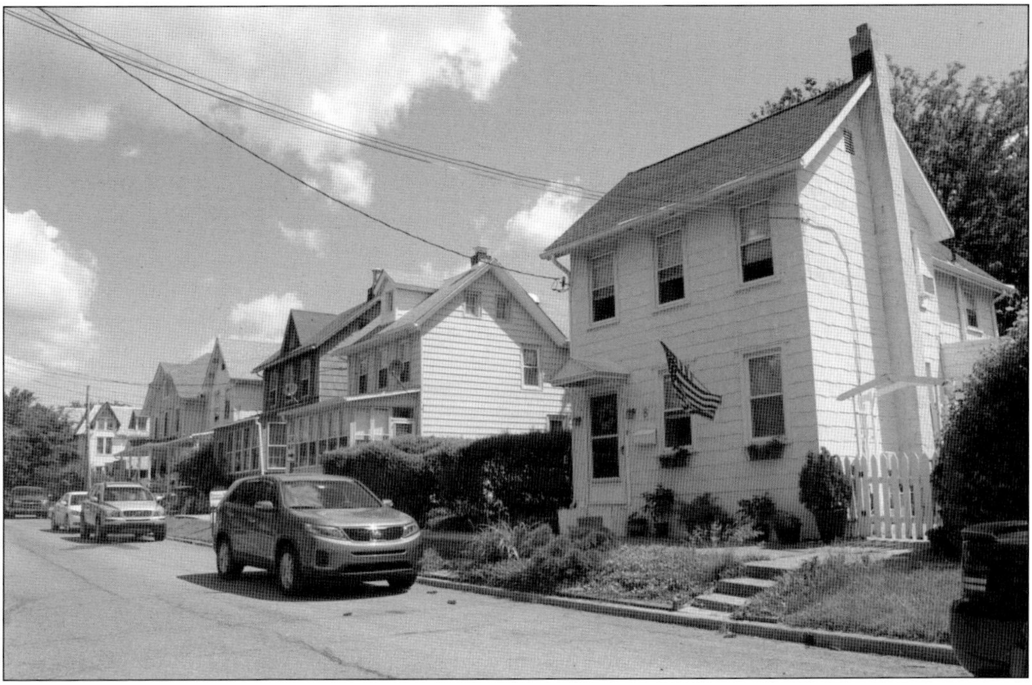

Pictured is a typical street scene in Newport, with Victorian vernacular houses built with a variety of different styles common at the turn of the 20th century. (Courtesy personal collection.)

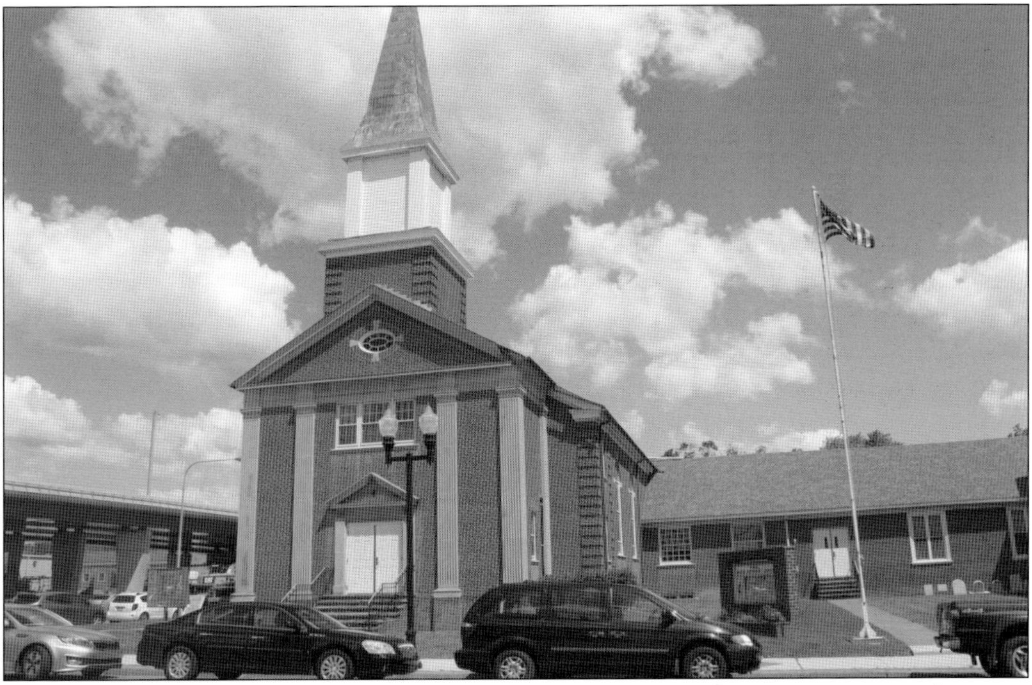

Across from the Masonic Hall, the Peniel United Methodist Church was constructed in 1842 on the same site of an earlier frame church, which was built in 1786. The edifice was remodeled in 1890 and an addition added in 1937. It has served the local community continuously since its dedication. (Courtesy personal collection.)

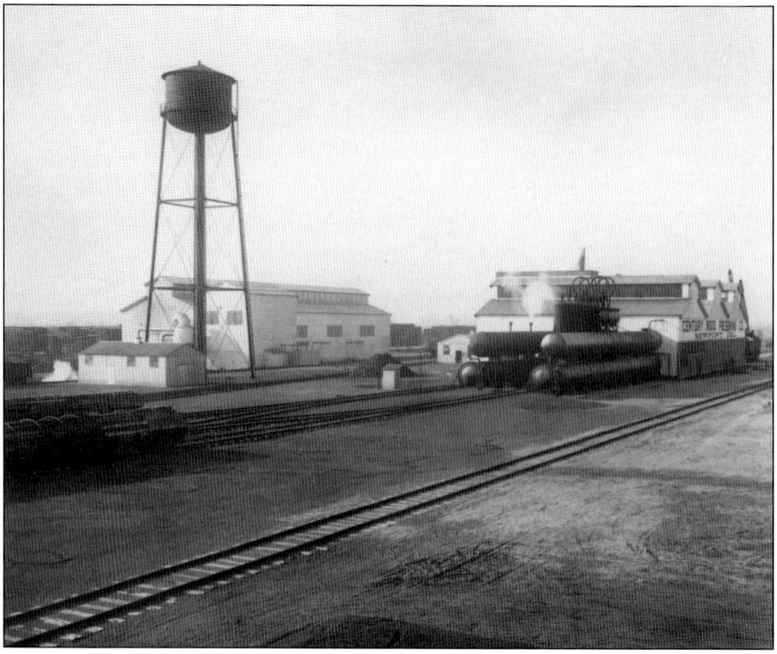

The Century Wood Preserving Company, formerly located just south of Newport on the Christiana River, specialized in manufacturing telephone poles and preserving them in creosote. Because of the nature of the business, the company's property became heavily contaminated with creosote. (Courtesy Delaware Public Archives.)

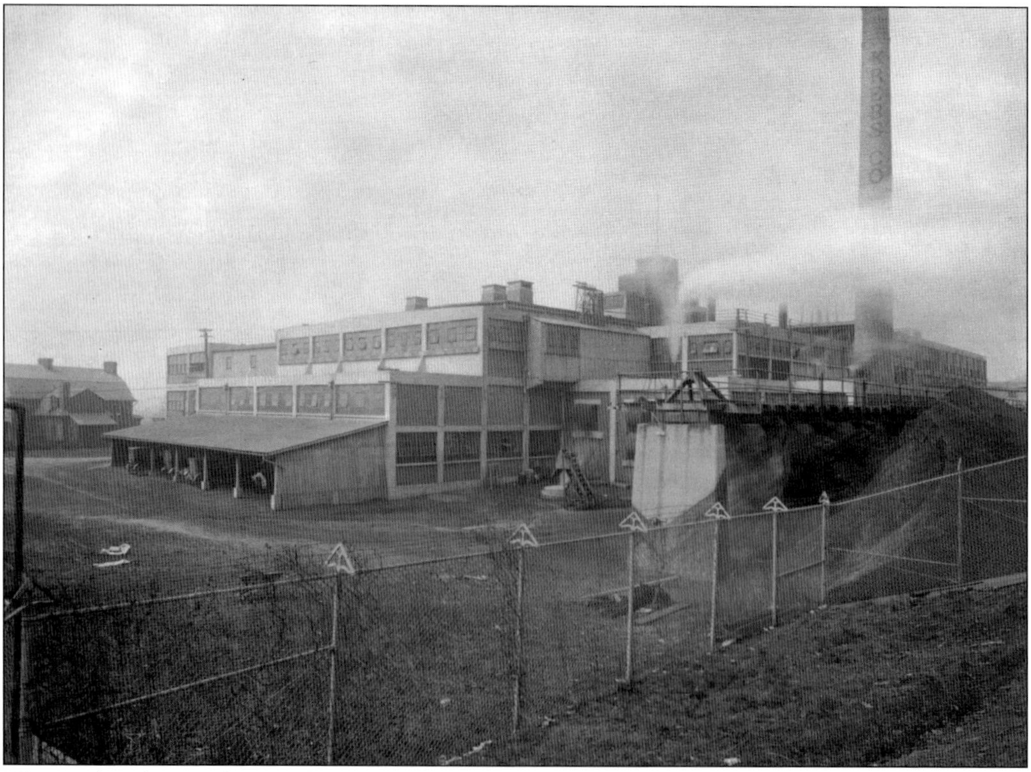

The Krebs Chemical Company, located next to the Century Wood Preserving Company, was later purchased by the DuPont Corporation for the manufacture of paint pigments. The company would dispose of the leftover paint in the adjacent marshes to the north of the factory. (Courtesy Delaware Public Archives.)

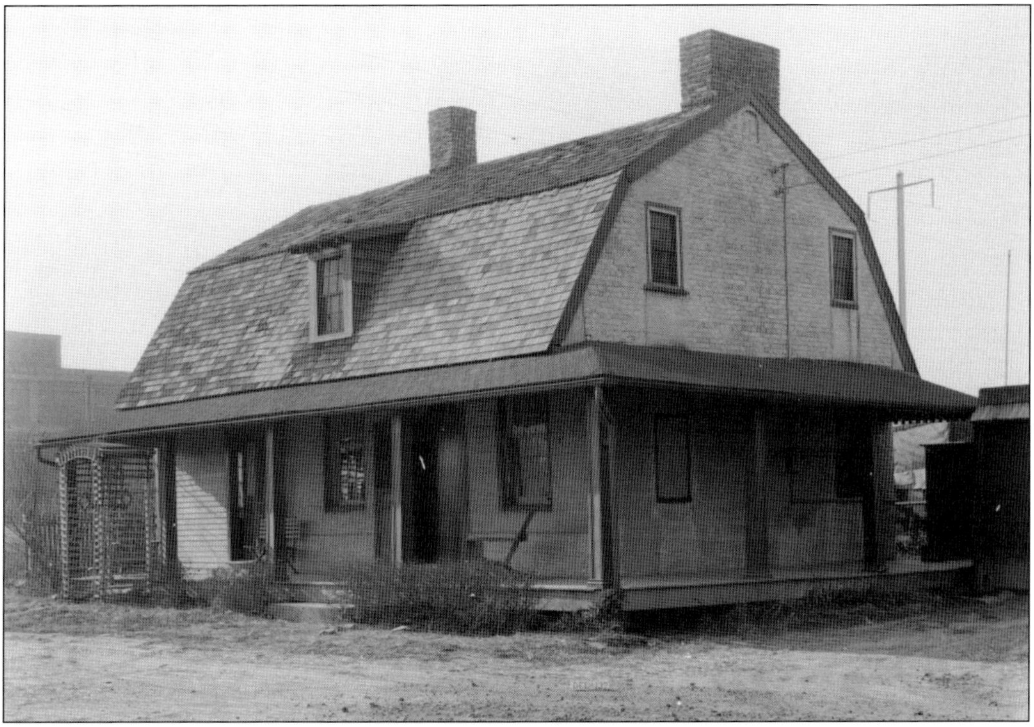

The original section of the Galloway-Walker House, built in the 18th century, is a one-and-a-half-story, three-bay brick dwelling with a gambrel roof. The house was expanded with a frame addition to create a fourth bay in the late 19th century. It is a hall-parlor-plan dwelling. (Courtesy Historic American Building Survey, Library of Congress)

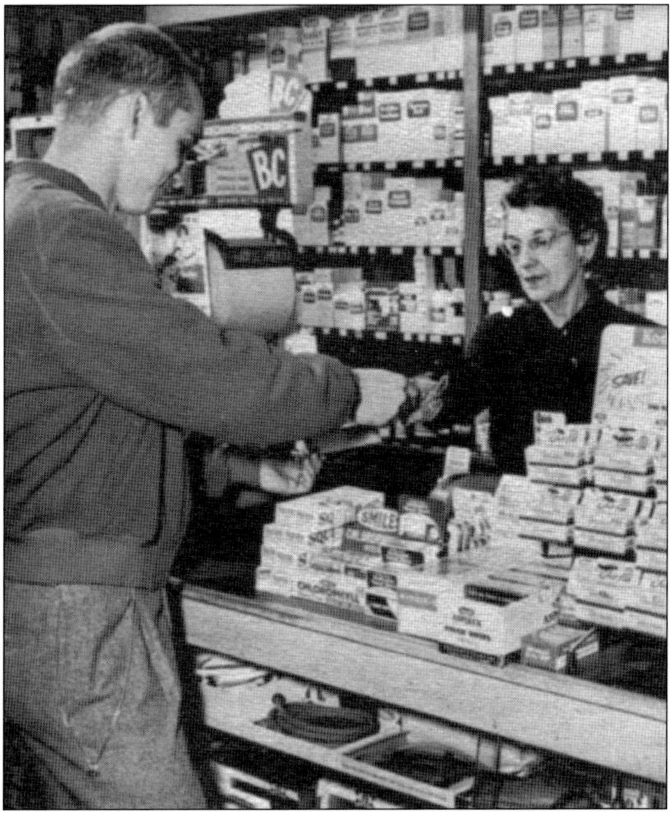

Massey's Drug Store in Newport was a popular venue in the 1950s. Pictured here is a Mrs. Massey waiting on a customer. It was eventually closed and no longer exists. (Courtesy Conrad High School Yearbook, 1955, personal collection.)

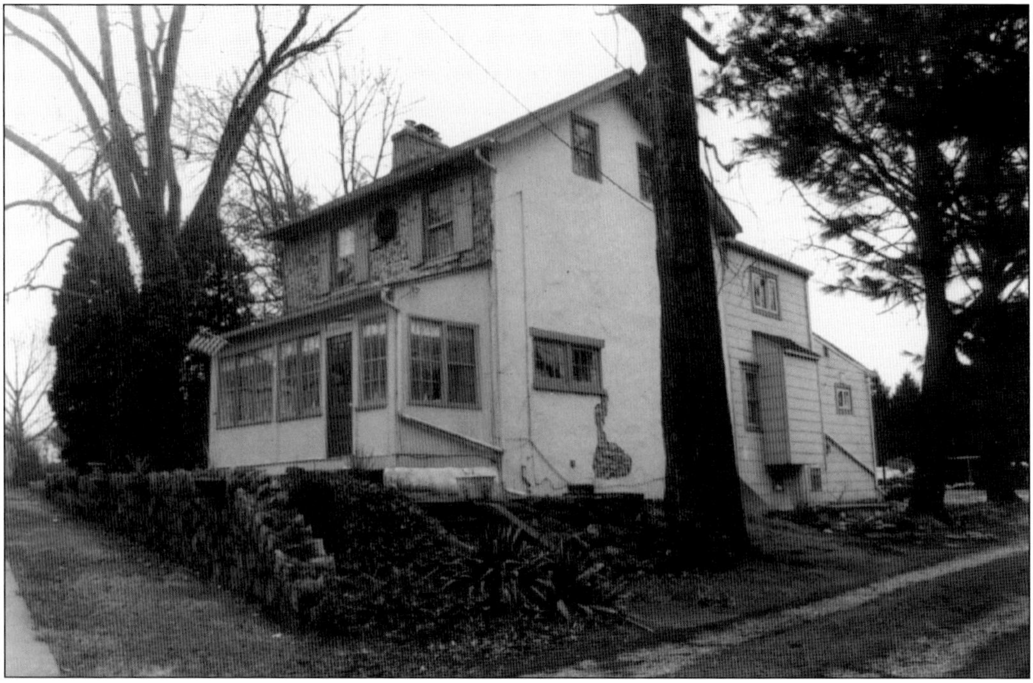

The Justis-Ayers House was the home of the founder of Newport. John Justis owned a large farm here but took the part close to the Christina River and laid out the town on it. His modest house features a large bake oven in the basement. (Both, courtesy National Register of Historic Places, National Park Service.)

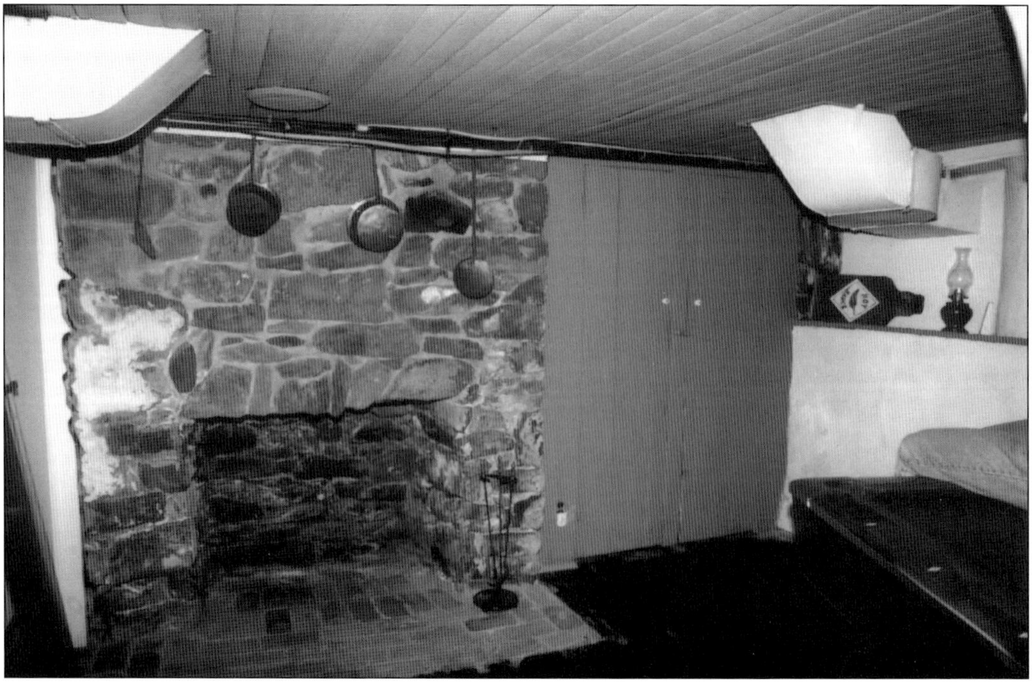

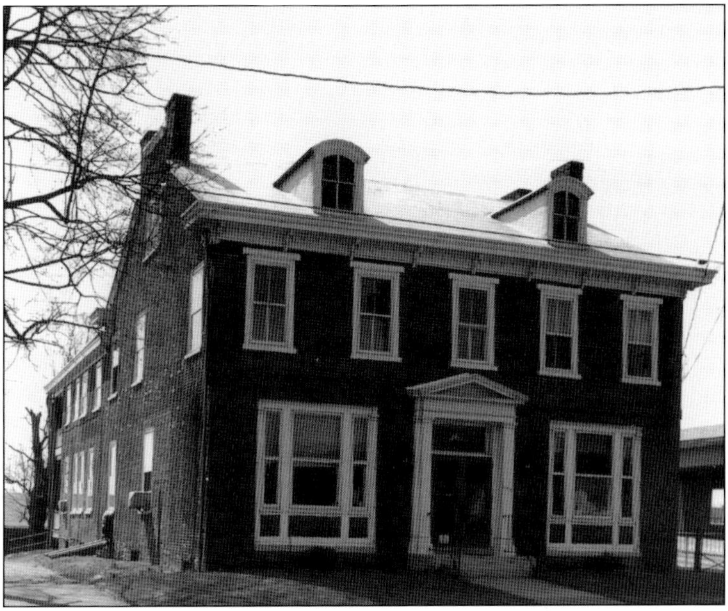

The Newport National Bank at 100 East Market Street was built in 1864 and is a two-and-a-half-story, three-bay, brick building. It was renovated in 1927 in the Colonial Revival style. The bank contained a residence because the cashier was required to live there as a security measure. It was added to the National Register of Historic Places in 1993. (Courtesy National Register of Historic Places, National Park Service.)

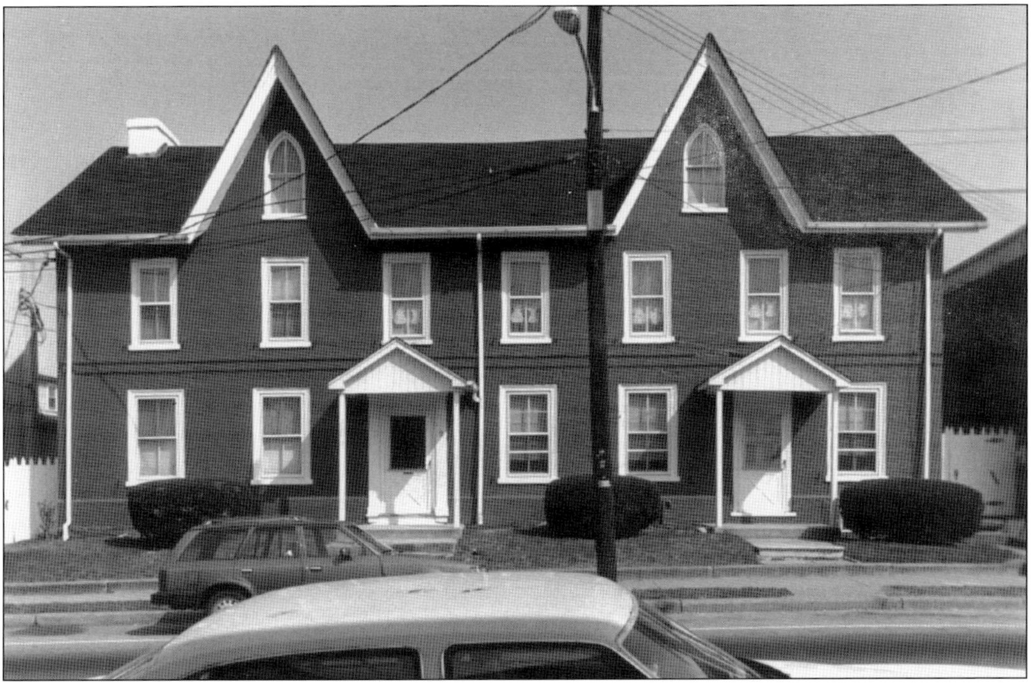

The Joseph Killgore House, built around 1860, is a simple two-story, three-bay saltbox house. It originally was a one-and-a-half-story building with a hall-parlor plan. Joseph Killgore added to his house as his fortunes increased with a commercial store that was next door. Although these two properties were listed in the National Register of Historic Places in 1993, they were demolished in 2000 to make room for the new Newport Fire Company. (Courtesy National Register of Historic Places, National Park Service.)

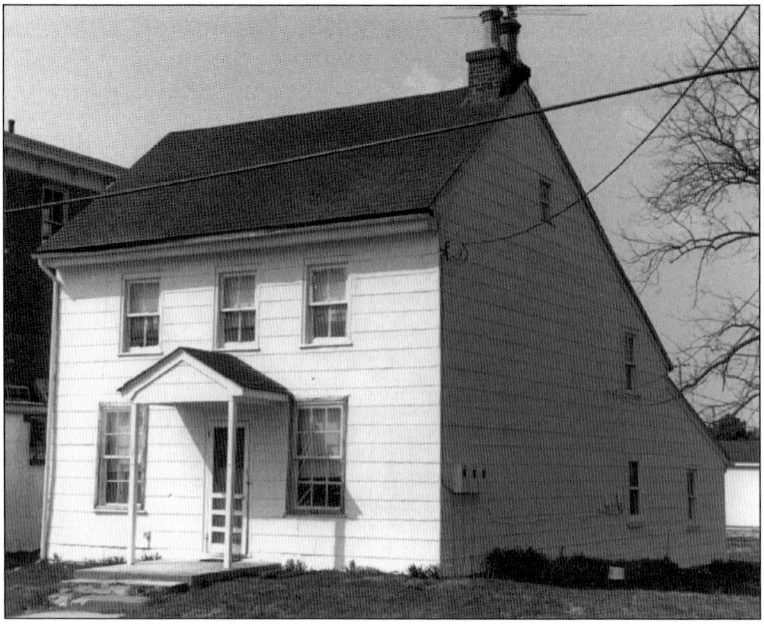

The Lewis Weldin House in Newport at 7–9 West Market Street was a two-story, gable-roofed, brick building that was seven bays wide. It was constructed in the late 18th century as a residential/commercial building and was renovated in 1863 by Lewis Weldin to serve as his residence. The building has been demolished. (Courtesy National Register of Historic Places, National Park Service.)

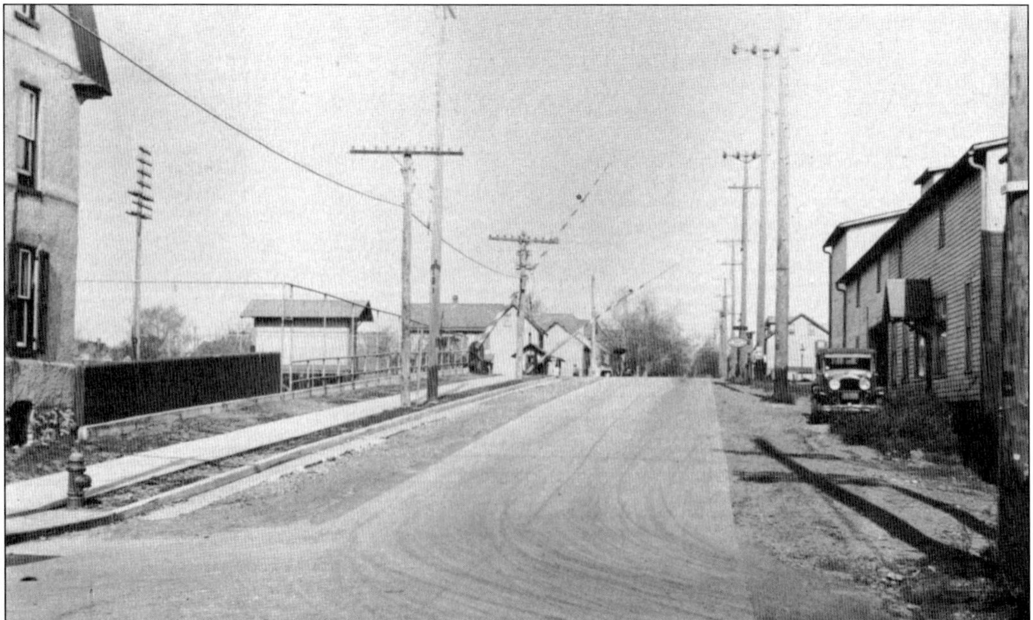

This photograph, dated to September 1961, shows a portion of Basin Road in Newport from the air. DuPont Highway is toward the top of the photograph. The DuPont Pigment Works, formerly the Krebs Chemical Company, is on the right. (Courtesy personal collection.)

Six

Stanton

The town of Stanton has become barely recognizable as a community since the dualization of Route 7 (Christiana-Stanton Road) through it; however, it was known by the derogatory name of Cuckholdstown as late as 1768 and later renamed after property owner Stephen Stanton. Gristmills and sawmills here operated under the waterpower of the White Clay Creek as early at 1679.

Across from the entrance on Route 7 to Delaware Park Racetrack is the site of fortifications that Washington's army occupied from August 28 to September 8, 1777. The Continental Army placed cannon "as thick as they could stand" and with pickets as far as Christiana Bridge. The heavy fortifications along the King's Highway forced the British to skirt the area after the Battle of Cooch's Bridge and delayed them while American reinforcements gathered for the Battle of Brandywine.

Locals will also fondly remember the railroad underpass in Stanton that was bypassed in the dualization of Route 7 and a new bridge was built, but semitrucks had a tendency to get stuck under the underpass frequently. Unfortunately, many of its historic homes and businesses were demolished when Christiana-Stanton Road was dualized in the 1980s.

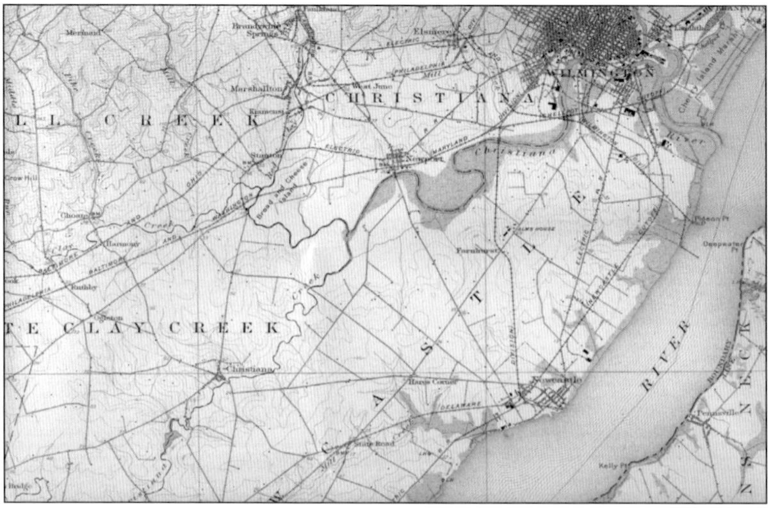

This map of the area from 1903 illustrates that prior to the beginning of suburbanization, the Old Post Road saw the most population at the cities and towns while widely separated farms and little crossroad communities were all that were found in between. (Courtesy personal collection.)

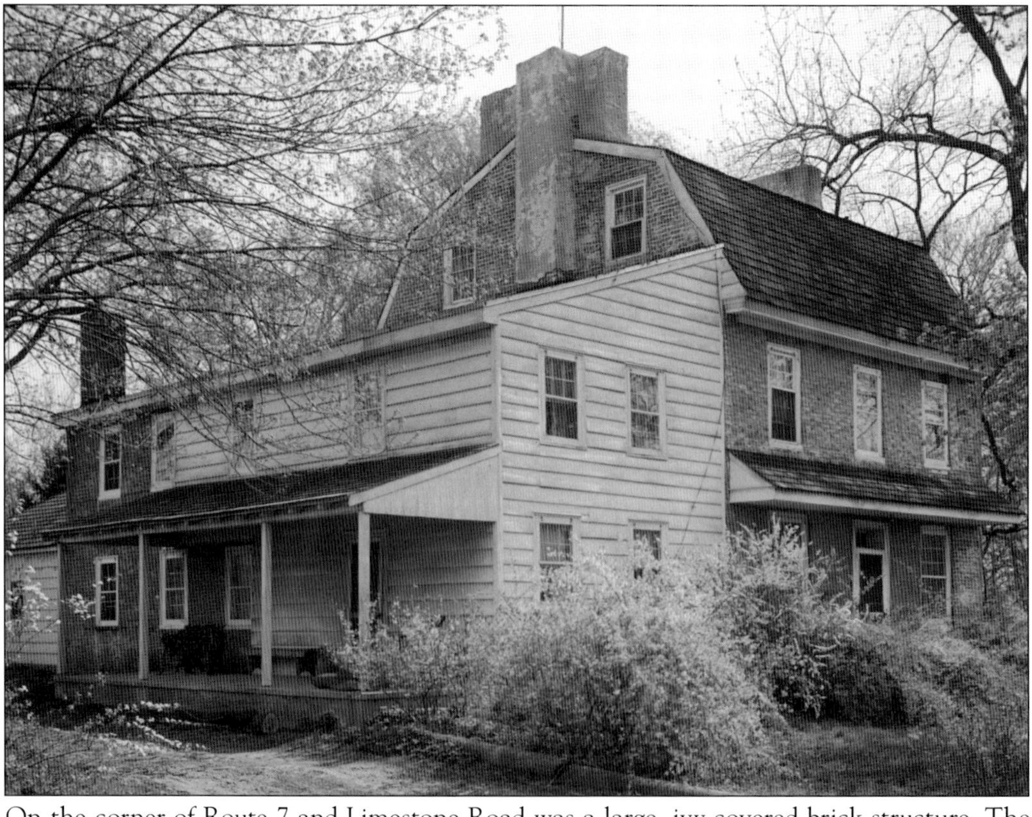

On the corner of Route 7 and Limestone Road was a large, ivy-covered brick structure. The Tatnall or Byrnes House was built of brick in 1750 in a Dutch Colonial style. It was erected by Peter Springer. (Courtesy Historic American Building Survey, Library of Congress.)

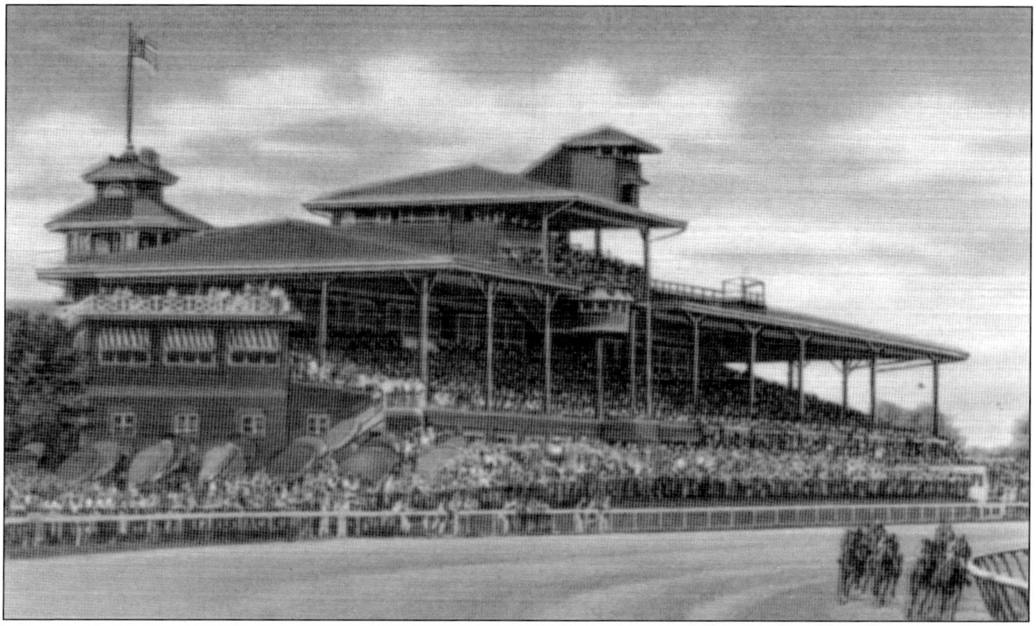

The Delaware Park racetrack opened in 1937 as one of the finest horse tracks on the East Coast. William DuPont, the founder of the track, led an effort to legalize gambling and won that victory in 1933. This 1937 photograph shows the Grand Parade that was held on opening day. (Courtesy personal collection.)

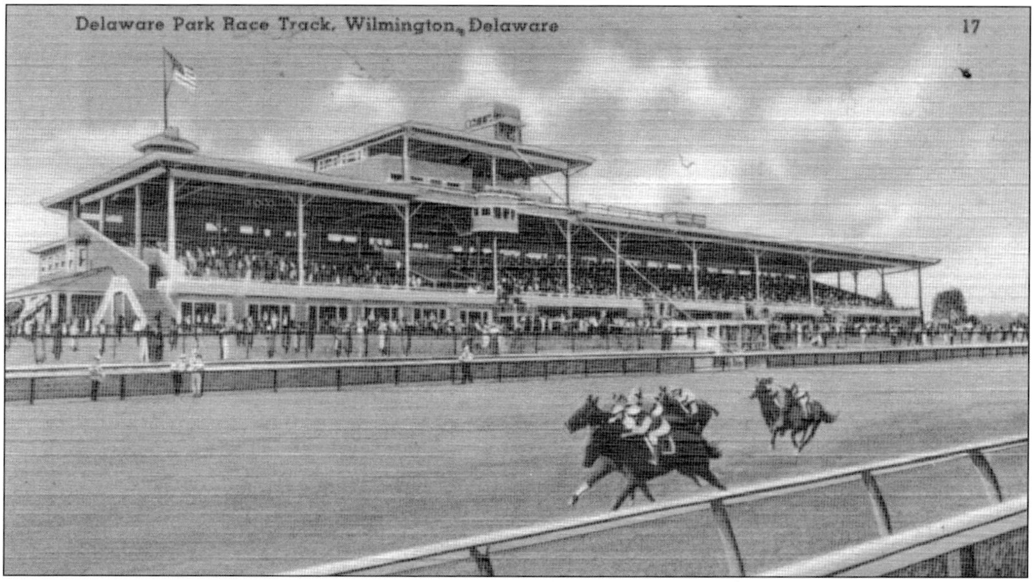

Delaware Park was popular in the 1940s for both flat-track and steeplechase racing. It also hosted semi-amateur boxing tournaments under the grandstand. Banker and philanthropist William DuPont designed the park to include a picnic grove to attract families to come to the races together. (Courtesy personal collection.)

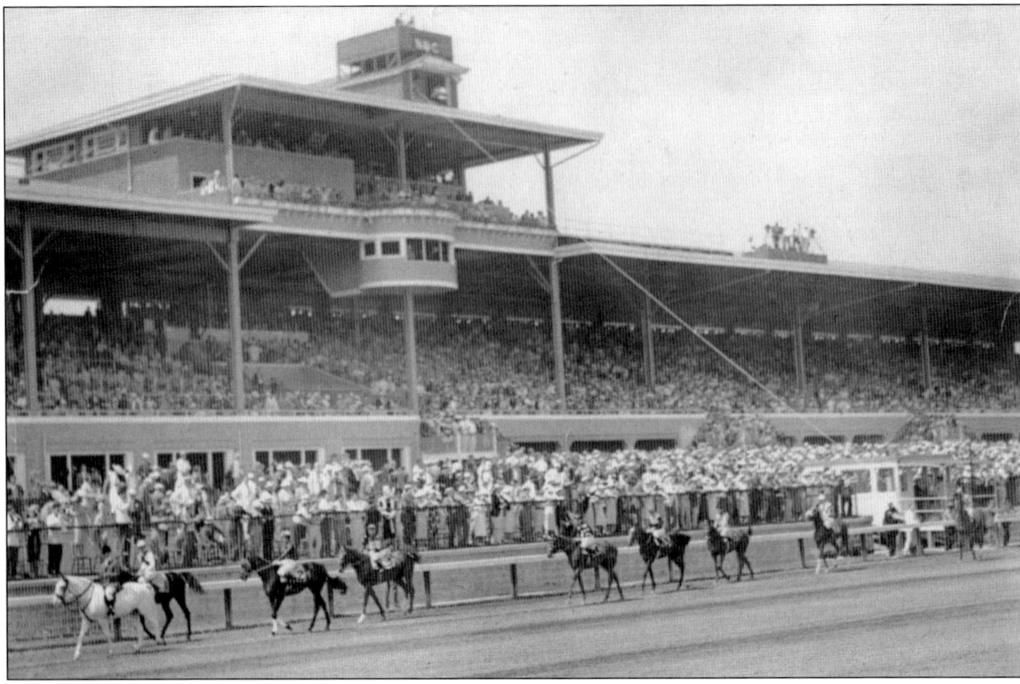

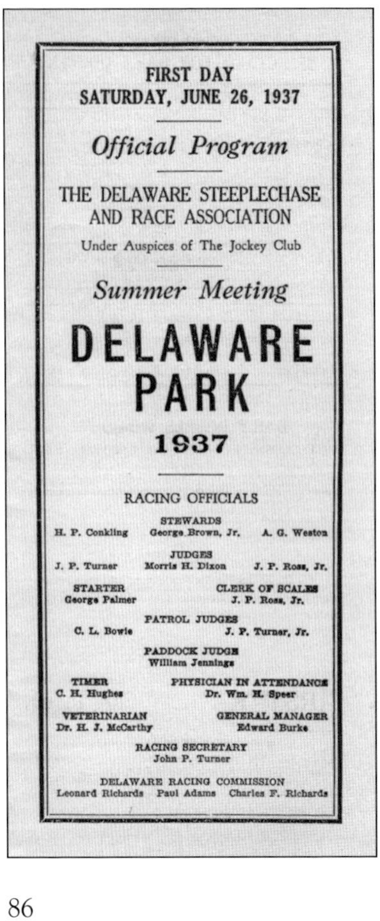

FIRST DAY
SATURDAY, JUNE 26, 1937

Official Program

THE DELAWARE STEEPLECHASE AND RACE ASSOCIATION

Under Auspices of The Jockey Club

Summer Meeting

DELAWARE PARK

1937

RACING OFFICIALS

STEWARDS
H. P. Conkling George Brown, Jr. A. G. Weston

JUDGES
J. P. Turner Morris H. Dixon J. P. Ross, Jr.

STARTER
George Palmer

CLERK OF SCALES
J. P. Ross, Jr.

PATROL JUDGES
C. L. Bowie J. P. Turner, Jr.

PADDOCK JUDGE
William Jennings

TIMER
C. H. Hughes

PHYSICIAN IN ATTENDANCE
Dr. Wm. H. Speer

VETERINARIAN
Dr. H. J. McCarthy

GENERAL MANAGER
Edward Burke

RACING SECRETARY
John P. Turner

DELAWARE RACING COMMISSION
Leonard Richards Paul Adams Charles F. Richards

The track was popular through the 1960s after a $2 million expansion in 1965, but it closed in the 1980s and was vacant for a number of years. The park was eventually was revived as a casino in 1995, which has helped bring back racing excitement to the area. (Courtesy personal collection.)

This program is from Delaware Park's opening day, June 26, 1937. Reports of opening day stated that the track was sold out and that many patrons arrived by train to a station built inside the park. At the time, most of the surrounding area was still farmland, but it is all now suburban developments. (Courtesy personal collection.)

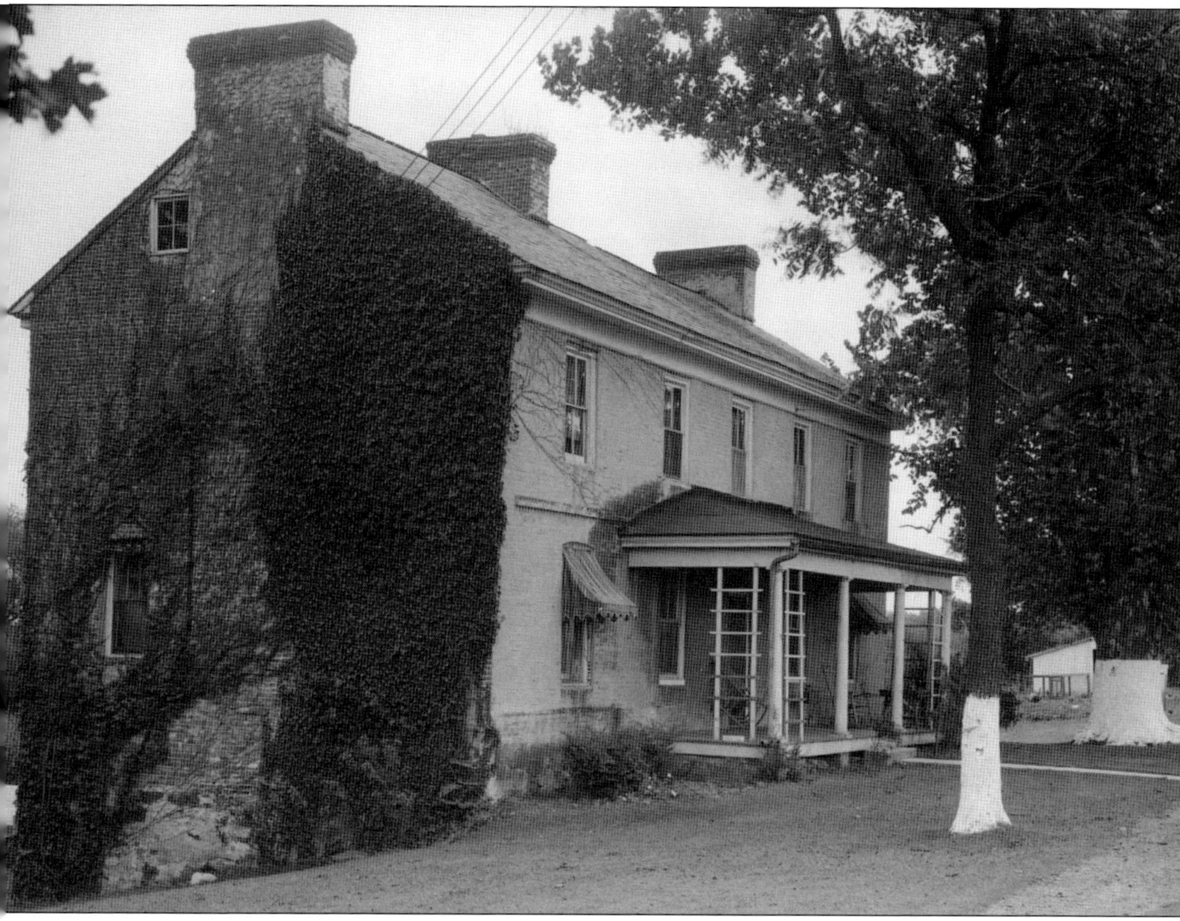

The Hale-Byrnes House at 606 Stanton-Christiana Road was built in 1750. It is a two-story, five-bay brick house. It was built by Samuel Hale, who sold it to Daniel Byrnes in 1754. The kitchen originally opened at grade on the creek bank, but it now frequently floods. With its broad chimneys, brick belt course, and water table, it is a notable example of Georgian Colonial architecture. (Courtesy Historic American Building Survey, Library of Congress.)

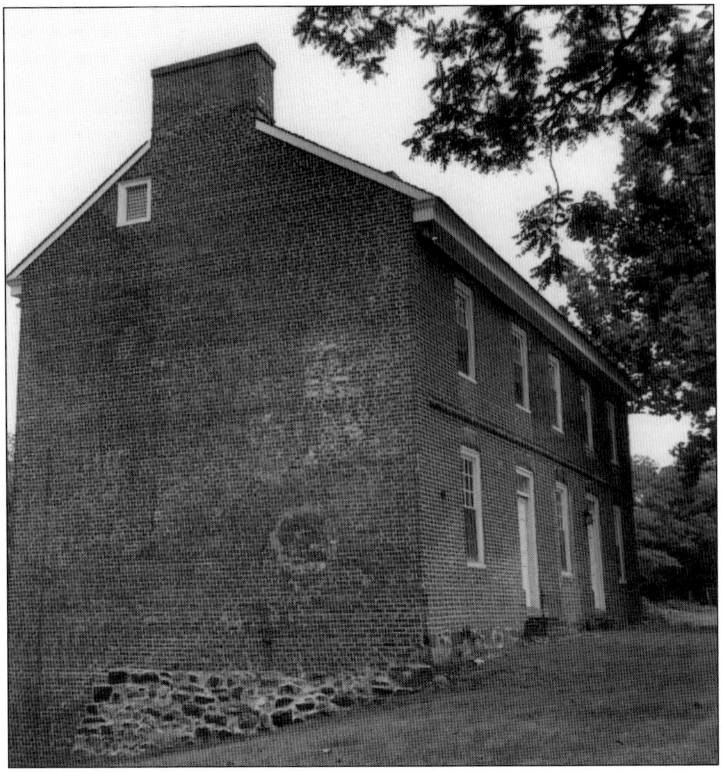

This view of the Hale-Byrnes House is from the 1960s. (Courtesy National Register of Historic Places, National Park Service.)

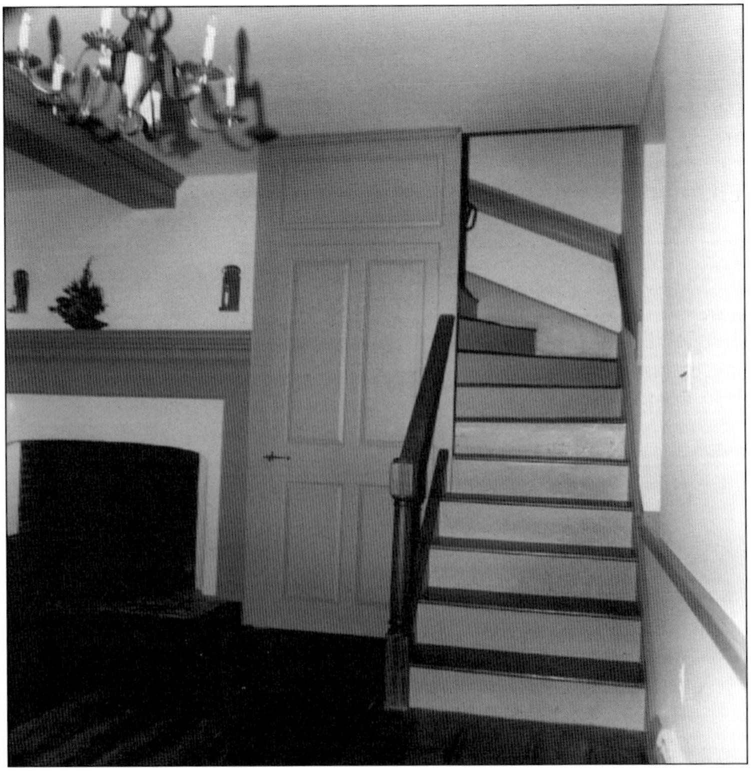

On September 6, 1777, American officers held a war meeting at the Hale-Byrnes House. "The general officers of American army September 6, 1777, were directed to meet at the brick house by White Clay Creek and fix proper picquets for the security of the camp" was recorded in an order book by Capt. Robert Kirkwood. The house is now a museum. (Courtesy National Register of Historic Places, National Park Service.)

Seven

CHRISTIANA

North of Christiana, the Old Post Road again changes its name. Here, it is Old Baltimore Pike. At the top of the hill north of the village, Christiana Mall, the largest mall in Delaware, takes its name from the sleepy little village.

The town of Christiana, originally Christiana Bridge, was first settled by John Ogle, a British soldier who received a land grant here as payment for service to the king's army. After his death, his son Thomas Ogle established the village of Ogletown a few miles north, and the Ogle land in Christiana was divided by Rees Jones and sold into smaller lots for housing.

At one point, Christiana was one of the most important shipping points in the county. The bridge that crosses the Christina Creek here was first built in 1686 as part of the road from the then capital at New Castle to the Nottingham Lots (now near Rising Sun in Maryland). An important landing was in Christiana, where sloops could load grain from the area for transport to Philadelphia. On the west side of the bridge were a number of warehouses for storing items for loading. It was also here that the American troops unloaded to establish perimeters before the Battle of Cooches Bridge during the Revolutionary War.

Because of its junction with the Old Post Road and Christina Creek, the town attracted many important visitors. It was a major stopping point along the Old Post Road, and it is known that President Washington and General Lafayette, among others, passed through this town. Mason and Dixon held a meeting here in 1768 to present the results of their boundary survey to representatives of the Penn (Pennsylvania) and Calvert (Maryland) governments.

The center of Christiana contains a number of important buildings dating to the 18th century. Because it was largely bypassed by alteration in the 20th century, the community still retains a Colonial feel and was listed as a district in the National Register of Historic Places in 1974.

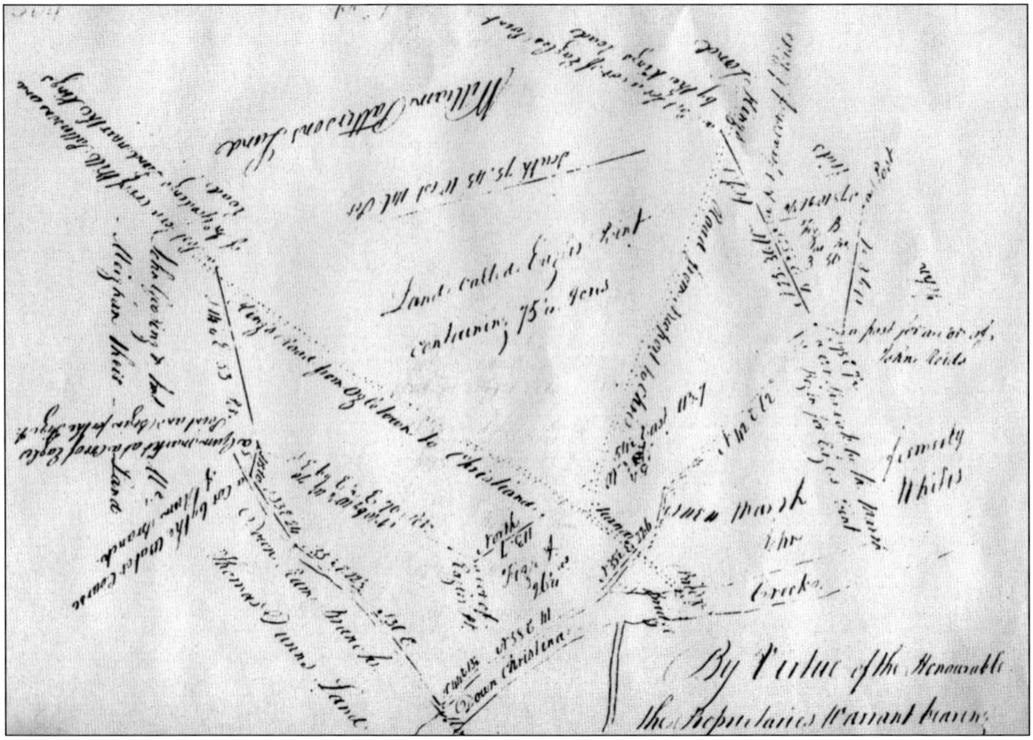

This plat was dated to 1752 but was a resurvey of the land given to John Ogle by the Duke of York in 1684 for military service. He called his estate Eagle's Point, a name still used today for a road that runs through the property. His land was the northwestern quarter of present-day Christiana, west of Old Baltimore Pike and north of West Main Street. (Courtesy personal collection.)

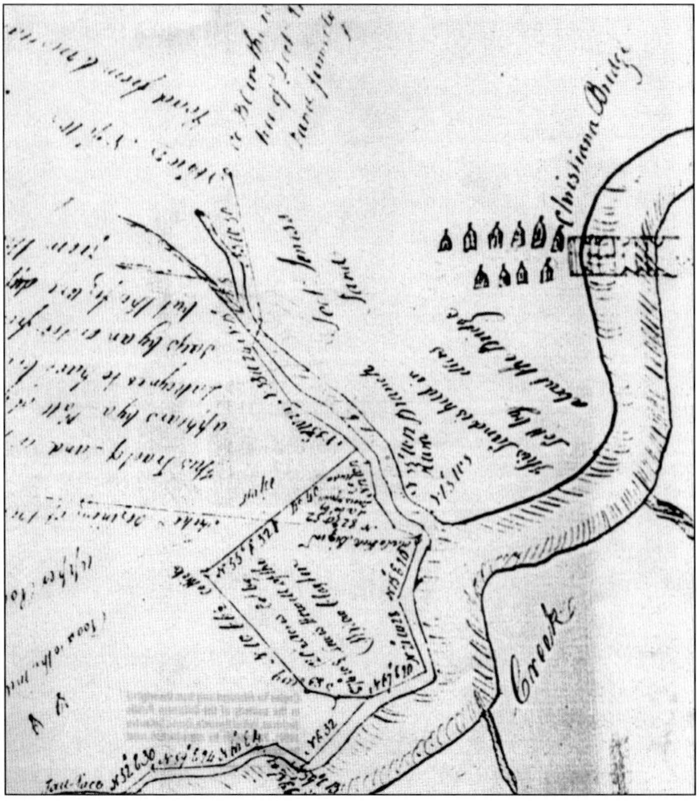

This map, dated to 1710, is probably the earliest map illustrating the village of Christiana and the bridge over the Christina River. It was included as part of a deed transfer. (Courtesy personal collection.)

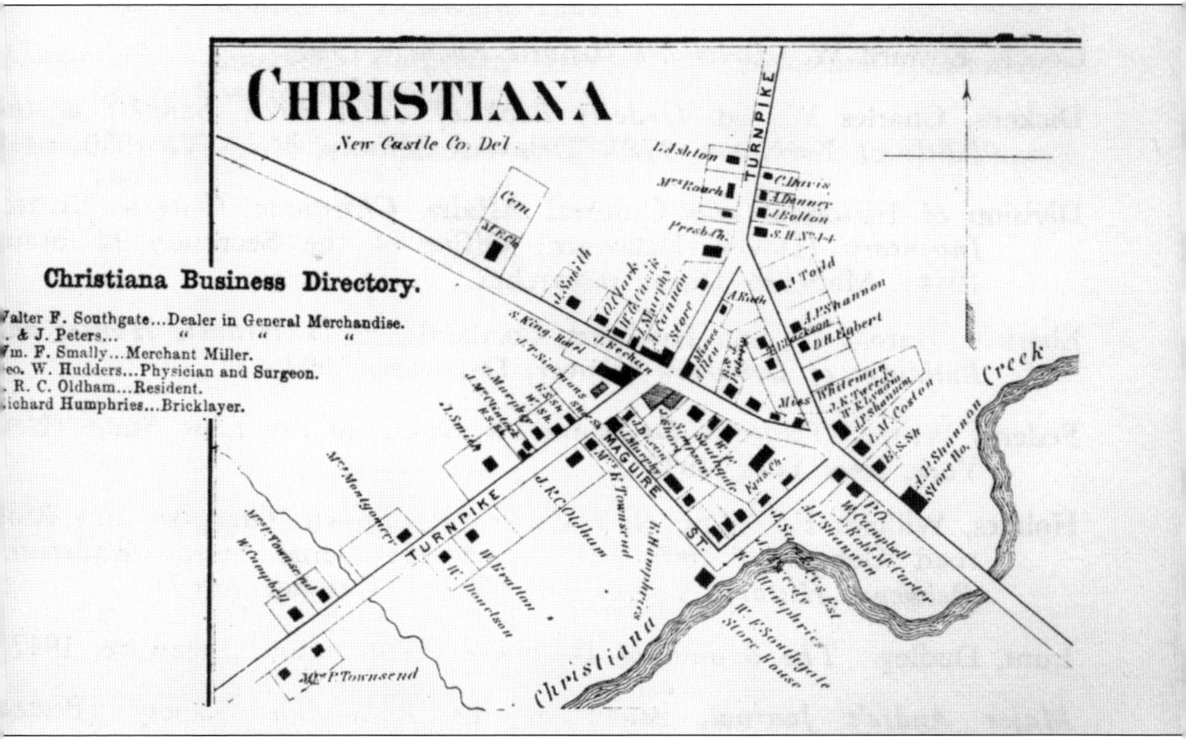

Beer's map of Christiana, published in 1868, shows the town in its heyday. There were shops, hotels, and storehouses, and it had its own post office. Most of the buildings shown on the map remain to the present day. (Courtesy personal collection.)

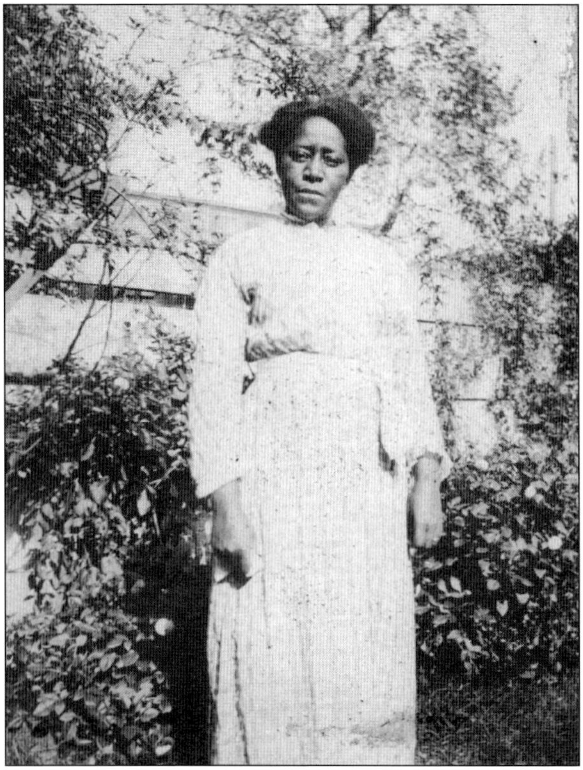

In the northern part of the village, one of the largest free black communities in early-19th-century Delaware developed around Brown's Lane. Many of the members of this community were in the Neal family. This late-19th-century photograph is thought to be a matriarch of that family. (Courtesy personal collection.)

The Brown's Lane community in Christiana was once one of the largest antebellum free black communities in the state. It contained a one-room schoolhouse, built in the late 19th century, that was operated by the local community. (Courtesy National Register of Historic Places, National Park Service.)

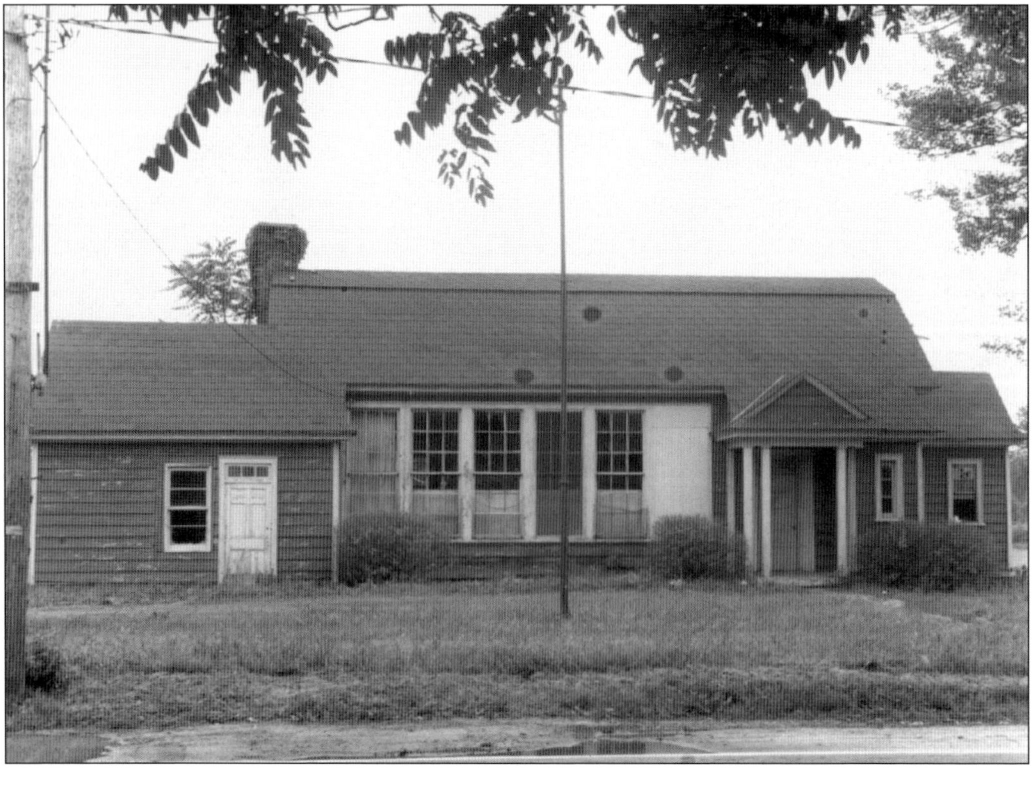

The DuPont schools were designed in 1920 by architect James O. Betelle of Trenton, New Jersey. They contained a single education room, a kitchen, and an indoor bathroom, unique for the time. (Courtesy National Register of Historic Places, National Park Service.)

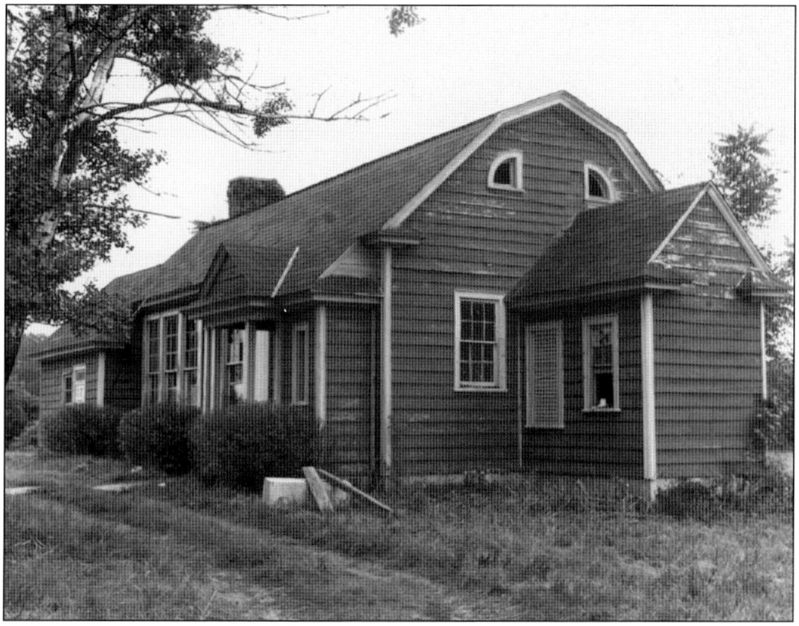

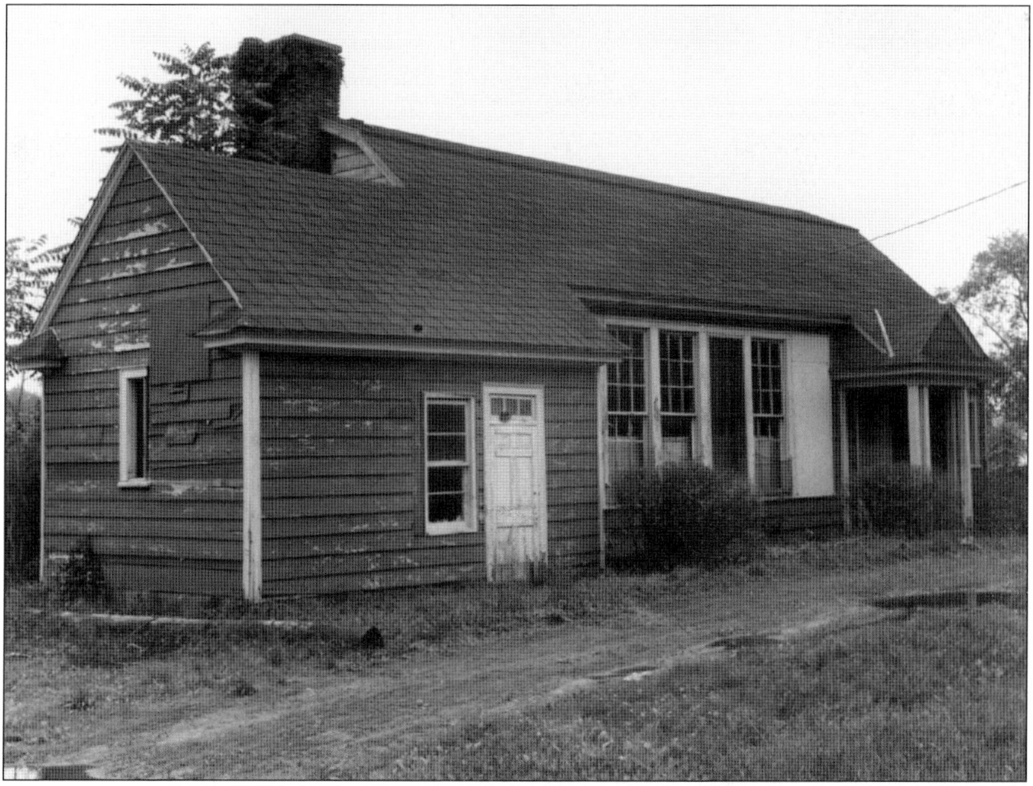

School 111-C was also the site of a protest against unfair taxation before *Brown v. the Board of Education* because the local residents were taxed after the school was closed and their children were being bused to Wilmington. The building is being renovated as a community center. (Courtesy National Register of Historic Places, National Park Service.)

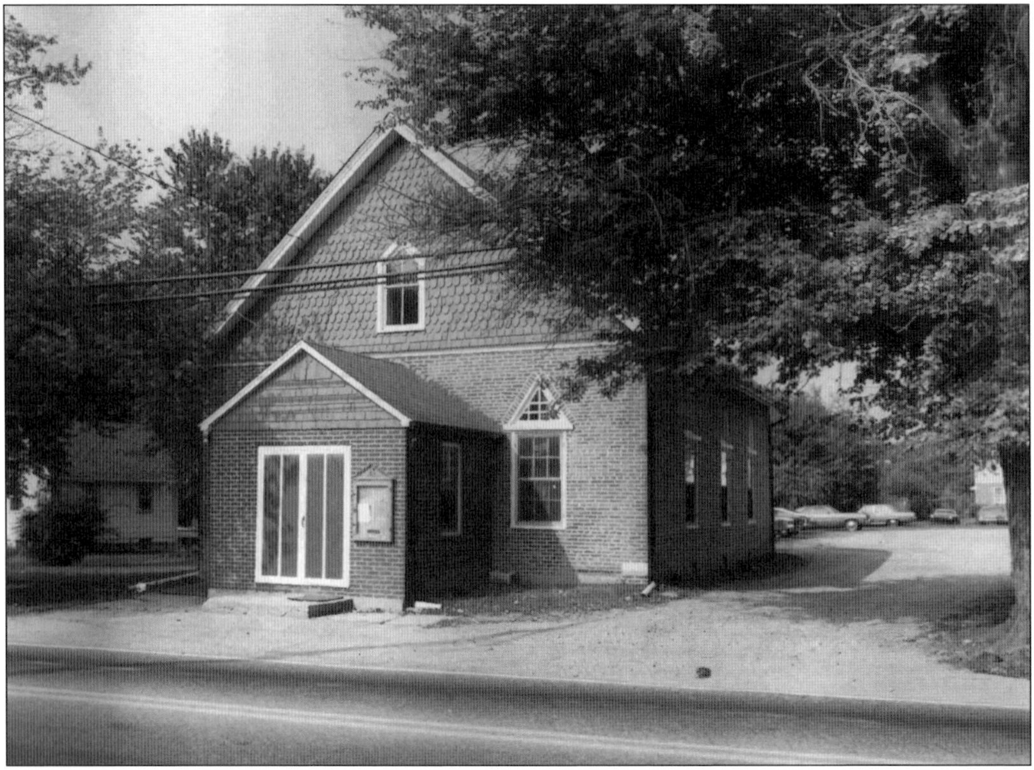

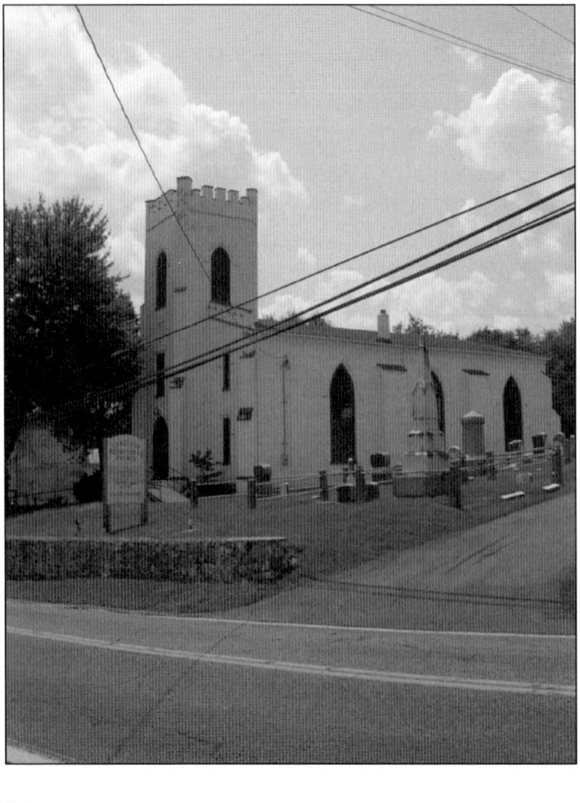

The Brown's Lane community was also served by the Old Fort Church. The brick church was built in 1850 adjacent to Schoolbell Road, but it was dismantled and moved to this location in 1897. Considered a "family church," many of its members are still related to the Neal family. (Courtesy National Register of Historic Places, National Park Service.)

The Christiana Presbyterian Church was built in 1858 on the site of an earlier church constructed in 1745. The church still holds regular Sunday services. (Courtesy personal collection.)

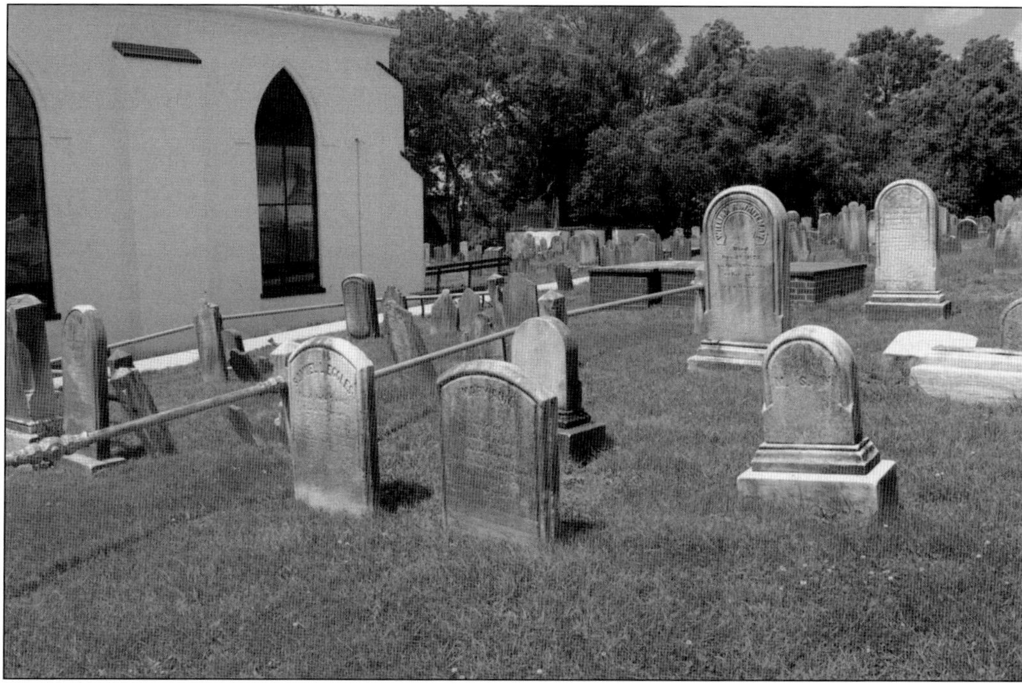

On the side and behind the Presbyterian church, a large cemetery holds the remains of hundreds of locals. Col. Samuel Patterson, a miller and officer in the Revolutionary War, is buried here, and his headstone is incorporated in the back wall of the present church. (Courtesy personal collection.)

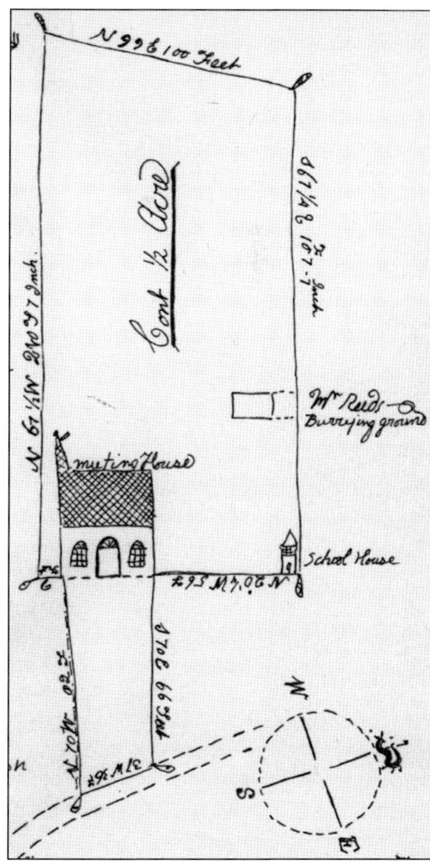

Col. William Read, father of a signer of the Declaration of Independence, and his wife are also buried in a crypt nearby. The limestone inscriptions have become almost worn smooth. (Courtesy personal collection.)

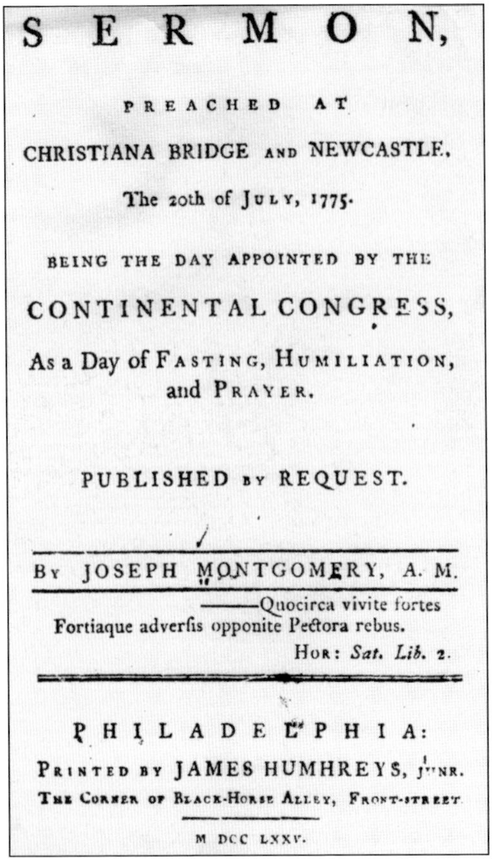

SERMON,

PREACHED AT

CHRISTIANA BRIDGE AND NEWCASTLE,

The 20th of JULY, 1775.

BEING THE DAY APPOINTED BY THE

CONTINENTAL CONGRESS,

As a Day of FASTING, HUMILIATION, and PRAYER.

PUBLISHED BY REQUEST.

BY JOSEPH MONTGOMERY, A. M.

——Quocirca vivite fortes
Fortiaque adverſis opponite Pectora rebus.
HOR: *Sat. Lib.* 2.

PHILADELPHIA:

PRINTED BY JAMES HUMHREYS, JUNR.

THE CORNER OF BLACK-HORSE ALLEY, FRONT-STREET.

M DCC LXXV.

This broadside announces the publication, in 1775, of a sermon recently presented at the Presbyterian churches in Christiana and New Castle. Broadsides were posted at taverns and other public places to advertise products for sale. (Courtesy Library of Congress.)

This seemingly insignificant piece of limestone on the church property has an important history. During the 18th century, roads were laid out by hand, with surveyors using a metal "chain" to mark distances. This was a mile marker, placed along the King's Road during an early survey. (Courtesy personal collection.)

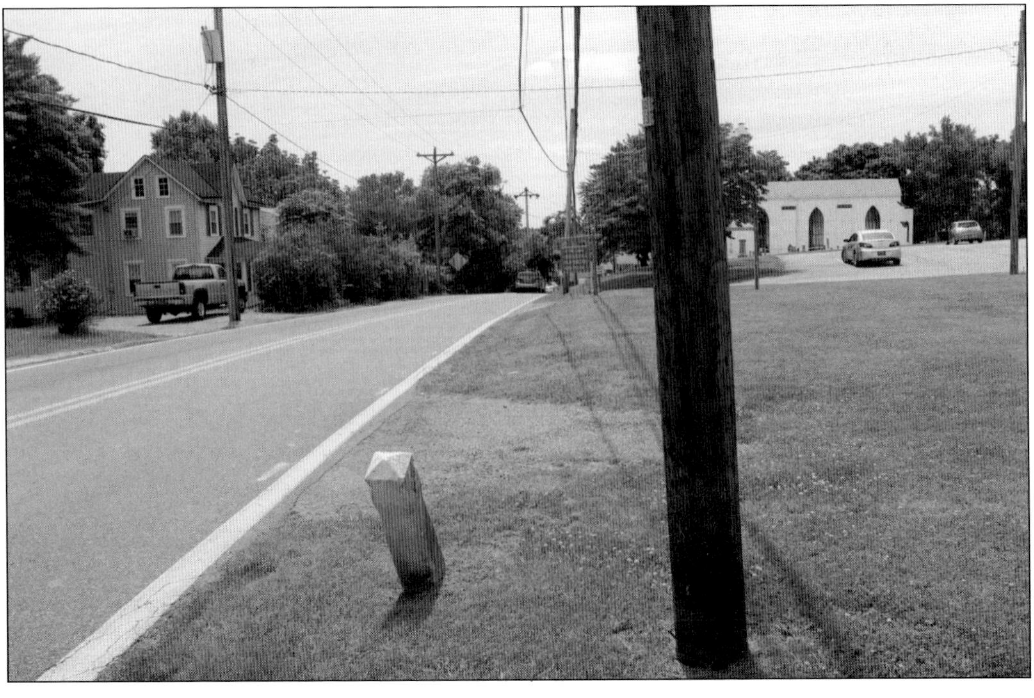

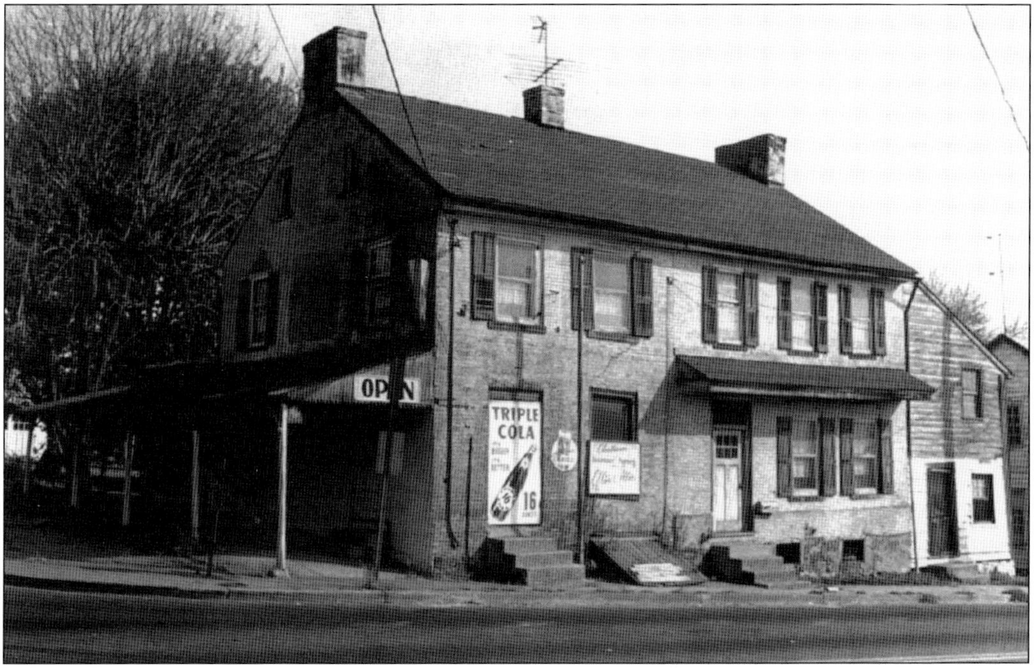

The center of Christiana contains two extant colonial taverns, the Shannon Inn on the northeast corner and the Christiana Inn on the southwest corner. At one of these taverns, surveyors Mason and Dixon met with representatives of Maryland and Pennsylvania to report the results of their boundary survey. The Shannon Inn is shown above in a 1936 photograph. (Courtesy Historic American Building Survey, Library of Congress.)

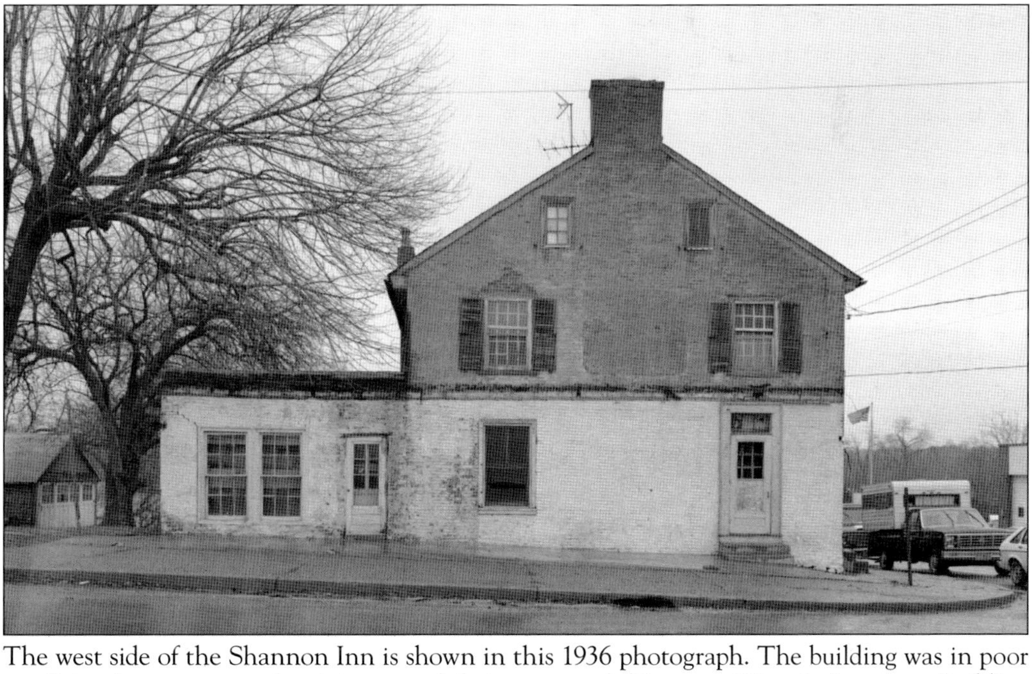

The west side of the Shannon Inn is shown in this 1936 photograph. The building was in poor condition for many years, but it is currently being restored. (Courtesy Historic American Building Survey, Library of Congress.)

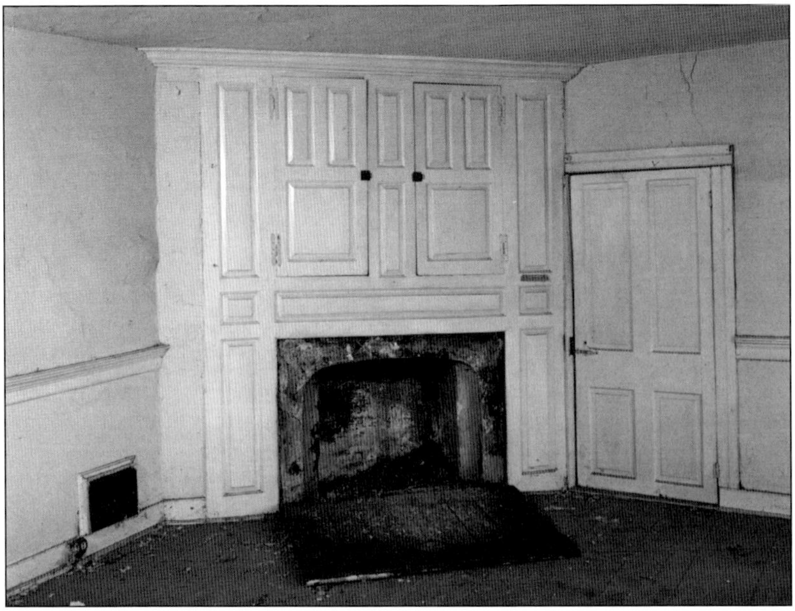

The interior of the Shannon Inn had a number of high-style Colonial features. This was a corner fireplace in one of the upstairs bedrooms. (Courtesy Historic American Building Survey, Library of Congress.)

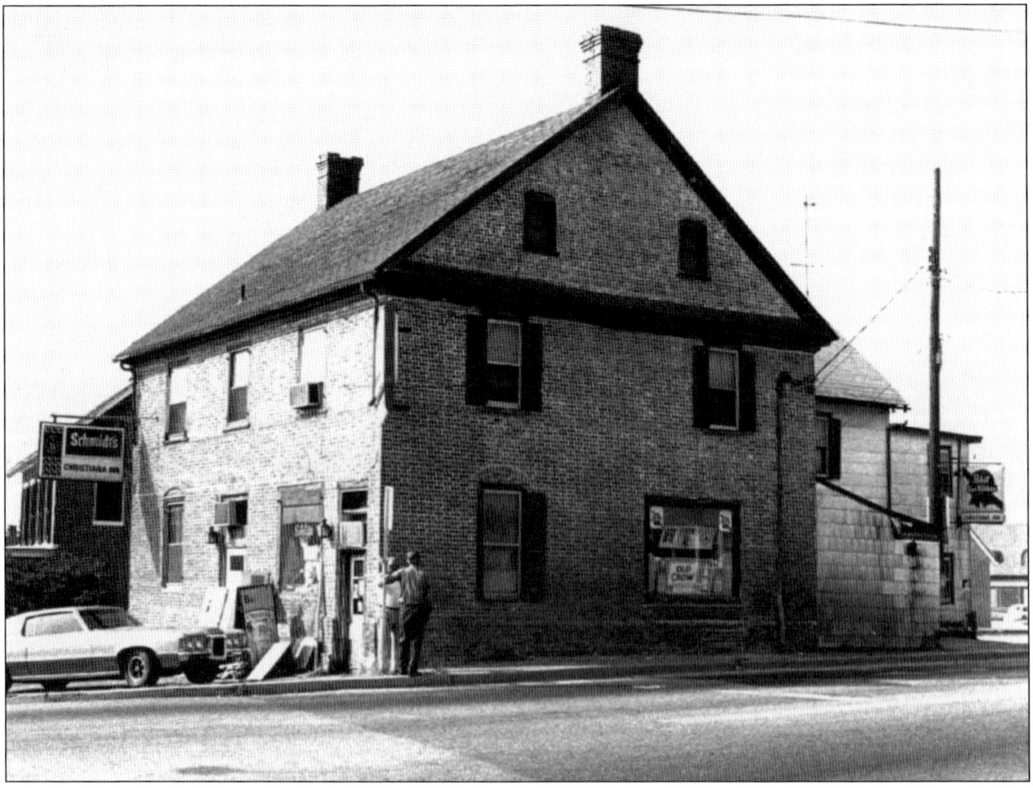

Across the street from the Shannon Inn is the Christiana Inn, which is pictured here as it was in the 1970s. It eventually was renovated and turned into office space. (Courtesy National Register of Historic Places, National Park Service.)

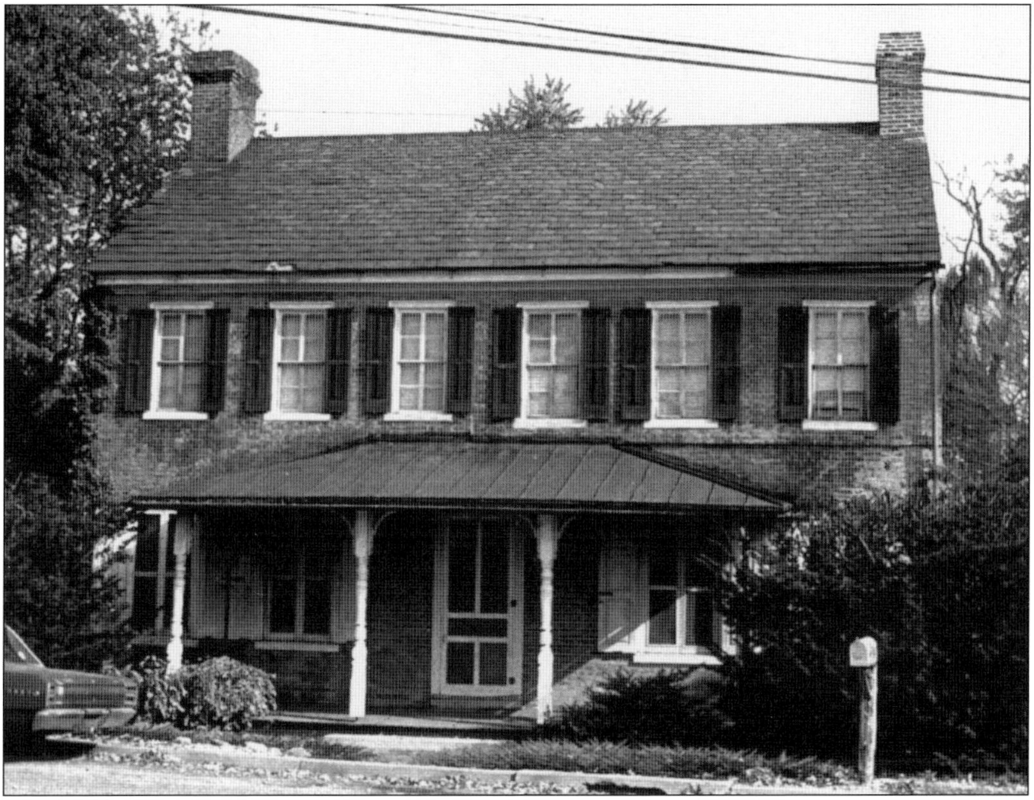

East of the Shannon Inn is the Rees Jones House, built about 1752. He was an early Welsh resident of the town and a member of the Welsh Tract Church in Pencader Hundred. He was largely responsible for dividing up the land and selling parcels that formed the town. (Courtesy National Register of Historic Places, National Park Service.)

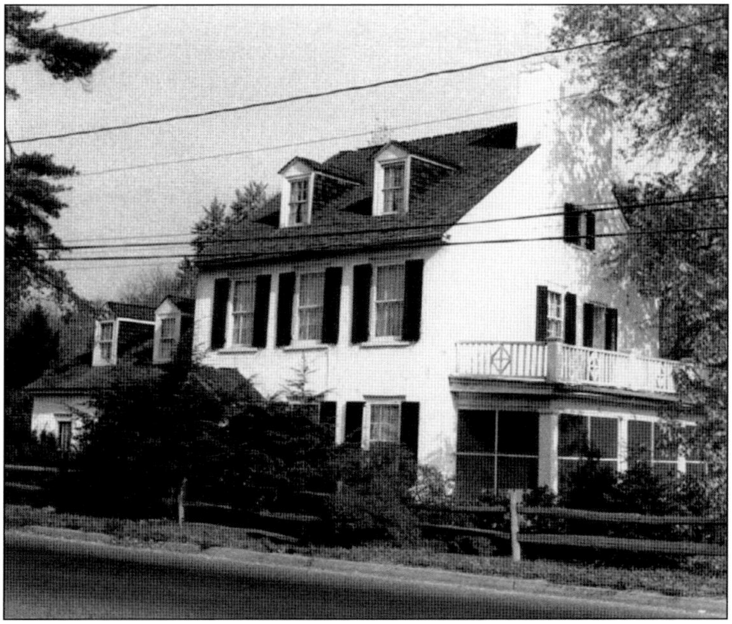

The last house on the north side of East Main Street is the Commodore Read House. He was the brother of George Read, who signed the Declaration of Independence, and was one of the first commodores of the new US Navy. His house features a second-story patio reminiscent of the bridge of a ship. (Courtesy personal collection.)

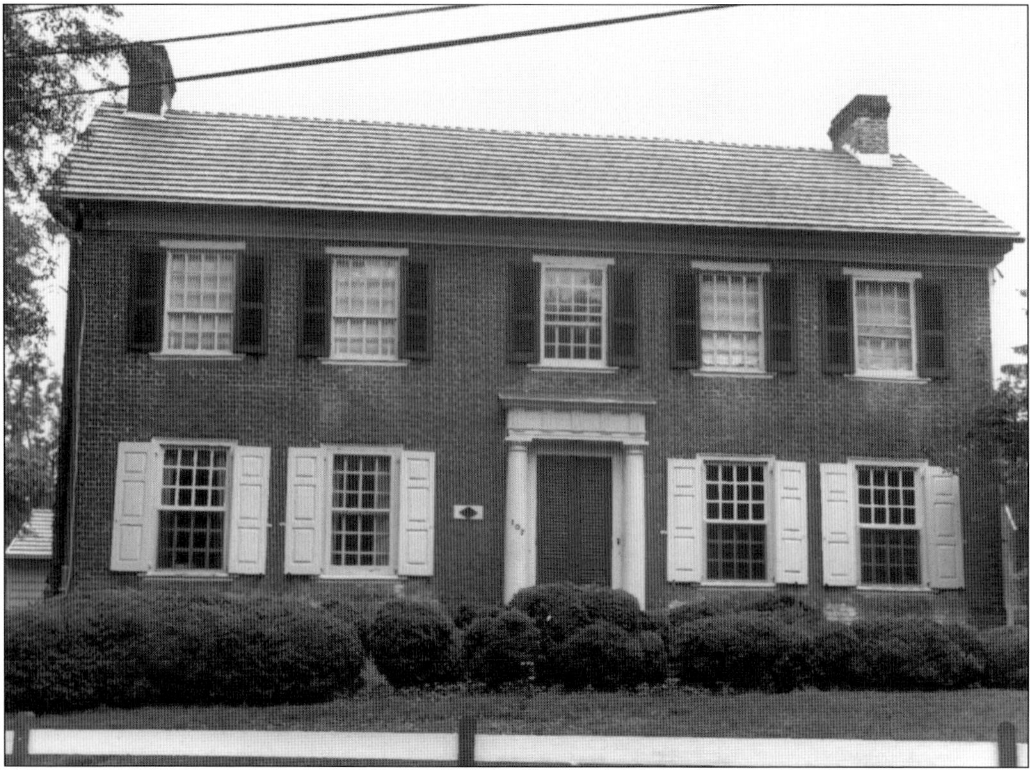

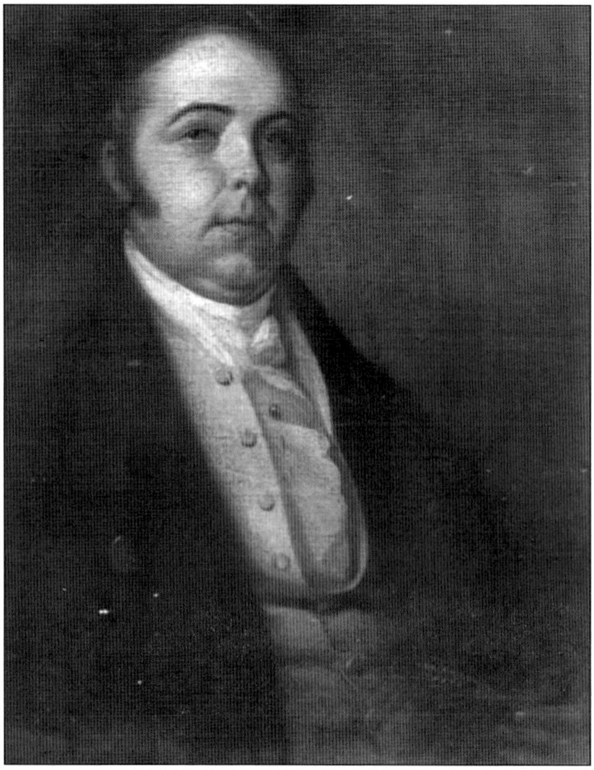

On the opposite side of the Christina, the Lewden House was built around 1770, and it is a fine two-story, five-bay brick dwelling in the Georgian style. The Lewden House remained in the ownership of direct descendants until the beginning of the 20th century. It was placed in the National Register of Historic Places in 1979 and has recently been largely restored. (Courtesy National Register of Historic Places, National Park Service.)

This painting of John Lewden, who lived at Lewden House in Christiana, dates to around 1825. He probably was the son or the grandson of the original John Lewden who built the house. (Courtesy National Register of Historic Places, National Park Service.)

The Lewden Mansion was highly furnished. The original John Lewden was a Quaker who operated a prosperous tanyard and farm on the large property, which went from the Christina River to Schoolbell Road. It has a center hall plan and the interior features original woodwork in the parlor and hall. These interior views of the Lewden Mansion, in 1936, show the entrance hall (right) and paneled fireplace (below). (Both, courtesy Historic American Building Survey, Library of Congress.)

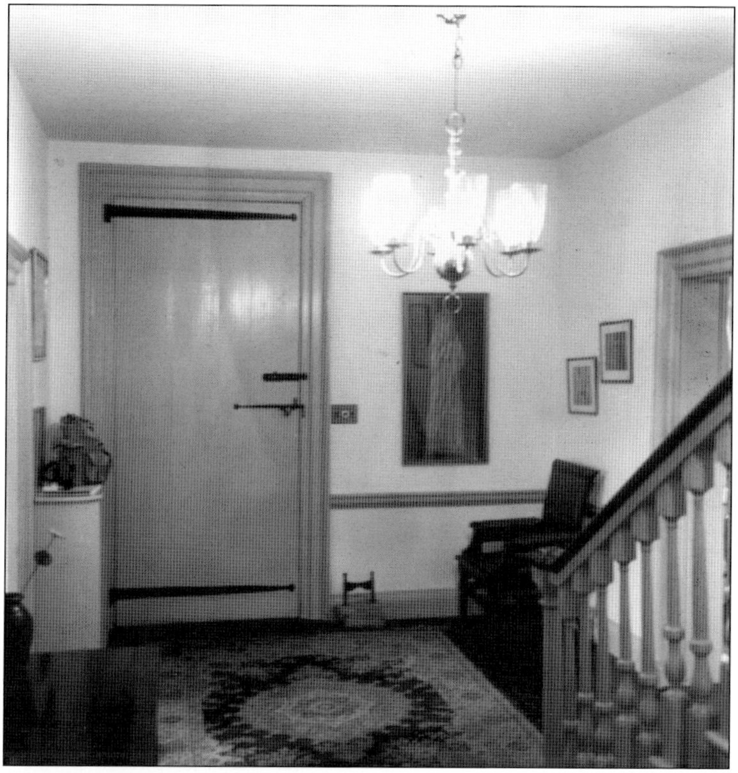

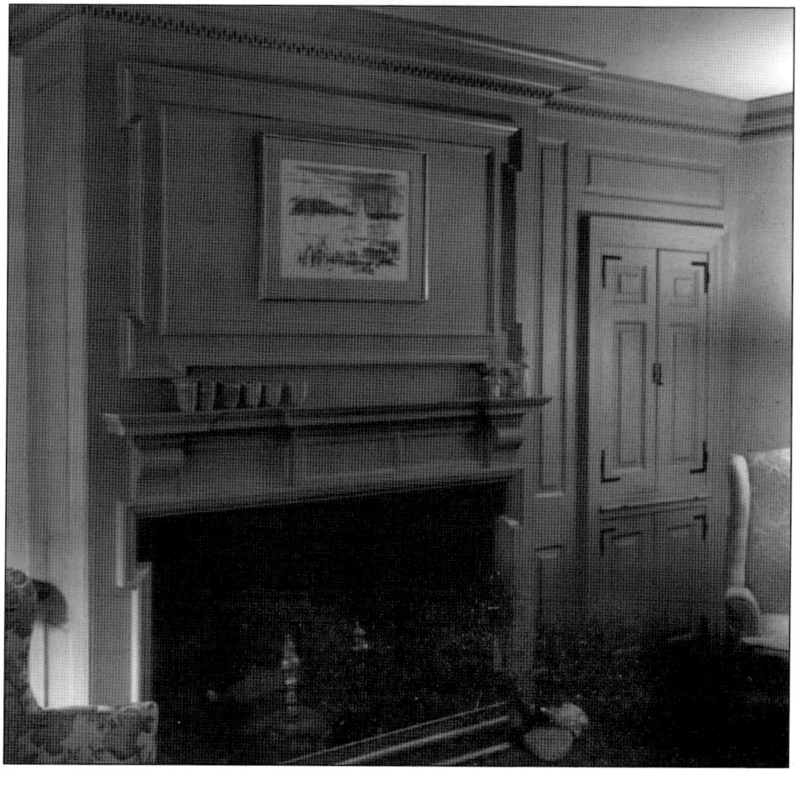

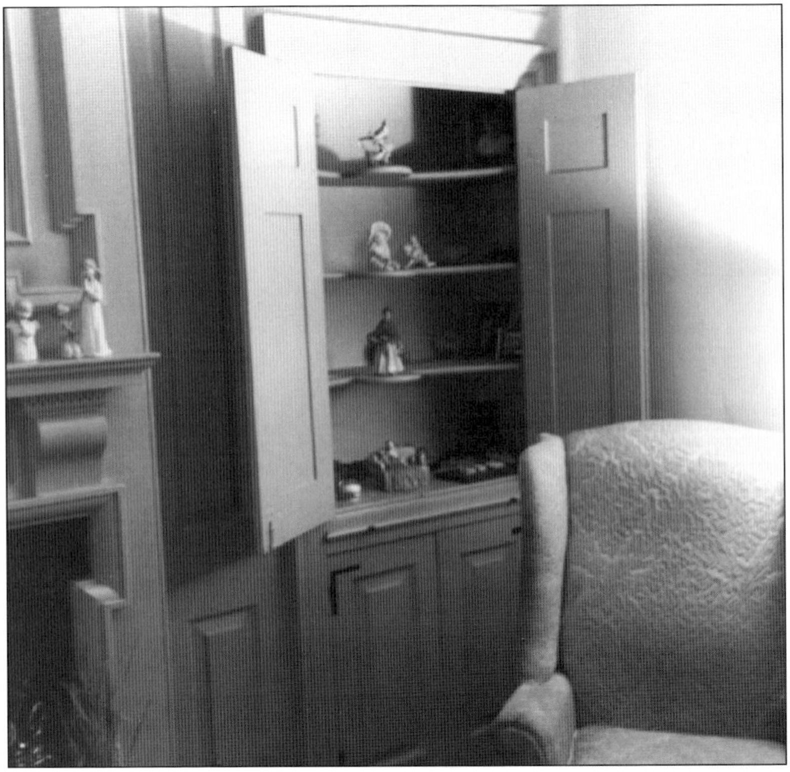

Also inside the Lewden Mansion was a cupboard built into a corner in the living room (left) and a Federal-period mantel above the fireplace (below). The building has been recently restored with the intention of establishing a bed-and-breakfast there. (Both, courtesy Historic American Building Survey, Library of Congress.)

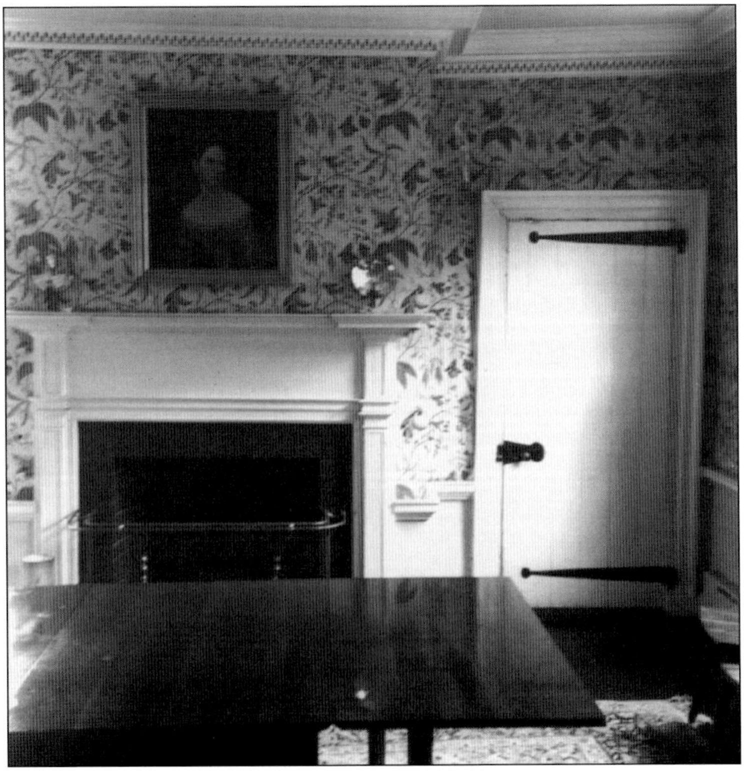

The Colonial entrance to the Lewden Mansion has been cited in several studies about Colonial architecture as a fine example of craftsmanship. (Courtesy Historic American Building Survey, Library of Congress.)

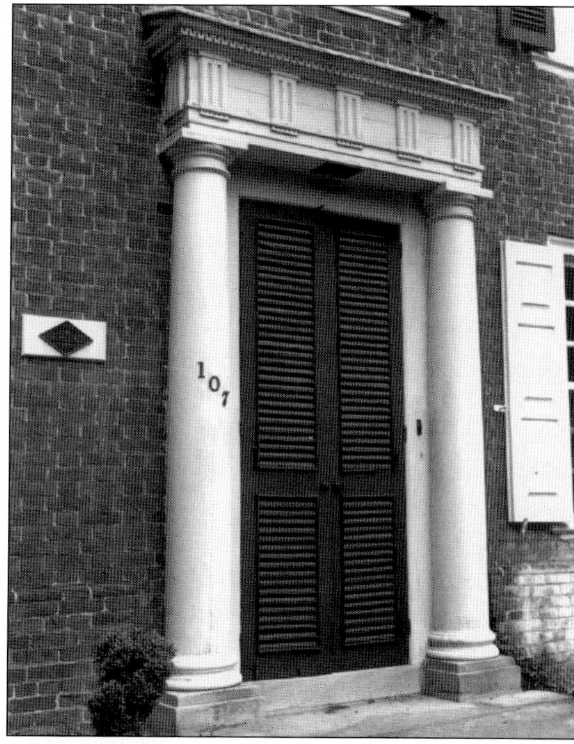

The 19th-century barn also survives on the Lewden estate, although the first floor was altered into a garage sometime during the mid-20th century. The second story, which once held fodder, has been converted into a studio apartment. (Courtesy Historic American Building Survey, Library of Congress.)

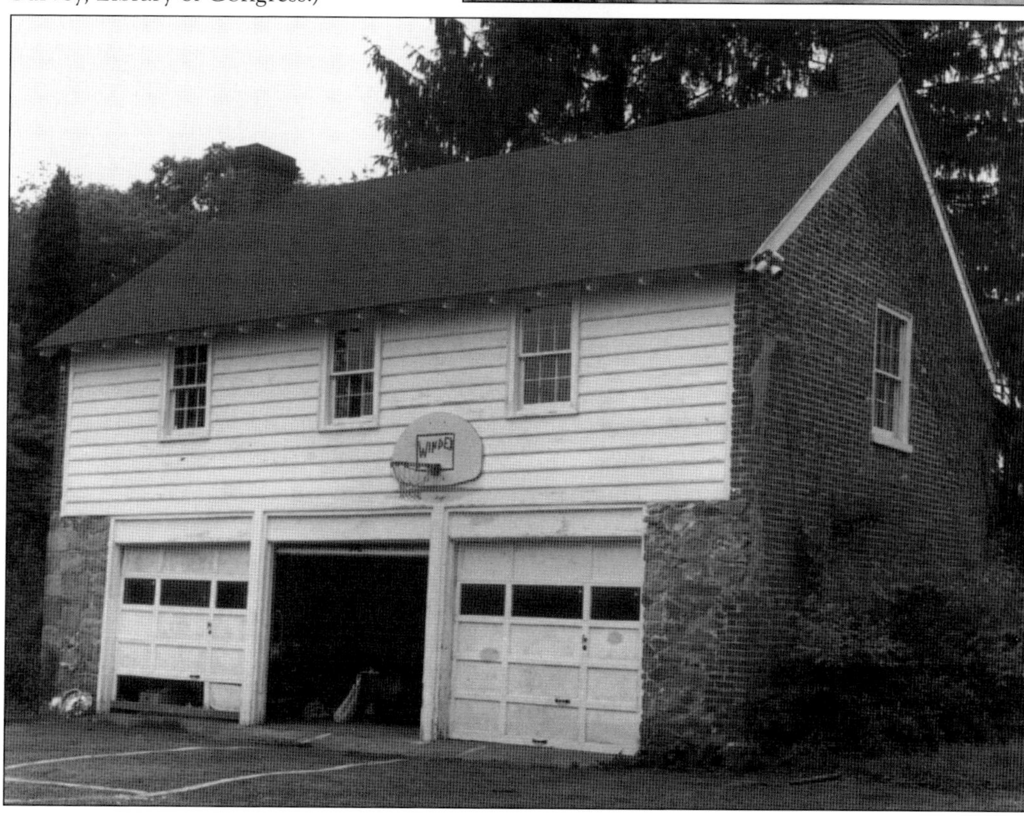

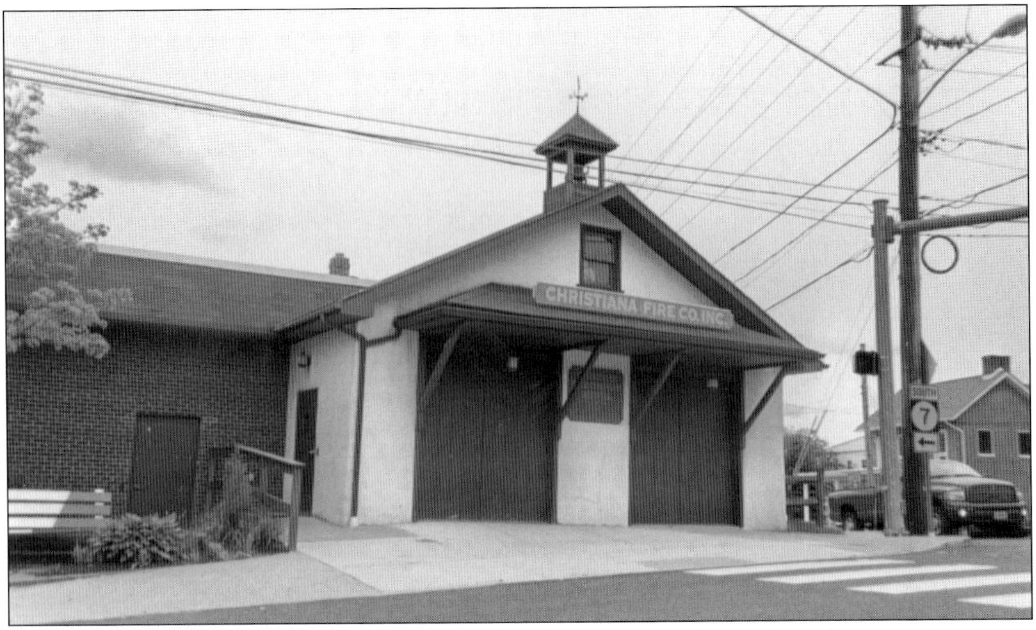

Back at Old Baltimore Pike, the Christiana Fire Company was housed on the opposite corner from the Shannon Inn in 1923. It has been a volunteer company for nearly 100 years and has served the community well with its expertise and bravery. The original 1930s firehouse is shown in this photograph. After the modern firehouse was added, the original part of the building was converted into a museum. (Courtesy personal collection.)

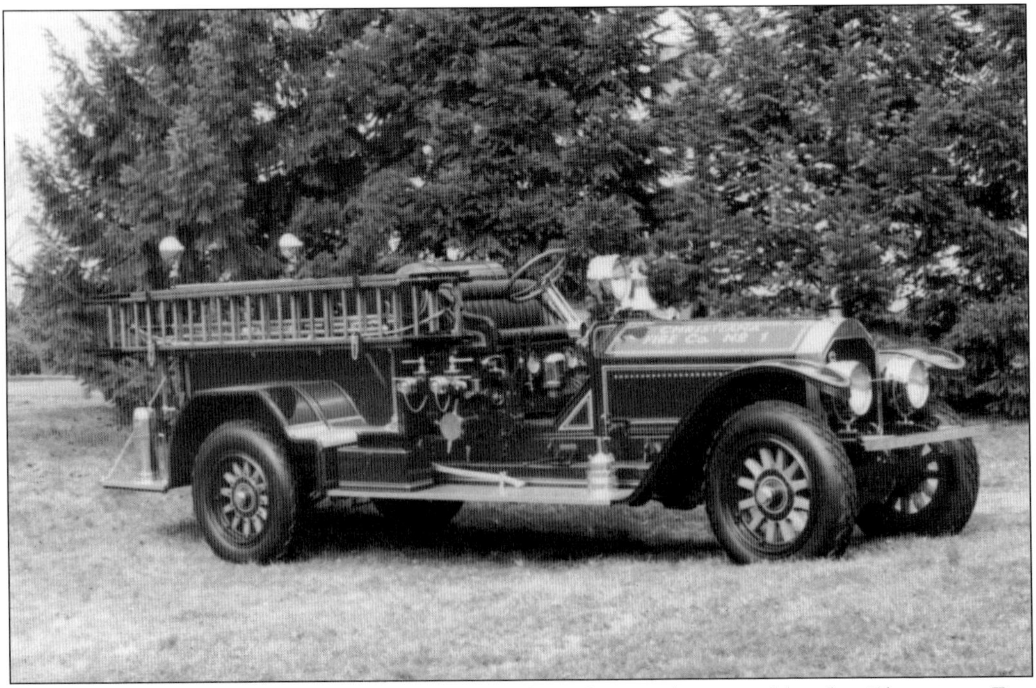

This image from the 1960s is of one of the earliest fire trucks owned by the Christiana Fire Company. Although at this time it had been long retired, it was maintained for use in parades and other celebrations. (Courtesy personal collection.)

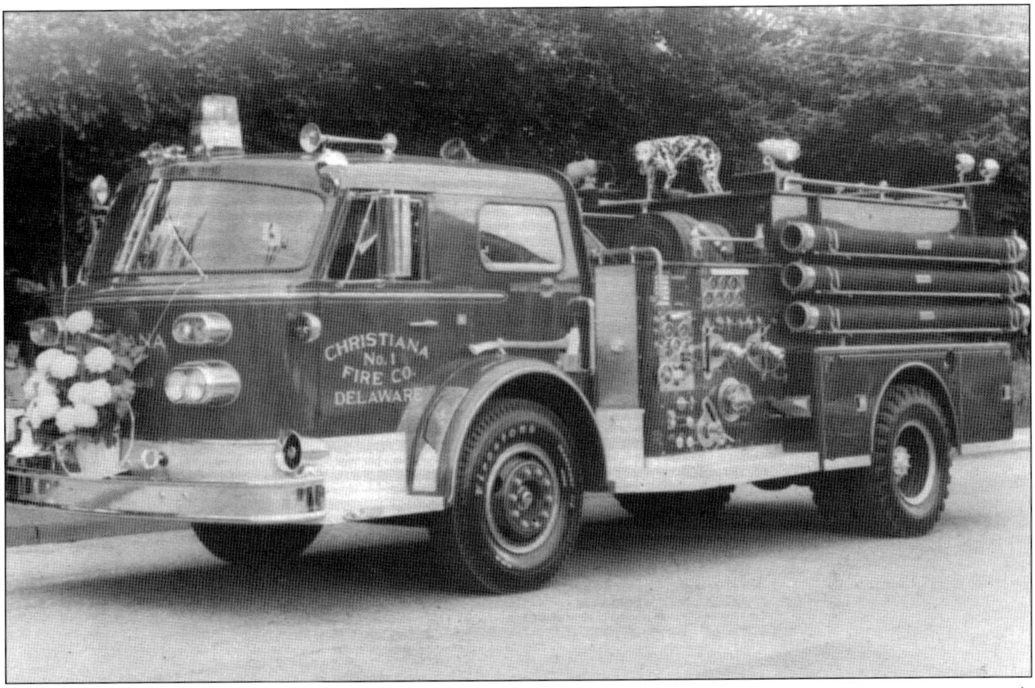

The traditional firehouse Dalmatian proudly rides on top of a Christiana Fire Company truck during a parade. (Courtesy personal collection.)

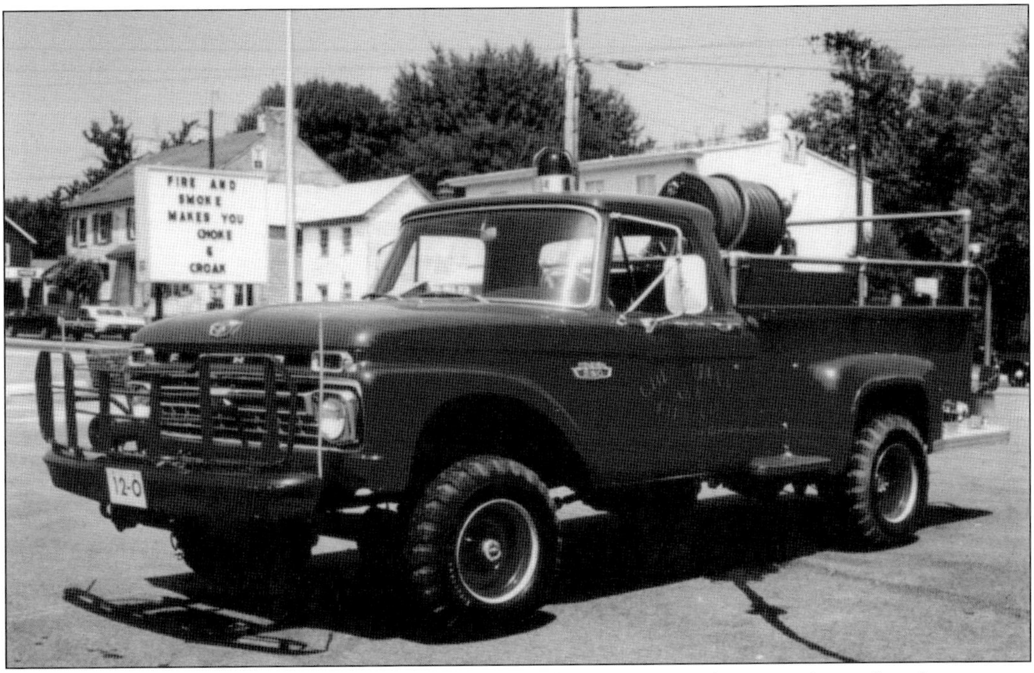

Seen in this 1960s photograph is another one of Christiana Fire Company's trucks, this one on East Main Street in front of the firehouse. The menu board issues a warning to the community at large. (Courtesy personal collection.)

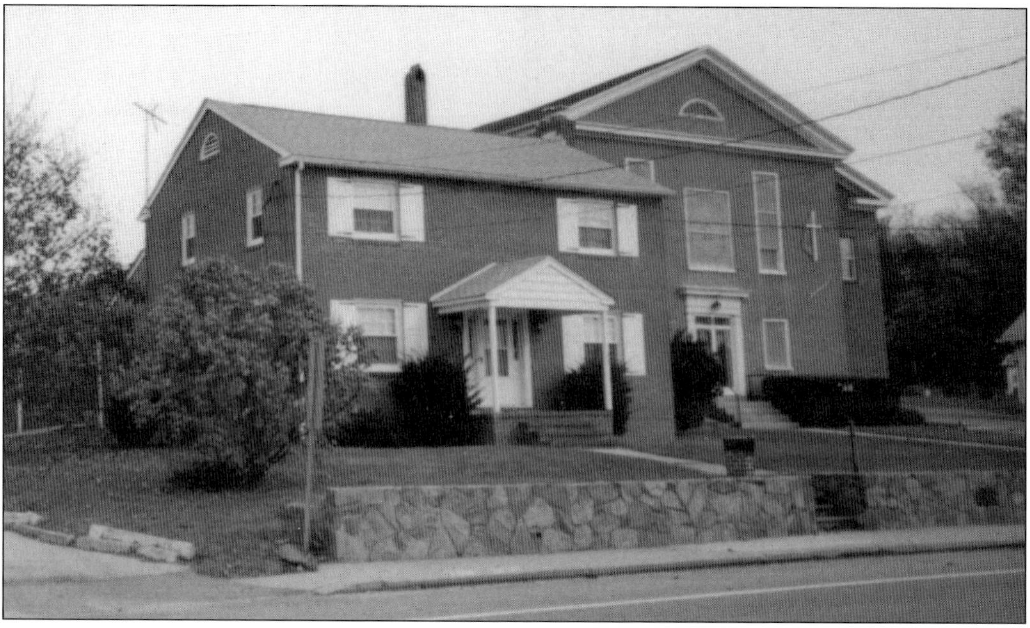

West of the intersection with Old Baltimore Pike is West Main Street, where the Christiana United Methodist Church, built in 1858, stands. On this site in 1771, Joseph Pilmore preached to a crowd outside. Converts met in homes and then at the church in Salem until they built this church in 1857. Civil War causalities are buried in the adjacent cemetery. (Courtesy National Register of Historic Places, National Park Service.)

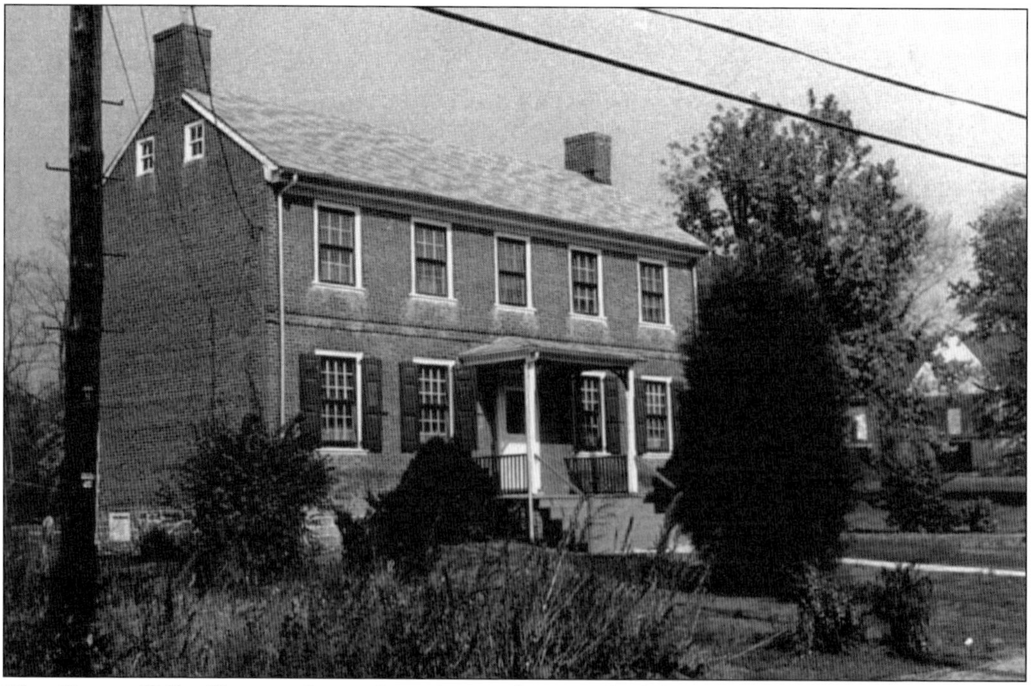

The George Hillis House is located on the southern end of the village on Old Baltimore Pike. This photograph was also used by the Christiana Historical Society in its 1976 bicentennial pamphlet. (Courtesy personal collection.)

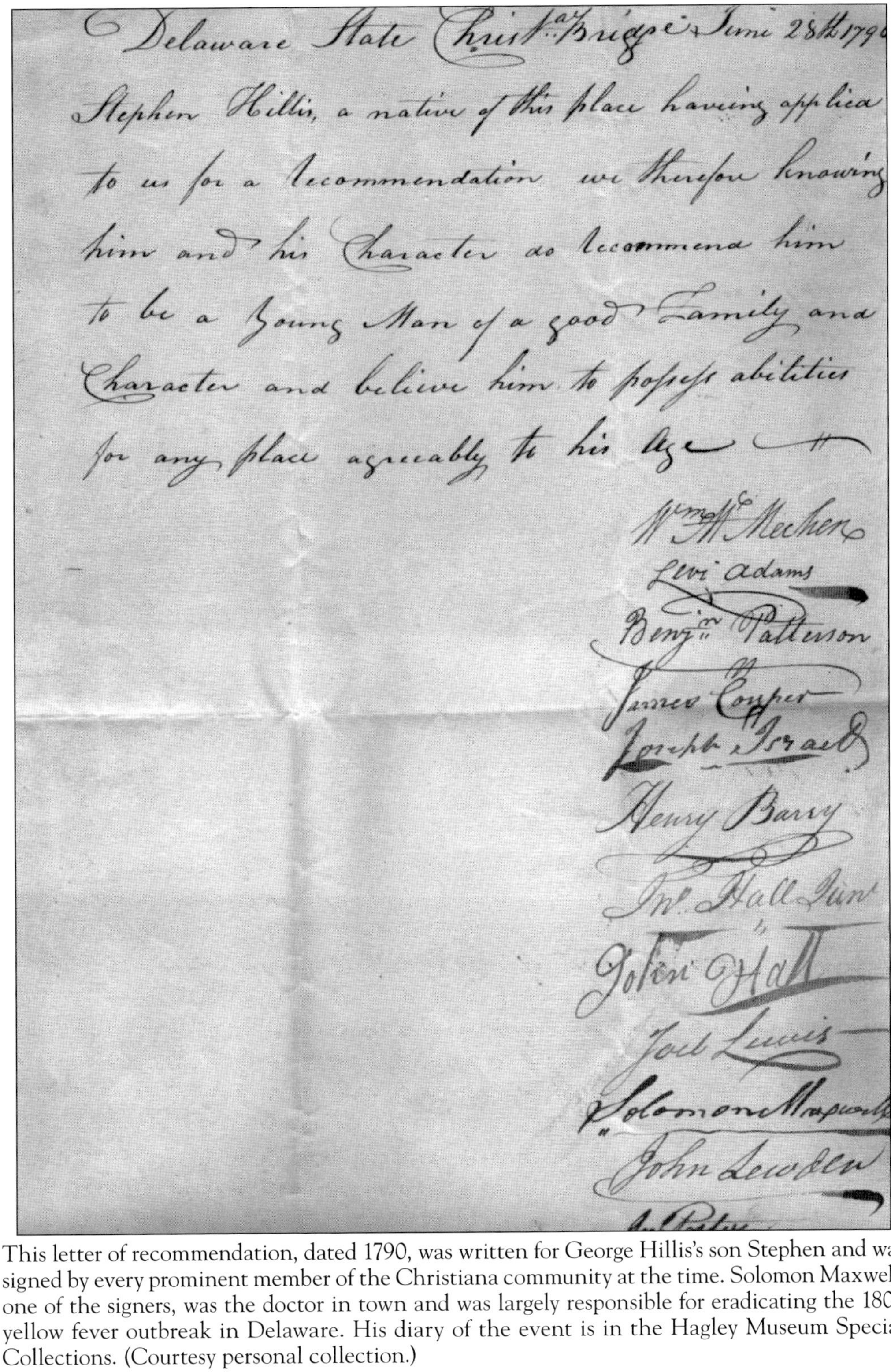

Delaware State Christ.a Bridge June 28th 1790

Stephen Hillis, a native of this place having applied to us for a recommendation we therefore knowing him and his Character do recommend him to be a Young Man of a good Family and Character and believe him to possess abilities for any place agreeably to his Age

Wm McMechen
Levi Adams
Benjn Patterson
James Couper
Joseph Israel
Henry Barry
Jno Hall Junr
John Hall
Joel Lewis
Solomon Maxwell
John Lewden

This letter of recommendation, dated 1790, was written for George Hillis's son Stephen and was signed by every prominent member of the Christiana community at the time. Solomon Maxwell, one of the signers, was the doctor in town and was largely responsible for eradicating the 1804 yellow fever outbreak in Delaware. His diary of the event is in the Hagley Museum Special Collections. (Courtesy personal collection.)

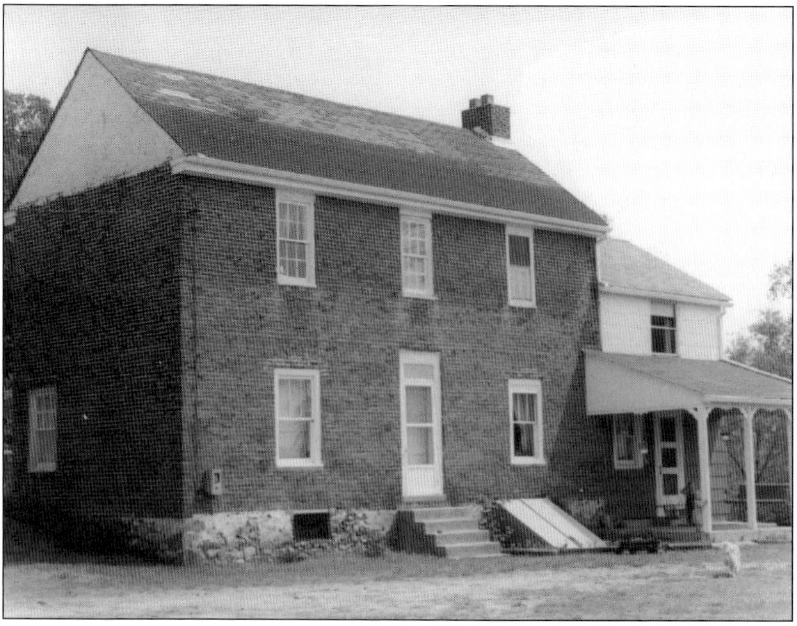

The Charles Allen house was built in the last half of the 19th century and is a two-story, three-bay brick home with a later one-story addition. It was listed in the National Register of Historic Places in 1983. (Courtesy National Register of Historic Places, National Park Service.)

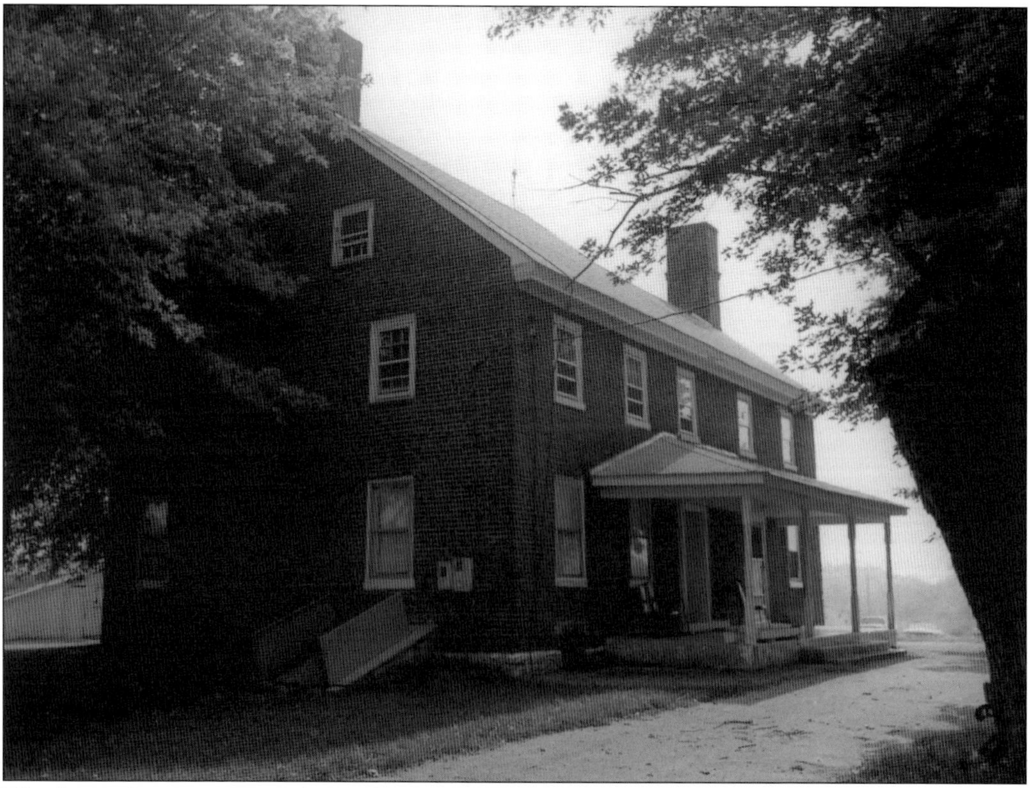

The James Stewart House, located outside the village, is a vernacular farmhouse with simple detailing. It dates to the 18th century. The porch was added at a later date. (Courtesy National Register of Historic Places, National Park Service.)

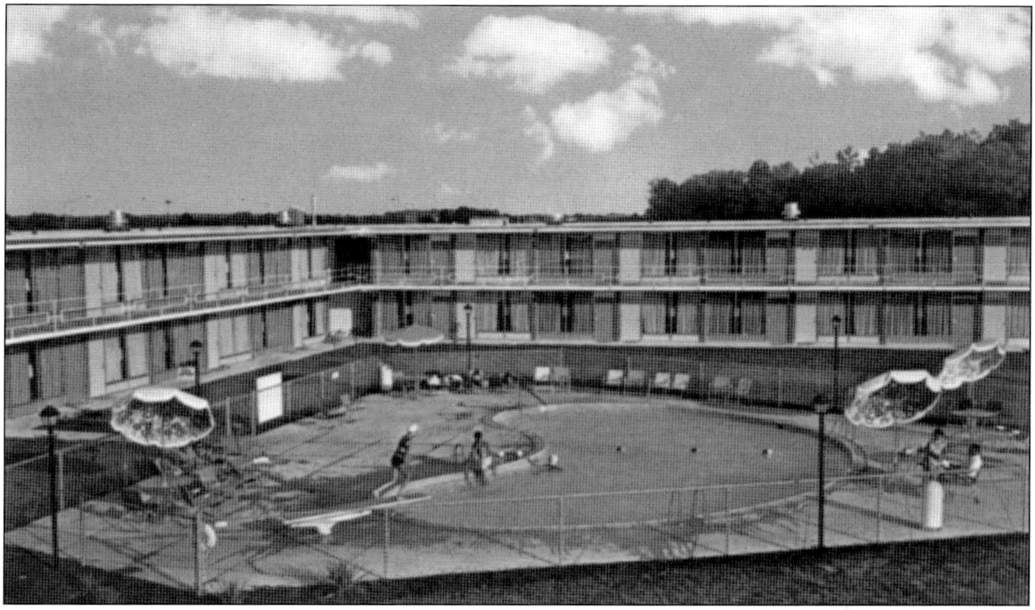

This 1960s photograph shows the inner courtyard of the former Holiday Inn Hotel, west of Christiana. This hotel was recently demolished and a new multistory hotel replaced it. (Courtesy personal collection.)

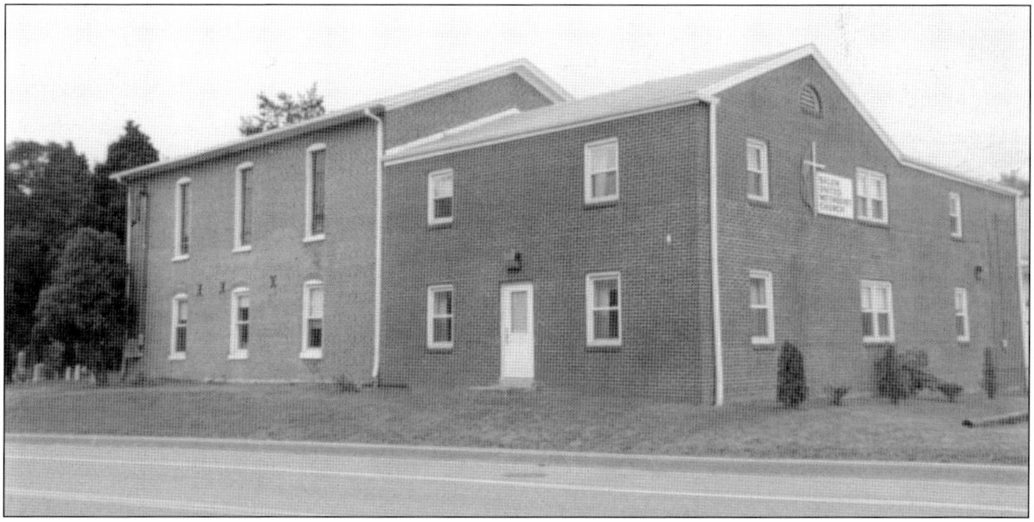

The Salem United Methodist Church, near the intersection of Old Baltimore Pike and Salem Church Road, was originally built in 1807 and has been remodeled a number of times since. Famed Methodist bishop Francis Asbury preached at this church a number of times. The adjacent cemetery holds many early residents. (Courtesy personal collection.)

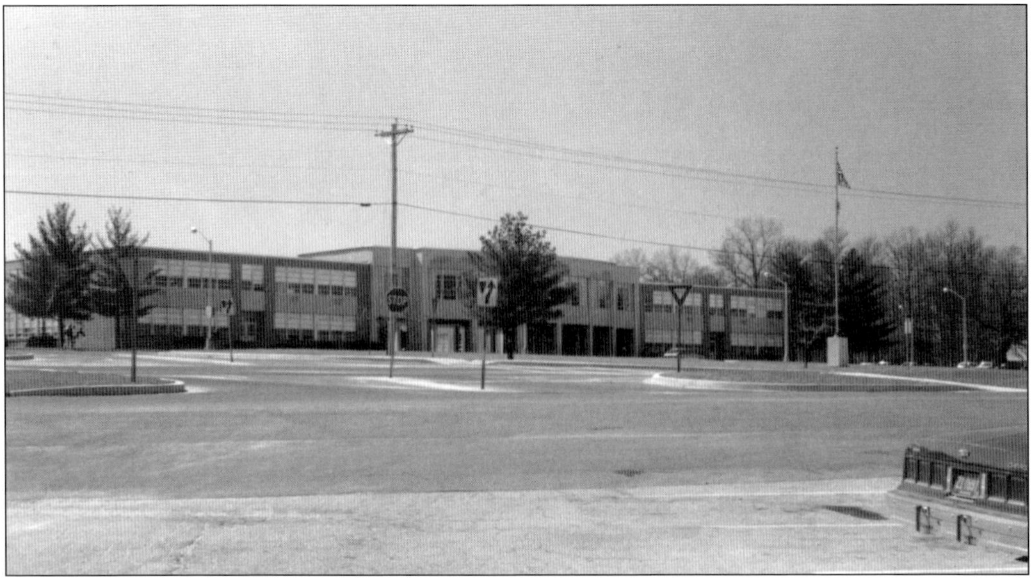

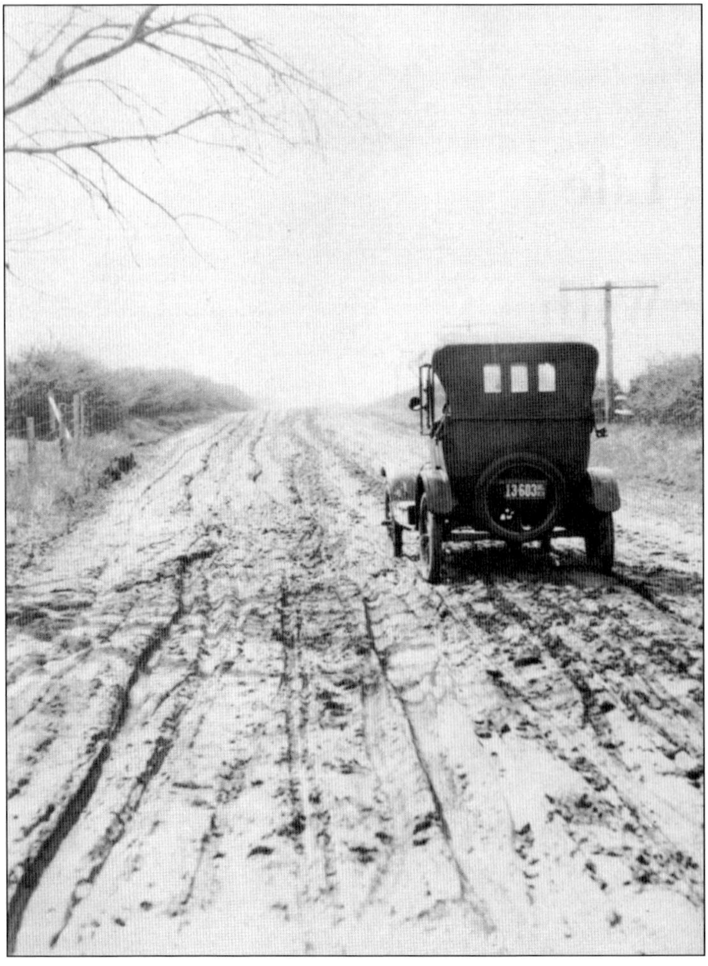

The suburban high school, Christiana High, was built in 1963 to respond to an influx of families moving into suburban neighborhoods in the area. The old Newark High School was no longer able to support the growing population. (Courtesy personal collection.)

This early-20th-century photograph is of the Old Baltimore Pike. Conditions on the road were certainly treacherous before the roads were paved. (Courtesy personal collection.)

Eight

Pencader Hundred

Pencader Hundred was settled in the late 17th century by a gift of land to the Welsh, who settled on the Welsh Tract and built a church there just north of Old Baltimore Pike. Until the 1990s, Pencader Hundred remained largely agricultural.

The prominent feature in the county is Iron Hill, one of the highest hills in the state. It was a site of iron mining during the 18th century, and the British camped on it during the Revolutionary War, as did Caesar Rodney in 1814.

The Welsh Tract Church was built in 1746 as the successor to the first Baptist church in Delaware, a log church at this location in 1706. The congregation now belonging to the Primitive Baptist Church was organized in Wales in 1701. The elevation of Iron Hill is said to have been what attracted them to this location, as well as the reason *pencador*, the Welsh word for "highest place," was used for the name of the area.

Old Baltimore Pike crosses through the middle of the Cooch's Bridge Battlefield, the only battlefield in Delaware. On September 2, 1777, a small company of Hessian dragoons began to move north along Cooch's Bridge Road and fought American troops, positioned in small groups along both sides of the road. British major John Andre later documented in his diary that "here the rebels began to attack us about 9 o'clock with a continued irregular fire for nearly two miles." The battle lasted all day, with 3 British and 20 Americans killed. It was also the first time that the new flag of the United States was flown in battle.

During the Battle of Cooch's Bridge, General Cornwallis seized the Cooch farmhouse as his headquarters. The event was memorialized with a monument and cannons placed at the entrance to the farm.

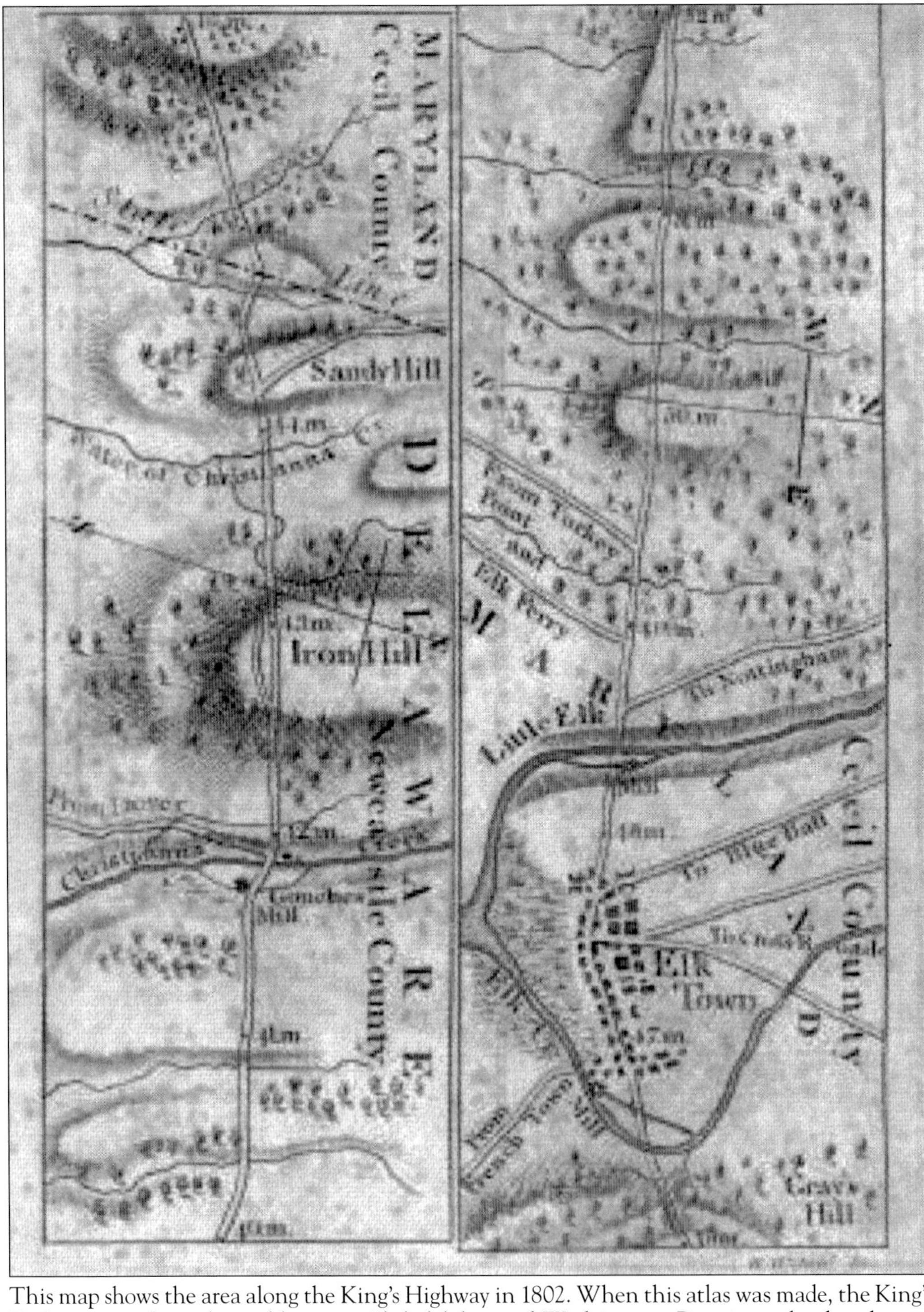

This map shows the area along the King's Highway in 1802. When this atlas was made, the King's Highway was the only road between Philadelphia and Washington. Prominent landmarks and inns helped travelers find their way. (Courtesy personal collection.)

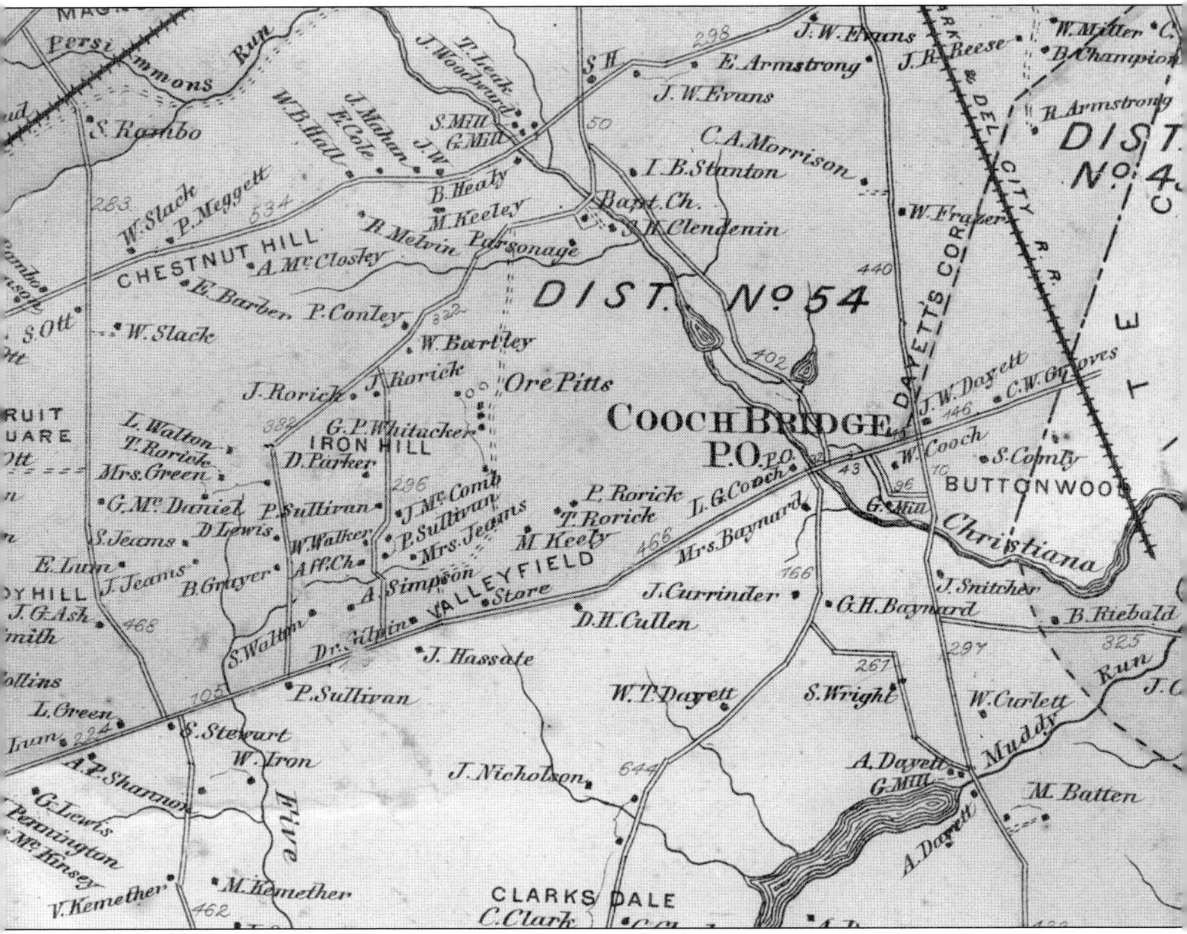

The 1868 Beer's Atlas of the state of Delaware details the Cooch's Bridge area. Cooch's farm, the milling complexes, and Iron Hill are all prominently displayed. (Courtesy personal collection.)

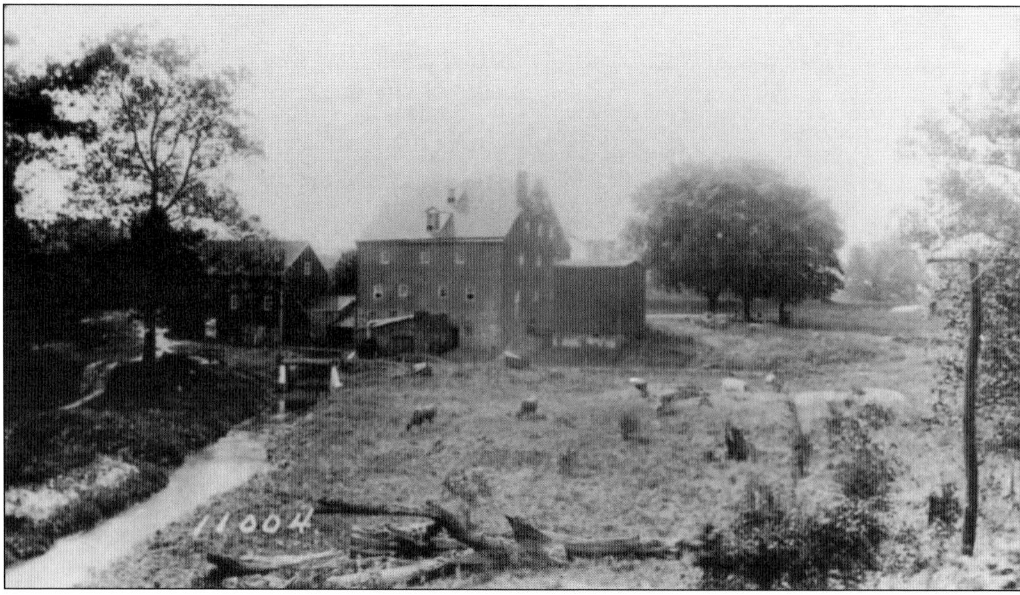

The Cooch-Dayett Mill, on the corner of Old Baltimore Pike and Route 72, was an important flour mill in its day and was owned by John W. Dayett. It was originally owned by Sir William Keith, Delaware governor, and was water powered until 1884. It suffered a terrible fire in 1903 and had to be largely rebuilt. This photograph predates the fire. It is now the home of the Pencader Historical Society. (Courtesy personal collection.)

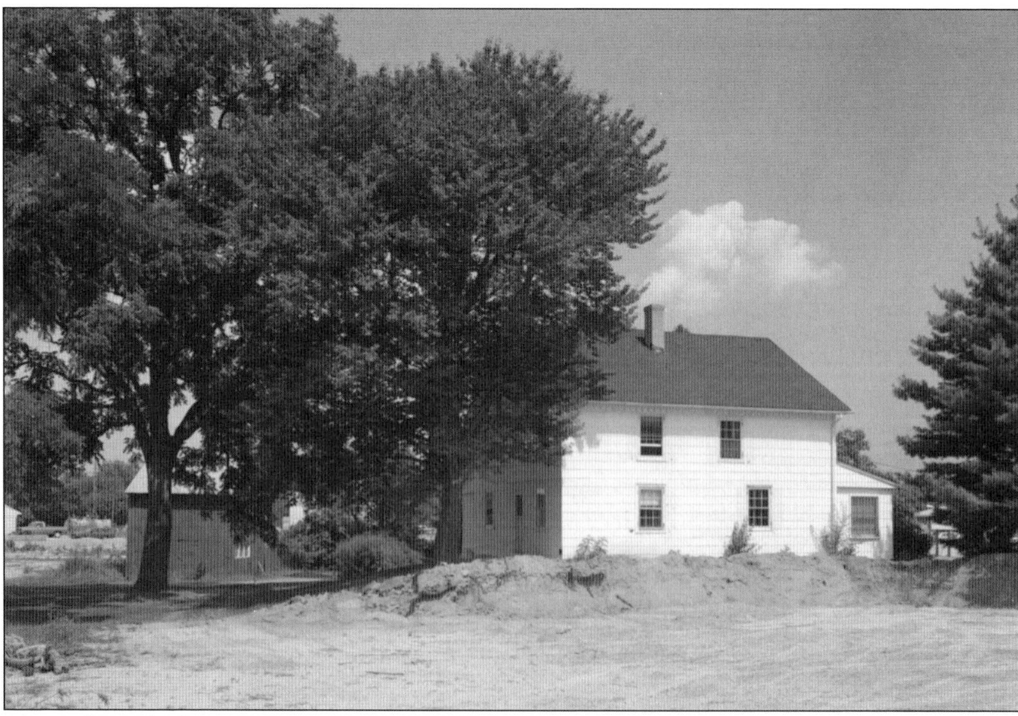

The Wilson-Slack Agricultural Works, located north of Old Baltimore Pike on Chestnut Hill Road, is another important example of the rich agricultural success in Pencader Hundred. (Courtesy National Register of Historic Places, National Park Service.)

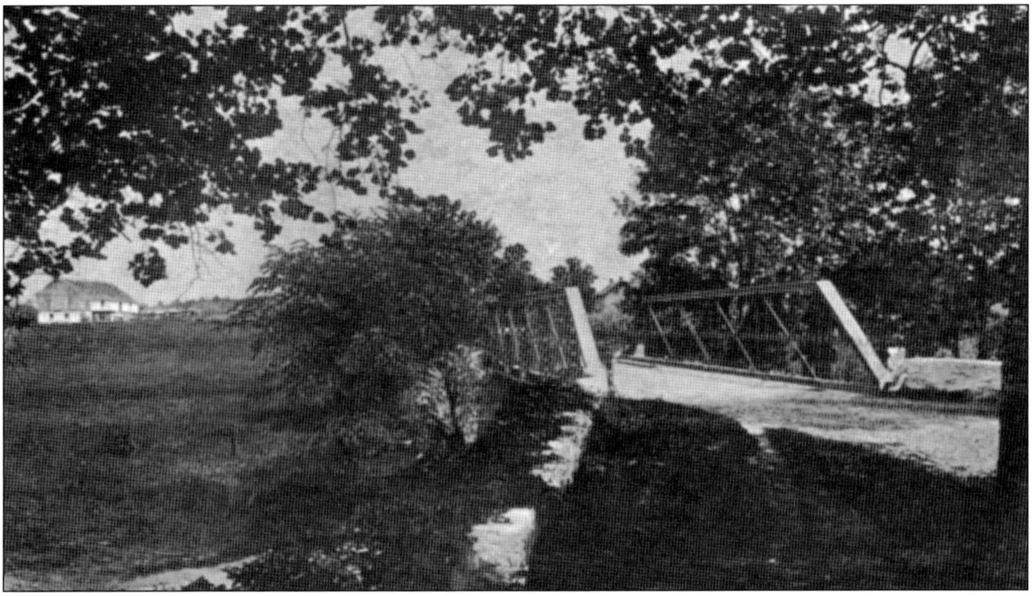
Cooch's Bridge was the location where the American and British forces met for the only Revolutionary War battle to be fought in Delaware. The American position before the skirmish was around the barn seen in this early-20th-century postcard. (Courtesy personal collection.)

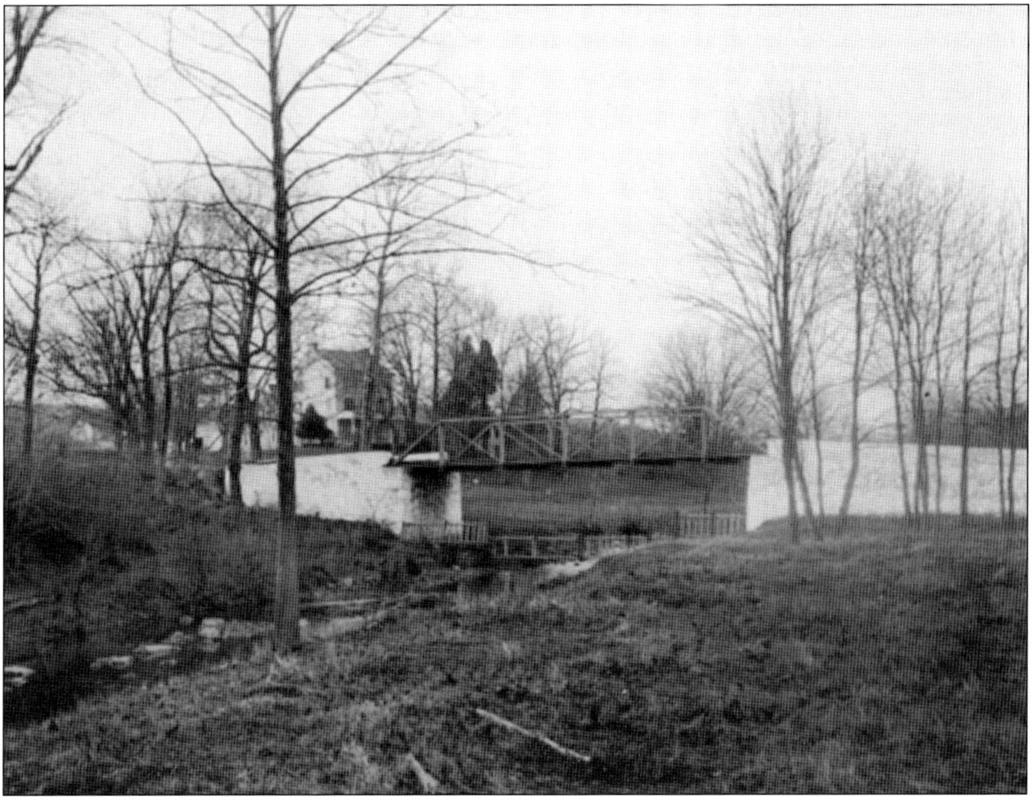
This photograph, dated to 1898, shows the British position during the battle, with the Cooch Mansion in the background. (Courtesy Delaware Public Archives.)

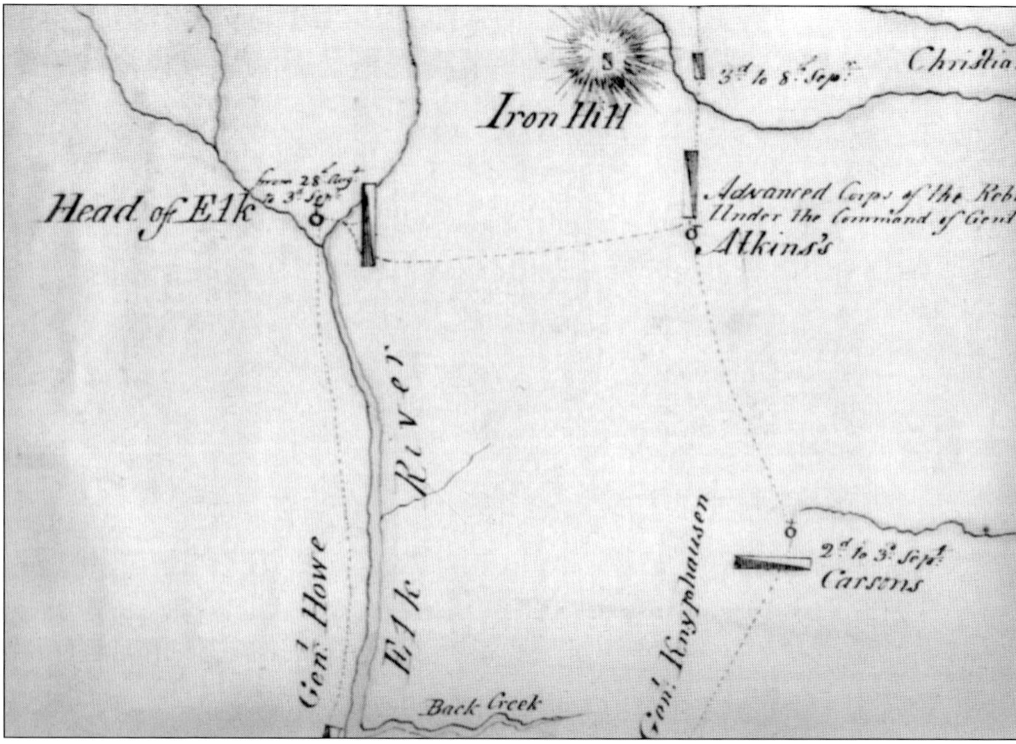

This period map shows the location of British and American troops during early September 1777. Aiken's Tavern, as shown on the map, is the village now known as Glasgow. Iron Hill is prominently shown on the map. (Courtesy Library of Congress.)

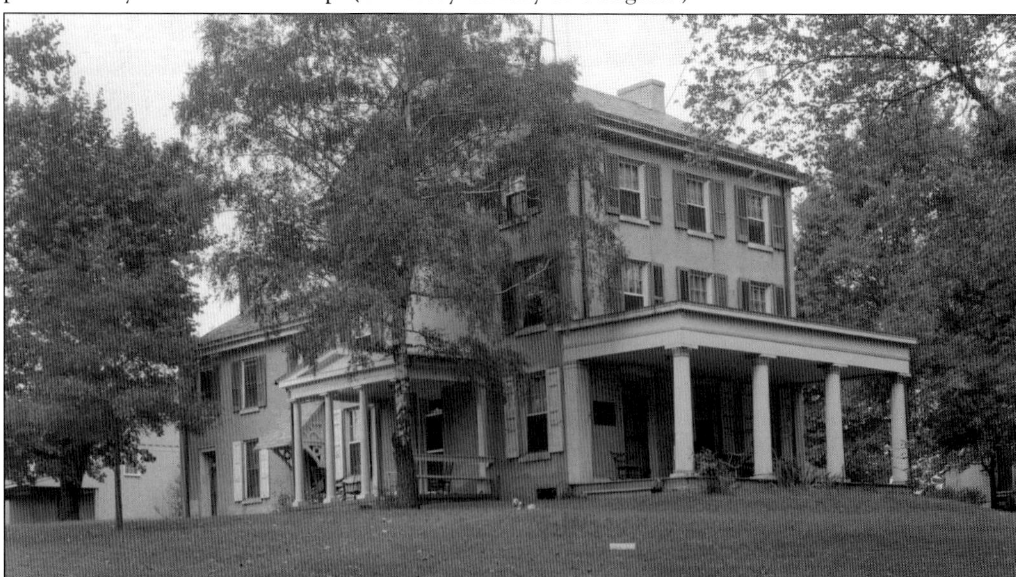

The Thomas Cooch House just north of the bridge was occupied by British forces during the battle. The house was in the ownership of a direct line of Cooch family members until 2011, when the farm was willed to the State of Delaware for the creation of a state historical park. (Courtesy Historic American Building Survey, Library of Congress.)

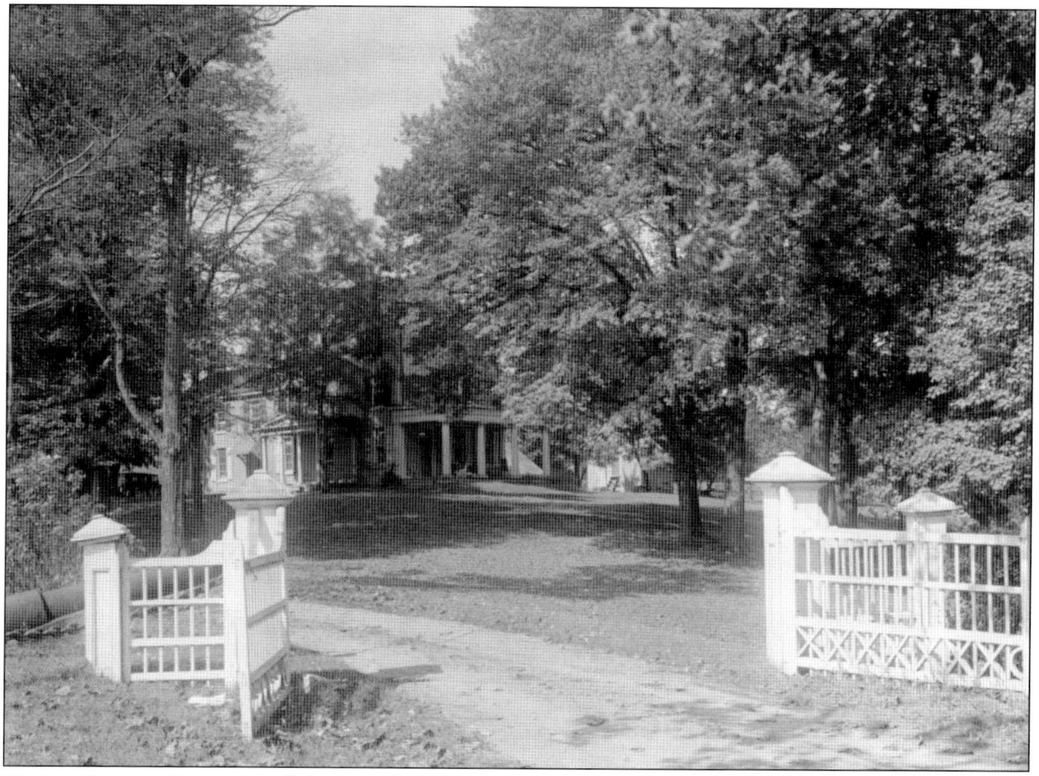

Pictured is another view of the Cooch House, dated to 1898, soon after the creation of the monument at the end of his driveway. (Courtesy Delaware Public Archives.)

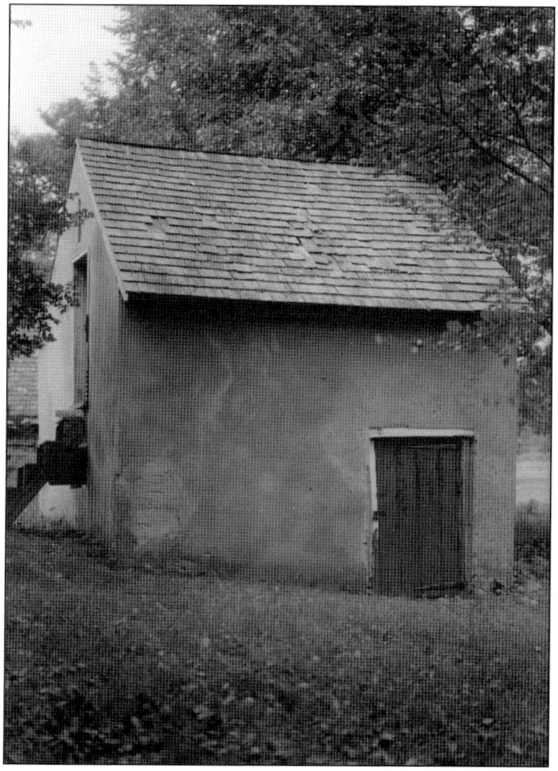

The Cooch Farm also featured this unique two-story smokehouse. (Courtesy Historic American Building Survey, Library of Congress.)

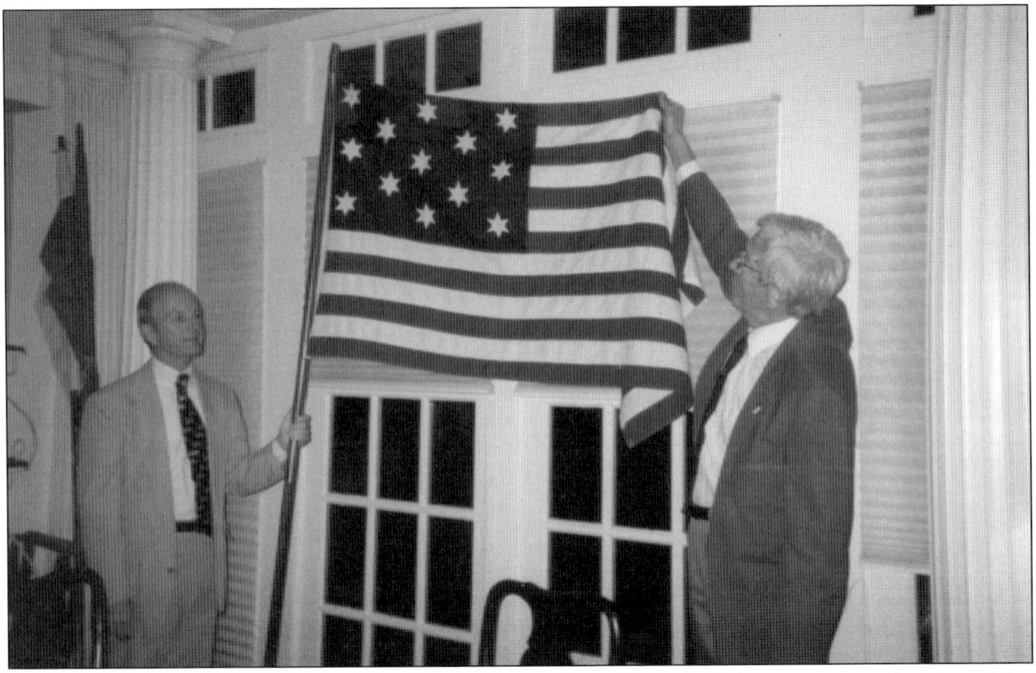

During a celebration of the Rochambeau Marchers passing through Delaware, a reproduction of the original US flag flown at the Battle of Cooch's Bridge was displayed for the audience. Cooch's bridge was the first battle at which the new American flag was flown. (Courtesy personal collection.)

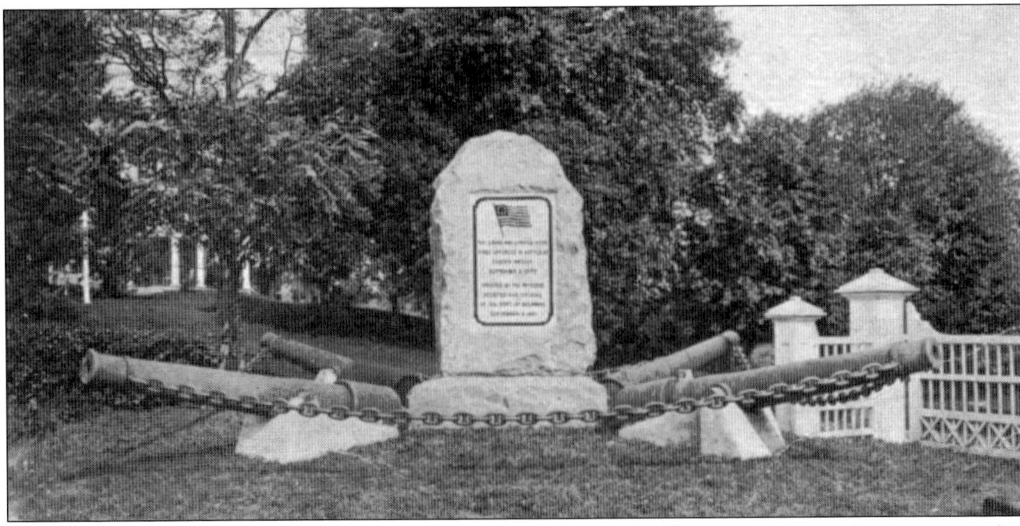

The Battle of Cooch's Bridge was memorialized in the early 20th century by a plaque set inside a large boulder and the placement of four cannons, as seen in this postcard from 1906. The memorial is still passed by many commuters to this day. (Courtesy personal collection.)

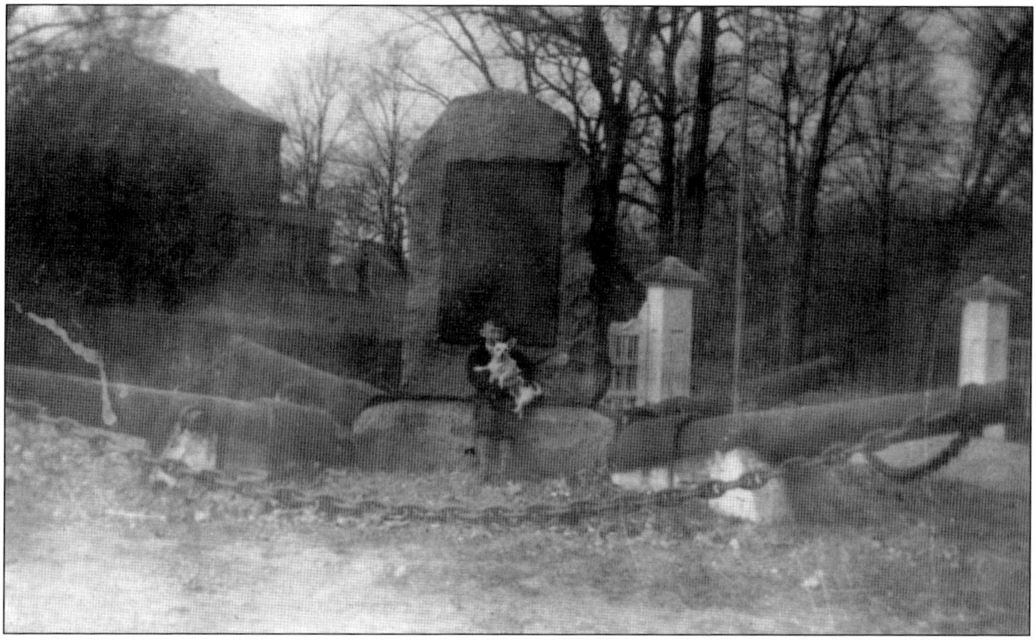

In this photograph from the late 1930s, the author's father and his dog visit the Cooch's Bridge Battlefield. (Courtesy personal collection.)

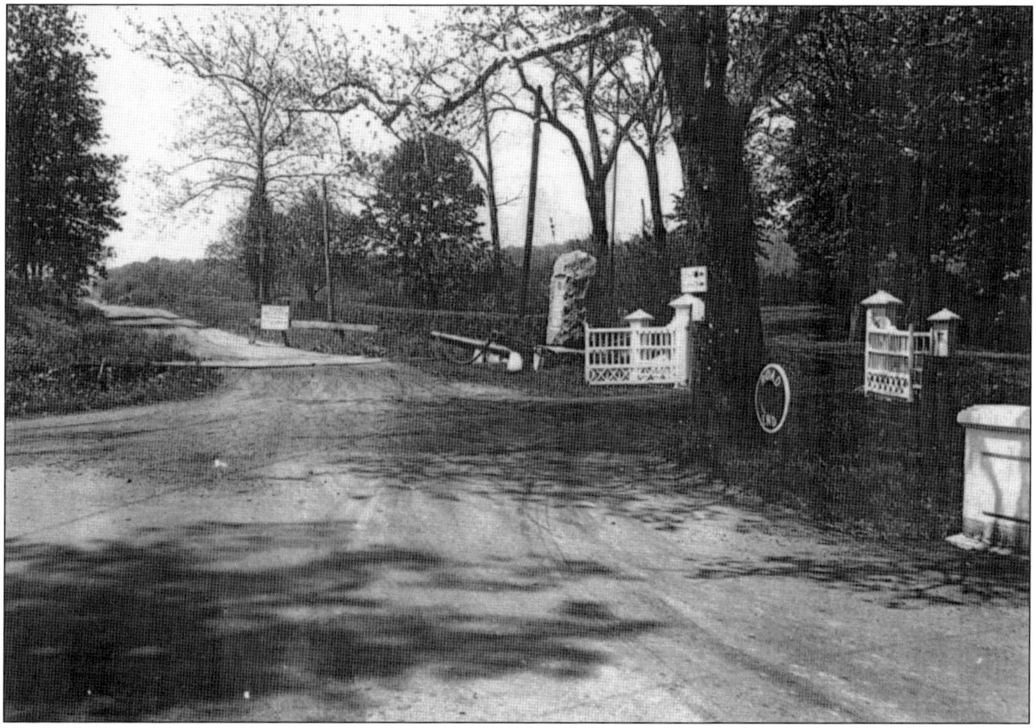

This view of Old Baltimore Pike at Cooch's Bridge shows the condition of the road in the early 20th century. Apparently, so many accidents had occurred from people crossing Old Cooch's Bridge Road and running into the tree on the other side that the homeowner placed a warning sign on it. It is still one of the more dangerous intersections in the county. (Courtesy personal collection.)

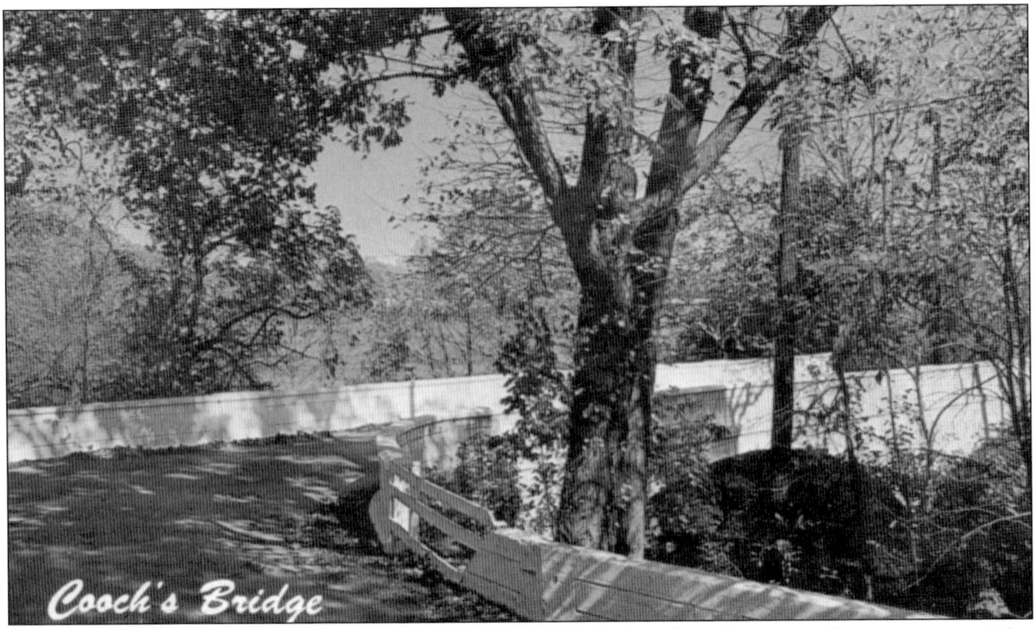

Like the Christiana Bridge, Cooch's Bridge has been replaced and improved many times. The bridge that was used during the Revolutionary War battle was destroyed before 1781, and it was replaced later, as seen in this postcard dated 1960. (Courtesy personal collection.)

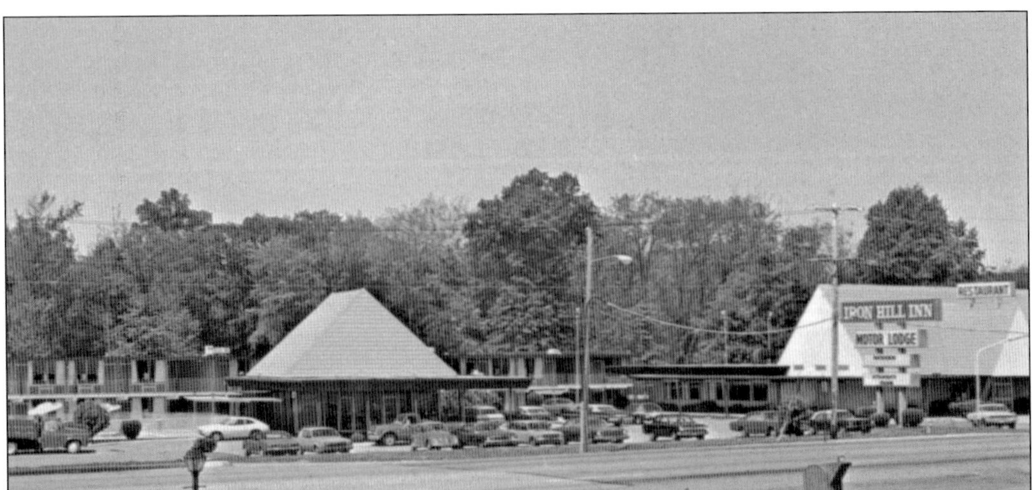

The Iron Hill Inn, located on Route 896 just north of the Old Baltimore Pike, is shown as it appeared in the 1960s. Many of the old motels along the major north-south routes were later eclipsed by more modern hotels that have been built along Interstate 95. (Courtesy personal collection.)

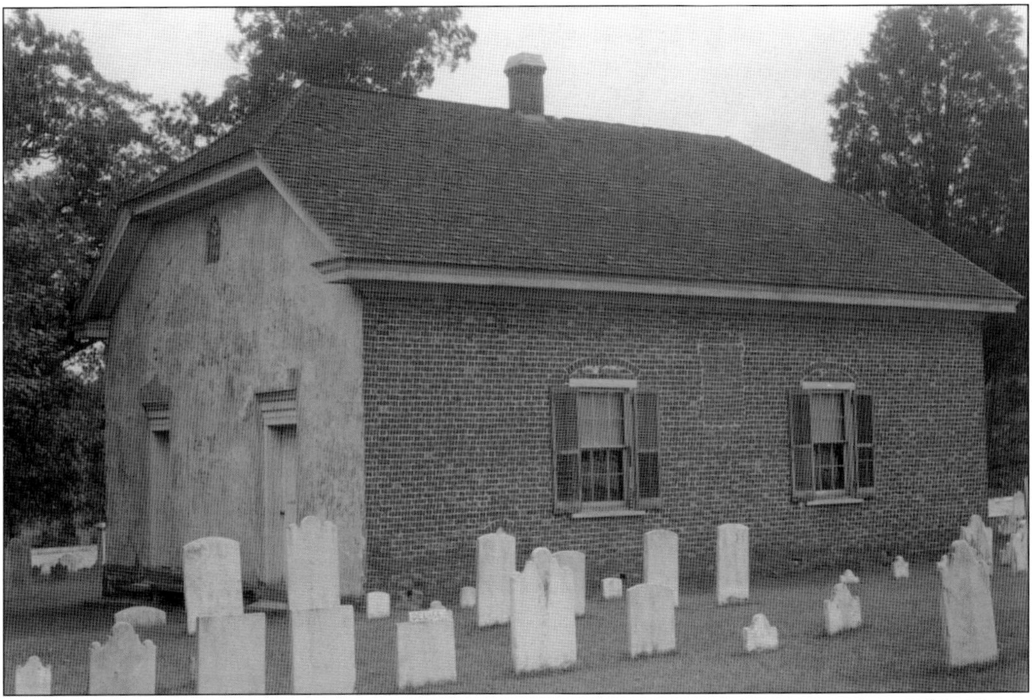

Just north of the Old Baltimore Pike south of Newark was the area known as the Welsh Tract. This photograph, dated to 1936, shows the Welsh Tract Church and its adjoining cemetery. The church was built of brick imported from England. (Courtesy Historic American Building Survey, Library of Congress.)

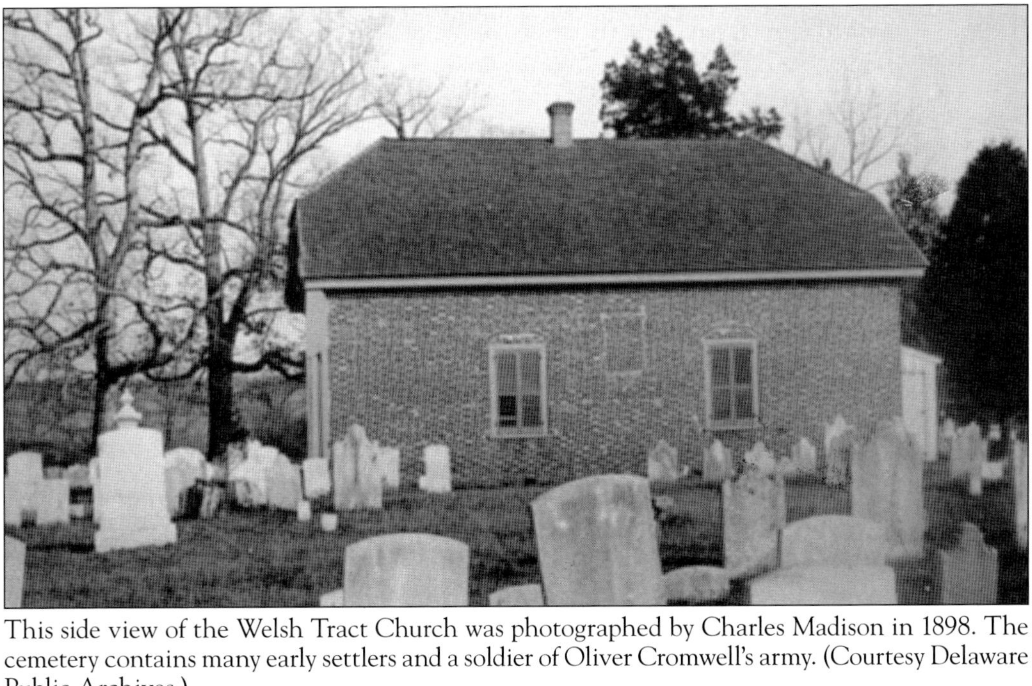

This side view of the Welsh Tract Church was photographed by Charles Madison in 1898. The cemetery contains many early settlers and a soldier of Oliver Cromwell's army. (Courtesy Delaware Public Archives.)

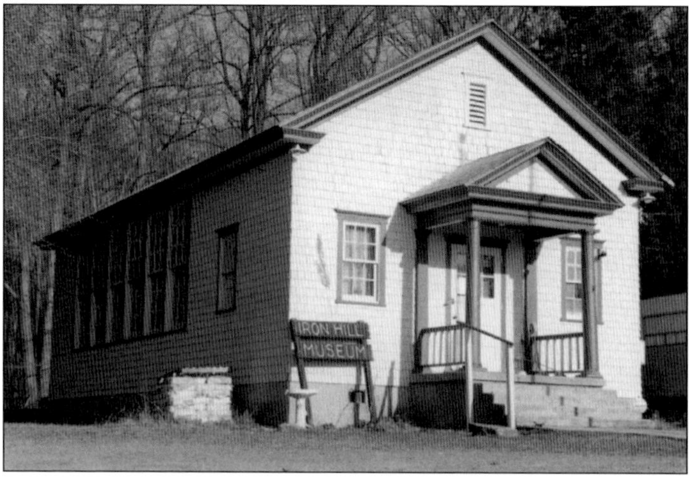

Iron Hill School No. 112-C was built in 1923 by noted architect James Oscar Betelle. It is a one-and-a-half-story frame building with pedimented portico on the front gable end. It served as a one-room schoolhouse for African American students, most of whom lived in the vicinity of the school. It was used until segregation was abolished in 1965. (Courtesy National Register of Historic Places, National Park Service.)

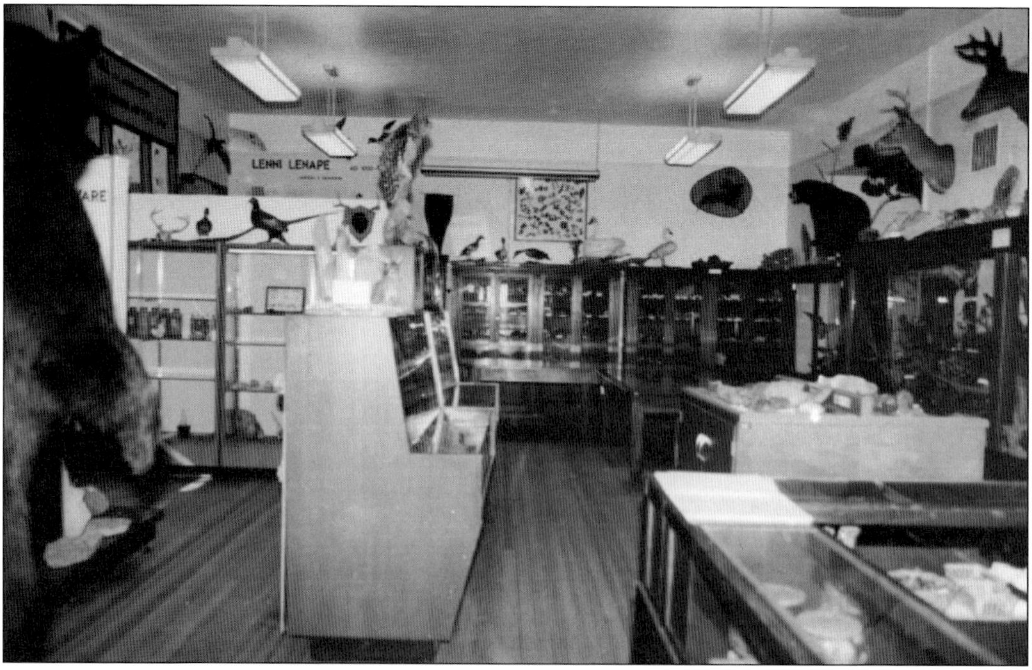

In the 1968, the Iron Hill School No. 112-C was renovated into the Iron Hill Museum of Natural History, an educational museum for children to learn about local history and nature. It has been a favorite tour site for elementary and middle school students. The museum has displays on local fauna, flora, geology, and mineralogy. (Courtesy National Register of Historic Places, National Park Service.)

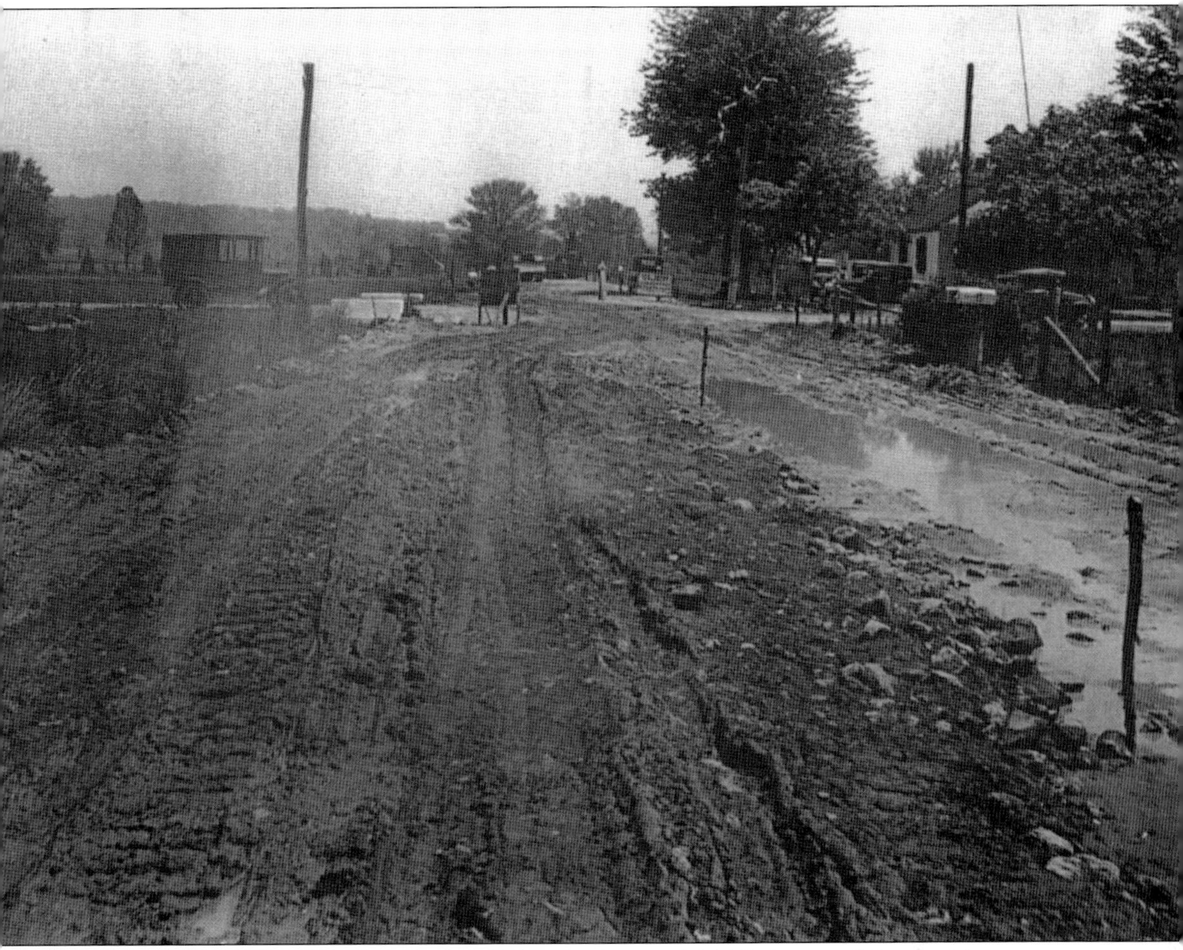

This late-19th-century photograph shows the condition of Old Baltimore Pike, looking west at the intersection with Pleasant Valley Road. (Courtesy personal collection.)

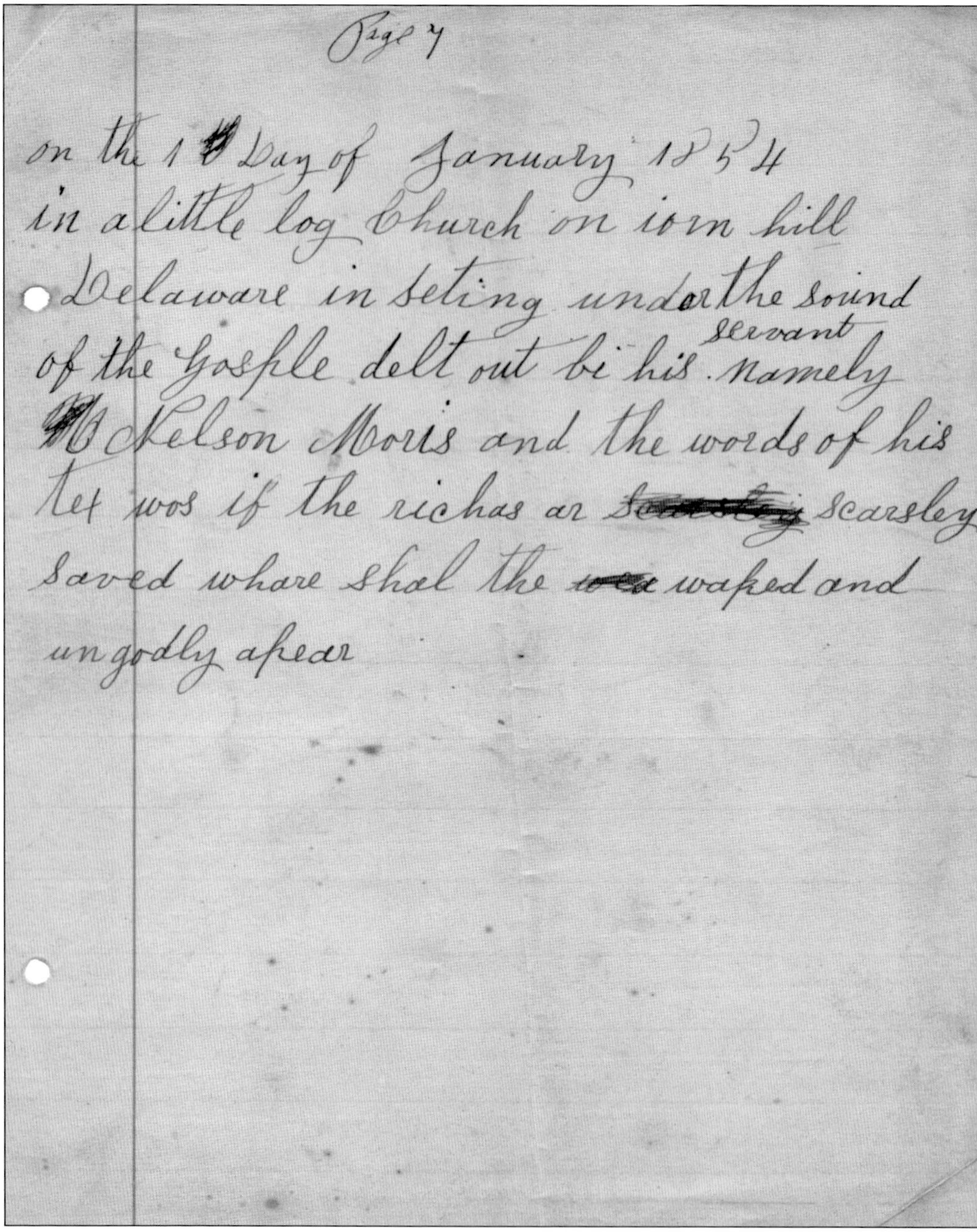

Page 7

on the 1 Day of January 1854
in a little log Church on iorn hill
Delaware in seting under the sound
of the Gosple delt out bi his servant namely
Nelson Morris and the words of his
tex wos if the richas ar scarsley
saved whare shal the waked and
ungodly apear

This handwritten autobiographical account by Rev. Nelson Morris in 1854 describes that "on the 1 day of January 1854 in a little log Church on Iron Hill, Delaware, in setting under the sound of the Gospel delt out be his servant, named Nelson Morris and the words of his tex was if the riches ar scarcely saved whare shal the waked [wicked] and ungodly afear." (Courtesy personal collection.)

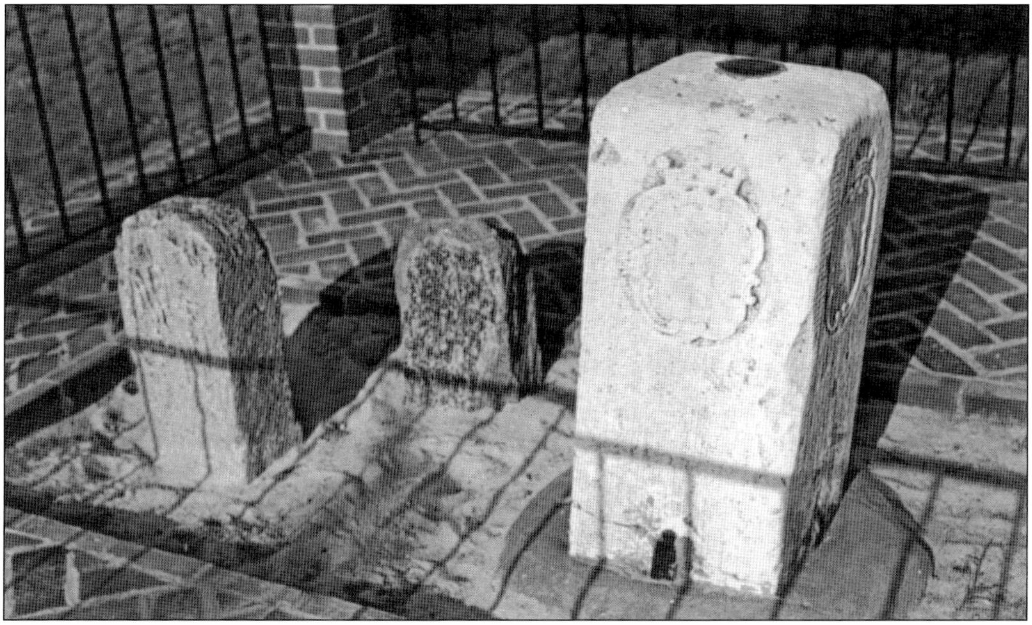

At the terminus of the Old Baltimore Pike in Delaware, the road crosses the line where Mason and Dixon surveyed the western boundary of Delaware, dividing it from Maryland and Pennsylvania in 1768. The marker, located on private property south of the road, is similar to the one pictured above, preserved and prominently displayed in Delmar, Delaware. (Courtesy personal collection.)

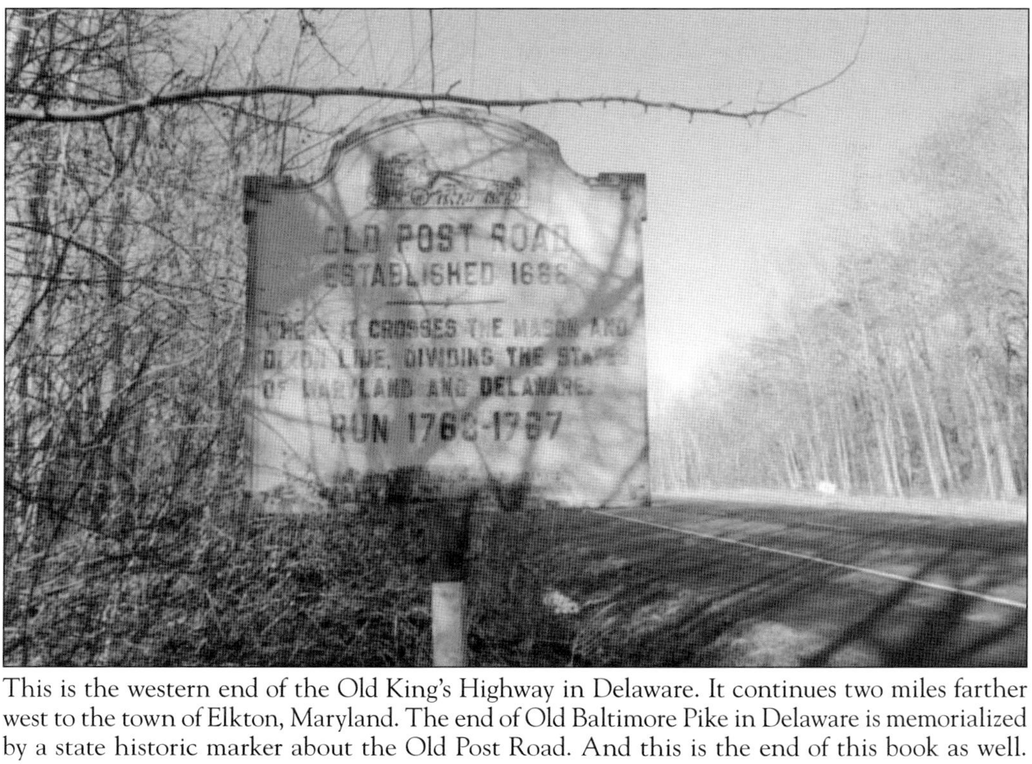

This is the western end of the Old King's Highway in Delaware. It continues two miles farther west to the town of Elkton, Maryland. The end of Old Baltimore Pike in Delaware is memorialized by a state historic marker about the Old Post Road. And this is the end of this book as well. (Courtesy personal collection.)

Bibliography

Bennett, Gordon and Joseph L. Copeland. *Early Architecture of Delaware*. New York: Bonanza Books, 1932.

Conradian. High School Yearbook Published by Conrad High School, 1955.

Cooch, Richard. *Christiana Bicentennial Brochure*. Christiana, DE: Christiana Historical Society, 1976.

Eckman, Jeanette. *Delaware: A Guide to the First State*. Federal Writers Project. New York: Hastings House, 1938.

Delaware Department of Transportation. *Delaware's Historic Bridges*. 2000.

Kronika. High School Yearbook Published by Christiana High School, Christiana, Delaware, 1970.

Index

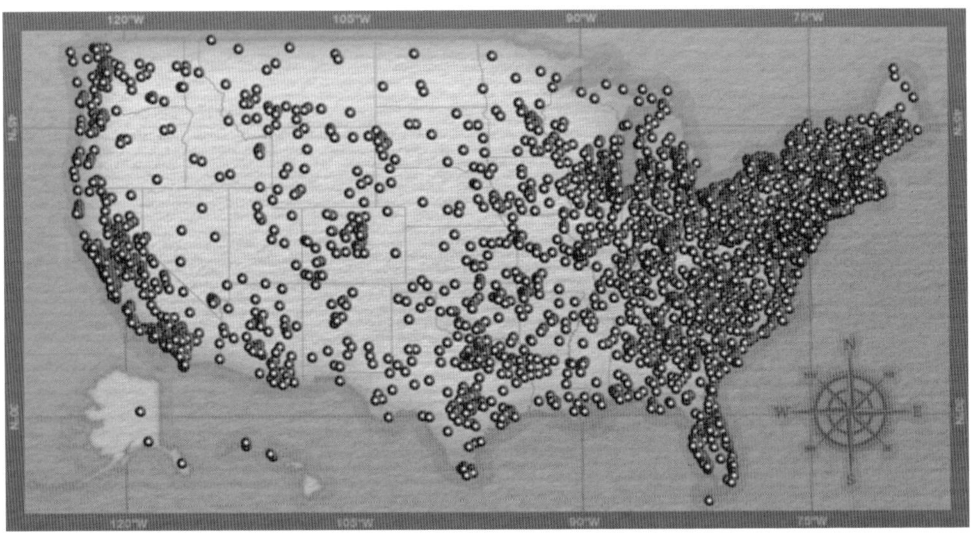

Consistent with our mission to preserve history on a local level, this book was printed in South Carolina on American-made paper and manufactured entirely in the United States. Products carrying the accredited Forest Stewardship Council (FSC) label are printed on 100 percent FSC-certified paper.